UPRISING OF THE FOOLS

UPRISING
OF THE FOOLS

Pilgrimage as Moral Protest in Contemporary India

VIKASH SINGH

STANFORD UNIVERSITY PRESS

STANFORD, CALIFORNIA

Stanford University Press
Stanford, California

Printed in the United States of America on acid-free, archival-quality paper

Library of Congress Cataloging-in-Publication Data

Names: Singh, Vikash, 1974- author.
Title: Uprising of the fools : pilgrimage as moral protest in contemporary
    India / Vikash Singh.
Other titles: South Asia in motion.
Description: Stanford, California : Stanford University Press, 2017. |
    Series: South Asia in motion | Includes bibliographical references and
    index.
Identifiers: LCCN 2016028825 (print) | LCCN 2016031633 (ebook) |
    ISBN 9781503600379 (cloth : alk. paper) | ISBN 9781503601673 (pbk. : alk.
    paper) | ISBN 9781503601741 (ebook)
Subjects: LCSH: Hindu pilgrims and pilgrimages—India—Haridwār. | Religion
    and social status—India. | Capitalism—Moral and ethical aspects—India.
    | India—Religion—Economic aspects. | India—Religious life and customs.
Classification: LCC BL1239.36.H37 S56 2017 (print) | LCC BL1239.36.H37
    (ebook) | DDC 294.5/35095451—dc23
LC record available at https://lccn.loc.gov/2016028825

Typeset by Bruce Lundquist in 10.75/15 Adobe Caslon

For Indu, Jhanvi, Shaurya
and Deependra

As soon as man comes to life, he is at once old enough to die.

A medieval homily, Heidegger, *Being and Time*

For the philosophical tradition of the West, every relation between the same and the other, when it is no longer an affirmation of the supremacy of the same, reduces itself to an impersonal relation with a universal order.

Levinas, *Totality and Infinity*

CONTENTS

ACKNOWLEDGMENTS

This is a book on gift, gratitude, of the impossibility of "returning." And perhaps this is so, because it is a gift by itself, say, in the form of the authorial name and its significance, real or imaginary. Thus, by definition, a certain appropriation of authority, surplus, capitalization based as much on others' generosity as on their being there. These were the others whom I saw walking, often in pain, with bleeding feet, traversing their traumas and desires, others who trusted a stranger with their stories, their realities. Insofar as they are the nameless subjects of this account, of these failings of representation, insofar as it is their works and words that I strive after, they are the body of this text, which gives me this name of author. Their abundant hospitality I must first thank. Then there are others who led me to these performances, helped me reach out to people, who carried my burden or suffered my occupation—Ankit of Chhaprauli, Indu, and Jhanvi. I am in their debt.

Before these, there was Deependra—a friend, guide, mentor—who taught me to read, found the books, tolerated me, and gifted from a faith of which only he knows the source, the possibility of my own faith, in the self, in others. In India's anomic social conditions, the near-pathological uncertainty of existence, trust is undoubtedly the hardest thing to find. For someone to conjure faith then, and gift it, is by all means a modern miracle—a "leap of faith," which must have distinguished the saint in another epoch. To Deependra, I owe everything. In those formative years, I also learned a lot from my interactions with other members of the "Bhopal school," including Madan Soni, Rustam Singh, Teji Grover, Udayan Vajpayee, and my friend, Sovendra Singh.

I am thankful to Jason Torkelson, David Peterson, Andrew Stroffolino, João Cowperthwaite, Crystal Bedley, Susan Kremmel, and many others. They helped me navigate a time (hand holding me, especially you,

David) while I was still in the shock of the American academic culture. This project itself would be inconceivable without the tremendous help and faith of Arlene Stein. Arlene devoted an inordinate amount of time and effort on this project, reading and editing proposals and large parts of the manuscript, brainstorming titles, and finally working out the title as it now stands. In addition, at Rutgers, I am also very thankful to the kindness of József Böröcz, and his remarkable ability to keep his passion for justice and intellectual honesty, and infectiously pass it on, in the face of all the objections and objectivities of the university discourse. And I am thankful to Karen Cerulo for her love and kindness; Karen is one to never miss a kind deed, and I have been on the receiving end of her kindness far too many times. Dianne Yarnell, Tamara Crawford, and Lisa Iorillo also played vital parts in the eventual realization of this project. Furthermore, the fieldwork for this project was made possible by the financial and academic support of the Rutgers South Asian Studies Program, the Graduate School of Arts and Sciences, and the Rutgers Sociology Department.

I am no less grateful to my colleagues at Montclair State for their unstinting support. The passionate conversations with Yong Wang; the calming influence of Janet Ruane, Susan O'Neil, and Ben Hadis; the enthusiasm of Sangeeta Parashar; and the moral support of Jay Livingston, Yasemin Besen-Cassino, and Chris Donoghue—they have all played their part in making this possible. I am also thankful for the generous financial help from the College of Humanities and Social Sciences at Montclair State and the Provost's Office in the past two years, which has allowed me to keep working on this project and bring it to fruition. I must thank our Dean, Robert Friedman and Provost, Willard Gingerich for this kindness. I would also like to thank Sumit Guha for first suggesting the Kanwar as a research topic, Arvind Rajagopal for his support and for several interesting discussions on the subject, and Paul Courtright for his continued moral support.

I am deeply grateful for the invaluable feedback and encouragement I have received from members of the New York Psycho-Social Group, including John Andrews, George Cavalletto, Patricia Clough, Tom DeGloma, Joshua Klein, Christina Nadler, Catherine Silver, and Ilgin Yorukoglu. They read several of these chapters, as I was still timidly writing them, and blessed them with the value they appeared to see in here. I must single out Lynn Chancer for her compassion, generosity, and help. Going far beyond the call of duty seems to be second nature to Lynn, and she surely did so in my case. I cannot thank her enough for her trust and bounteous supply of kind words and deeds.

Beyond these people I know personally, I have received invaluable suggestions from many anonymous reviewers along the way—through Stanford University Press and the journals *Ethnography*, *Subjectivity*, *Sociological Forum*, and *Culture and Religion*.[1] These reviews gave me ideas, some of which became chapters and key themes of this work. If this book lands in the hands of these reviewers at some point, I want them to know that their kind readings and generous gifts of ideas have made it possible. I also must thank Jenny Gavacs for making the publication process a wonderful and seamless experience. From the first discussions on the proposal, Jenny made my first experience in book publishing refreshingly efficient and smooth. What Jenny began, others carried on! I owe much to the excellent editors at Stanford University Press—Anne Fuzellier Jain, Kate Wahl, Cynthia Lindlof, and James Holt. It has been wonderful working with Kate in the later stages of the project, while Anne has been patient and thorough in bringing this work into production. I also must thank Cynthia for her painstaking and precise copy editing. And, I am surely grateful to Thomas Blom Hansen as much for bringing this book out as for making room for Lacan—perhaps the most important influence on my intellectual career—in South Asian Studies.

I would also like to express my gratitude for the unspoken yet foundational role of my parents, Ilam Singh and Satbiri Devi, and their sacrifices in this adventure.

Finally, I should not fail to mention the gift of those works, the pathbreaking reflections on the human condition, on the "other" that have shaped my life of the mind—the radical empathy of Kierkegaard, the writing acts of Derrida, the affects and teachings of Lacan, Heidegger's company in angst, the rebellions of Marx and Foucault, the analytical feats of Sudhir Kakar and Ashis Nandy, and the many wonderful ethnographies of pilgrimages across the world.

Having benefited from all this generosity then, is it any surprise that this book should turn out to be but a work on the gift?

UPRISING OF THE FOOLS

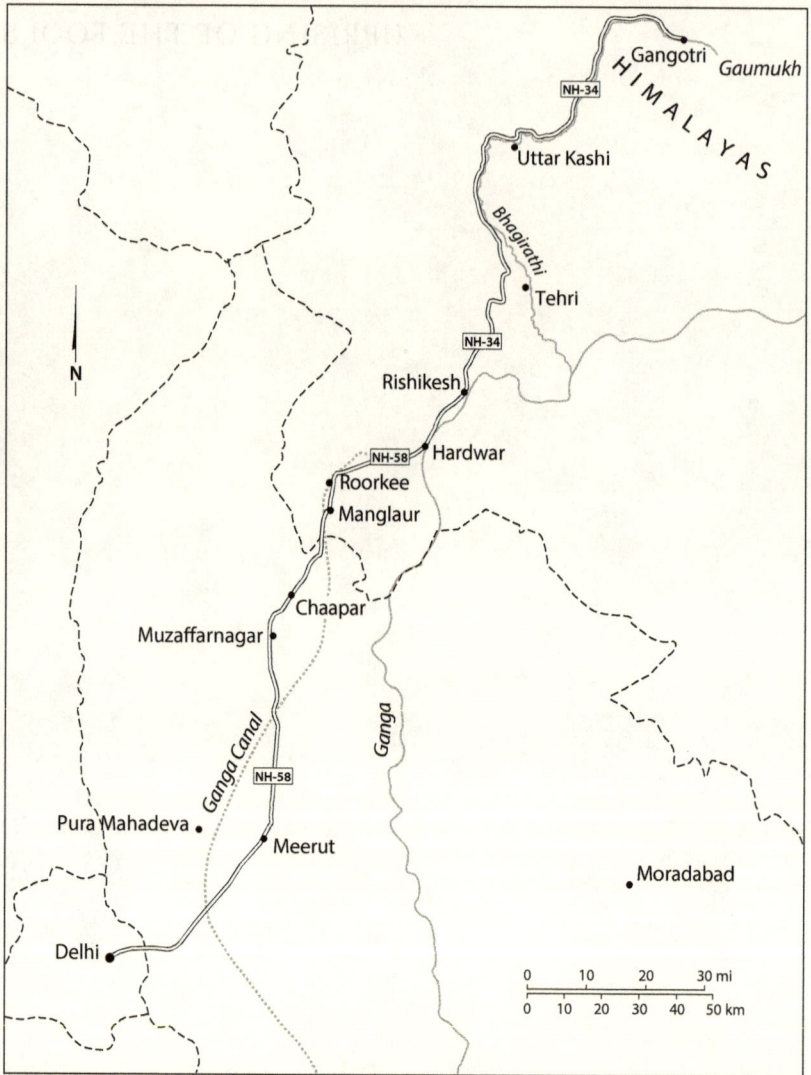

MAP 1. *The geography of the Kanwar pilgrimage*

INTRODUCTION
Illegitimate Religion

SEVERAL WEEKS before *amāvasyā* (new moon) in the month of Sāvan, millions of Kanwar pilgrims stream into the holy city of Hardwar to return with sacred water from the river Ganga.[1] They often walk hundreds of miles ceremonially carrying the water for libations in various Śiva shrines across northwestern India. The journey is long and arduous, with devotees carrying water vessels hanging on a wooden pole; often walking on bare, bleeding feet; and following elaborate rituals. Frequently, the pilgrims will aggravate their travail by pledging, for instance, not to remove the apparatus from their shoulders throughout the journey or to cover a segment of the journey on the ground, moving one body length at a time. The *kānwar*, the structure comprising the pole and the water vessels after which the pilgrimage (Kanwar Yatra) itself is named, is usually decorated with tinsel, streamers, wicker baskets, tridents, and pictures of gods and topped with iconic Styrofoam artifacts.[2] In addition to the walking pilgrims—profusely sweating, in pain, and often under the effect of *bhāng* or *sulfā* (cannabis products)—the Kanwar spectacle includes cavalcades of heavily decorated tableaux illustrating mythic tales in various art forms such as sculpture, paintings, and *tableaux vivants*. Camps are available at various places along the route, where volunteers provide the pilgrim, called *bholā* (simpleton/fool/idiot) after the patron deity Śiva (Bhola), with food, refreshment, and medical assistance.

There were only a few thousand participants until the 1980s, but the Kanwar has emerged as India's largest annual religious congregation over the years; there were as many as twelve million participants in 2011.[3] Young adult men of poor or lower-middle-class backgrounds from both rural and urban areas of the neighboring states of Delhi, Uttar Pradesh, Haryana, and Rajasthan constitute a disproportionate share of the participants. On their journey to Hardwar, pilgrims generally use public transport, while they walk following ritual conventions during the return journey.[4] Thus, for several weeks during the pilgrimage, the busy social landscape between Delhi and Hardwar is replaced by a vibrant community, a moving sea of enraptured pilgrims in ochre clothing, carrying kānwaṛs with all manner of ornamentation.[5] According to common (though loosely defined) beliefs, it is mandatory for participants to make at least a pair of pilgrimages; they, however, usually complete many more. In previous years, a majority of the libations would be performed at noted Śiva shrines, but as these sites have become unbearably crowded in recent years, an increasing number of pilgrims now perform these rituals at their local temples. While the Kanwar obviously has a wide following, these participants are frequently ridiculed, indeed reviled, by the urban liberal middle class, who find such vulgate religiosity disgusting.

For most scholars of religion and globalization, such movements reflect a "reaction" against social change. To proponents of the "religious fundamentalism" thesis, in particular, they amount to a reactive assertion of "identity" in the face of the inevitable, if rapid, changes of globalization. Peter Berger, previously an eloquent voice of secularization, summarizes:

> [This is] one of the most important topics for a contemporary sociology of religion, but far too large to consider here. I can only drop a hint. Modernity, for fully understandable reasons, undermines all the old certainties; uncertainty is a condition that many people find very hard to bear, therefore, *any* movement (not only a religious one) that promises to provide or to renew certainty has a ready market.[6]

The explanation may appear hurried, but it is nevertheless widely shared. It brings alive a wide body of literature that could as easily claim the structuralist corpus of Ferdinand de Saussure, Claude Lévi-Strauss, and

Émile Durkheim as it articulates itself through contemporary theories of identity and Anthony Giddens's neofunctionalism. Globalization, this explanation goes, causes anomie, which pushes people into seeking the security of traditional groups, based, for example, on ethnicity, nationality, or religion. Religious movements thus arise in "reaction to globalization"; they are reactionary expressions of collective solidarity as long-held traditions, worldviews, and beliefs struggle to stay aboard amid the tumultuous exchanges of globalization[7]—religion "originates from a world of crumbling traditions."[8] This is a dogged if futile obstruction of the wheels of history, the inevitable progress of modernization. Prophetic binary battle lines are thus drawn: "the twenty-first century will pit fundamentalism against cosmopolitan tolerance."[9]

The dubious epistemology of this notion of "fundamentalism" has taken a lot of criticism in interdisciplinary scholarship in recent years. Several theoretically complex and ethnographically situated accounts of religion, community, economy, and the profound diversities and sufferings of everyday life across the world have shown that the "modern" is a much more complex, variegated, and contested ground than abstractly represented here.[10] These schematic treatments of religion have likewise been proven fanciful.[11] In sociology, too, "fundamentalism" has surely become a fraught term; yet beyond a certain slant of appropriate symbolism, sociological discourse continues to be intrinsically defined by the vector of modernization and the apparently infallible logic of the market society as Reason.[12]

The strong thrust of such inferences, however, is fraught with many perils. An unusually felicitous combination of common sense and scholarly deliberation, the perspective is deceptive. Abstracting globally and authoritatively, at a distance—on the fly, as it were—such cognitive reasoning fails to reckon with the participants' finite lives and their lived circumstances. It is a perception circumscribed, perpetuated, and patrolled by disciplinary mandates and interests that lead into a singularly one-dimensional understanding. This dominant analytic, as this book demonstrates, is bound by a teleological morality of "progress" referencing putatively "universal" social collectives existing in abstract, endless time. This is a pervasive tendency of modern epistemology; it is precisely this imperative that impelled Martin Heidegger's monumental critique of Western metaphysics and explains the historic significance of his work. Heidegger states, "But what does this 'reifying' signify? Where does it arise? . . . Why does this reifying always keep coming back to exercise its dominion?"[13]

In South Asian studies, such renewed attraction of religion is usually elaborated in reference to the anxieties of Hindu identity and nationality in a modernizing social context. This explanation often complexly weaves together historical specificities, such as postcolonial anxieties, Muslim-Hindu relations, and issues of Hindu identity. Yet the core focus on the reactionary character of such interest in religion persists—it represents an unwillingness to change, surmount past affects and prejudices, and face up to new social realities and horizons. This book instead directs attention to the lived dilemmas and social conditions of participants dynamically embedded in social relations and obligations, navigating concrete material realities. It proposes an analytic grounded in the finite character of human life—that is, one that reckons with anxieties and moral obligations rooted in the finitude of actual human existence and the immediacy of social circumstances and expectations.

Listening to my respondents, closely considering their life accounts and compositions of the rituals, and participating in the journey, I found little of the chimeras of religious fundamentalism or dogmatic opposition to social change and modernity—conceptions apparently self-evident, second nature to scholarly as well as journalistic, statist, and activist readings. Instead of a fundamentalist reaction to social and economic changes, I witnessed practices that enable participants to *perform, practice, and prepare for* a new configuration of social and economic obligations. They reflect anxious social and psychological preparation for the norms, scarcity, and unpredictable outcomes of poor, informal economic conditions at a critical point of transition into adulthood.

These were young adults and teenagers anxiously preparing to deliver on their social expectations and moral obligations to loved ones in social conditions that were often as precarious as they were hierarchical and humiliating. In conditions where the overwhelming majority of workers are informally employed, with few employment, social, and health safeguards, and the prospects of stable and respectable employment or life course are for most faint and illusive, for many the steps in the pilgrimage rehearsed their first daunting steps into adulthood. At the margins of the economy, the religious phenomenon provided an open and freely accessible, yet challenging, stage—a definite and alternative field—for participants to practice and prove their talents, resolve, and moral sincerity.

To practice and prepare, however, are only part of the figure of repetition. To repeat is also to strive to master—to use the word in all its philosophical polyvalence and sociopsychic significance as Freud has demonstrated. The religious event is also a means to contest the symbolic violence and social inequities of a hierarchical society now dominated by a neoliberal social ethic, as imposing as it is exclusive.[14] This work thus dwells on the paradoxes of performance and recognition in an informal economy; questions of morality and the violence of everyday life in emergent neoliberal conditions; issues of gender and sexual anxieties; and aesthetic conflicts that invite rethinking "caste" and "race" in addition to relations between everyday social anxieties, globalization, and the politics of "religion" and "nation."

RELIGION'S ILLEGITIMATE CHILDREN
Subtending the life of the mind, the transcendental reference of its certainty as much as its immanent medium, for a long time at least in the Indo-European world, religion was both the limit and the medium of the consciousness. In these civilizations, notes the eminent French linguist Émile Benveniste, "everything is imbued with religion, everything is a sign of, a factor in, or the reflection of, divine forces," and hence there was no term to separately designate it.[15] Where Enlightenment philosophy may have aspired for a religion within the limits of reason alone, it was religion that had traditionally defined the limits of both reason and understanding.[16] Religion was the self; it was also the disavowal, the mortification of the self in the face of the other, as well as its solidarity with this other; a term for scruples, hesitation, misgivings, out of an apprehension of offending the gods. In another interpretation, *religio* could mean being bound to God by a bond of piety.[17] Now, in the dominant mood of late capitalism, this once "omnipresent reality" is but a frighten-

ing apparition, the sinister presence of a substance persistent beyond its death. Any sign of religion—a man carrying a Koran, a woman wearing a hijab, pilgrims on a journey, a person praying in public—stirs suspicion and fear. It represents madness, a threat of irrational action and blind faith, incomprehensible to instrumental rationality. Religion represents a power of violence, which this instrumental, market rationality, conveniently aloof to its own law-preserving and law-making violence, finds intolerant and intolerable.[18] The war against religion must proceed by explaining the origins of this monster that has come from the dead—a hybrid, atavistic creature crossing illegitimately with modern social and industrial technology.

Of course, the demise of religion (often seen as an alienating world of illusions based on human projections of their emotions and experiences) in the face of scientific evidence and bureaucratic systemic rationalities has been a truism of modern thought. Religion belongs to that figure of "self-incurred minority," a lack of courage and understanding where man is unable to use his own reason from which the Enlightenment exhorted him to come out. "'Have courage to use your own understanding!'—that is the motto of the Enlightenment."[19] Breaking free of the chains of Christianity, its grip on the mind as much as on custom and society, in favor of the freedom of ideas is so important to the Enlightenment philosophers that Peter Gay is right to call them pagans.[20] Here, religion, "of the priest," for example, "is so evidently bad that it would be losing time to demonstrate its evils."[21] For the sociologist, who inherits the guardianship of the Enlightenment from the philosophes, secularization is a teleological, historical fact and often a moral imperative. By nature, sociologists have said, religion cannot limit itself but has to encompass every other function, which is not practical in a modern society, characterized by highly differentiated functional systems.[22] Religion thus more and more becomes a case of personal belief as spirituality and disappears from the public sphere, with some of its moral sentiments informing modern state form as "civil religion."[23] In any case, the gobbledygook of magic, mysteries, and miracles, which make up the sum and practices of religion, must succumb to rational thinking. In his 1967 work, *The Sacred Canopy*, Peter Berger thus boldly predicted the final triumph of knowledge, of industry, the commerce between objects where religion itself, if it does not subside completely, will remain only another commodity in the marketplace.

Although positive about modernist social change, classical sociology of religion, especially of Max Weber, had a sober view of science's ability to meaningfully respond to the moral dilemmas, existential agonies, and the many contingencies of human life. "Science's own self-misconceptions, as the path to true art, to true nature, to God, or to happiness, would reveal themselves as so many illusions."[24] Thus, for Weber, rationalism can mean many different things, and most soteriological religions have been quite rational. "In general, all kinds of practical ethics that are systematically and unambiguously oriented to fixed goals are rational" because of their formal method and their distinction between valid norms and empirical evidence.[25] Notwithstanding his functionalist understanding, Durkheim was likewise cognizant of the moral value of religion and the limitations of market societies.[26] Persuaded by the ideological power of the market and the dominance of the economists, later sociological studies have habitually shirked off any such care, seeing market exchanges as synonymous with reason.[27] Quite in sync with the purposive rationalization of every domain of society by market forces and bureaucratic order, social scientists definitively buried religion as an irrational and archaic thing that did not belong to the modern public space.

In the 1980s, when religion demonstrated a new vitality in one country after another, in politics as much as in popular practice, breaking out of the "private" in which it had been interred in conflict with the power and reason of the state and market, sociologists were surely caught off guard.[28] True believers in reason, they hurriedly probed for rational explanations to this unexpected development. Some galvanized new defenses for a stronger secularization thesis, and others found it wiser to substantively qualify it; yet others, including Berger, famously rejecting his previous prophecies, argued that secularization itself had provoked this "worldwide resurgence of religion."[29] Notwithstanding the apparent differences, a near consensus aligned to the dominant contours of a normative sociological model soon evolved. "Modernity tends to undermine the taken-for-granted certainties by which people lived through most of history," says Berger without quite explaining this term "certainty."[30] Clearly, "uncertainty" here is predominantly perceived as a cognitive quality; for, of course, who would say, for example, that there were no material uncertainties before capitalism?[31] Uncertainty, in this discourse, is caused by the disturbance of the sense of belonging in stable social practices. This cognitivist explanation of the function that religion is called on to serve amid the dynamism of modernity, its industry and radical sociopolitical achievements, receives a more assured voice in Bauman as he argues that the appeal of religious fundamentalism—and indeed contemporary religion—lies in its promise to "emancipate" from the "agonies of choice . . . those who find the burden of individual freedom excessive and unbearable."[32]

According to Bauman, in the paradise of consumerism that is the postmodern world, all mysteries of death and experience have become routine and regulated, and eschatological concerns no longer occupy people who, when not actively seeking peak experiences, ultimate sensations, are only wishing or obliged to go about business as usual. Religion, in its postmodern form—that is, religious fundamentalism, which "usually refers to any sort of passionate religious movement"—appeals only to those unable to compete in the great game of the market, "left behind in the scramble for entry tickets to the consumers' party."[33] Thus, Bauman cites Gilles Kepel to describe such religious subjects as

> true children of our time: unwanted children, perhaps bastards of computerization and unemployment or of the population explosion and increasing literacy, and their cries and complaints in these closing years of the century spur us to seek out their parentage and to retrace their unacknowledged genealogy.[34]

These scholars could not have been more true to the extensive genealogy of children and miscegenation in Enlightenment thought. From John Locke to Immanuel Kant, man's entitlement to freedom has been argued based on his status as a rational adult. The savage, the nonwhite, on the other hand, is an irrational child who could hardly be trusted with freedom. We thus have quite an epistemological tradition to take stock of such children, the other "races"—Thomas Hobbes's savages in justifiable servitude since they would not resist to death, Locke's irrational individuals and captives of a just war, David Hume's "naturally inferior," James Mill's "hideous," and Kant's "stupid."[35] These savages, these children, like some fictitious dwellers of a Platonic cave, are unable to bear the light of the sun and rush back to find solace in the embryonic darkness of the cave.

These misbegotten, illegitimate children—Bauman, the sociologist, never really cares to ask how many of them there are. In this social order framed by the peak experiences of hyperconsumerism—their thoroughbred quality, of being true representatives of their epoch—any inability or unwillingness to immerse themselves in this particular game (of which Bauman can claim to know everything insofar as this is offered as a transparent, shining game) can only be a sign of miscegenation, of illegitimacy, of unworthy parentage. However, let us not forget the numbers here: about half of the people in the world live on less than $2.50 a day; more than 80 percent, on less than $10.00 (95 percent in non-Western countries), a brazen minimum one may benchmark for being a part of this world defining hyperconsumerist party.[36] Except, arguably, for Western Europe and a small proportion of the global elite, Berger notes in his new orientation, the world is as "furiously religious" as it has ever been.[37] We then have a world brimming with illegitimate people, people of doubtful parentage, the merit of whose choices and practices is hard to recognize in any legitimate ancestry—political, economic, ideological, or biological.

According to Bauman, the possibilities of postmodern culture have put the peak experiences, "once the privilege of the 'aristocracy of culture'" (saints, mystics, ascetic monks, etc.) "in every individual's reach . . . as the product of a life devoted to the art of consumer self-indulgence."[38] Referring, however, to peak sensual enjoyment in the hyperconsumerist culture portrayed in Bauman as the only genuine representation of this epoch, an entity fascinated by and performing to reflections in an object-world—of course, at work in the background is the neoliberal hyperrationality of the state and the corporation—one has to ask whether this involves a complete absorption as presence, an instantaneous identification, that is, if the entity has ceased to be temporally extended. Has the pleasure of these sensations been dissociated from any sense of pain, suffering, any prospect or possibility of relation to others, to the world, or to death; is this power, "infinite human potency," without a trace of any "weakness," any lack; is it a complete eclipse of lived time, of being-in-the-world?

In this consumerist utopia, one may indeed see how the symbolic order addresses, incorporates human experience; however, to describe this as a true representation of the Real is perhaps as misplaced as the comparison that Bauman makes with the past through the sweeping characterization of religion as focused on the "perpetual insufficiency" of the human.[39] Insofar as in this "postmodern culture" there remains any concern for others, for an otherness beyond all others, any acknowledgment of a lack of absolute knowledge, insofar as there still resides the possibility of a sociality that is not completely mesmerized by the order of the system or the object, insofar as the object itself remains a product of work and labor, are we not already in the realm of the religious?

This book tells the story of one such group of "children"—religion's illegitimate children that reason matured must dismiss as "hooligans" and "miscreants," with no ethics and "rules to follow," hardly capable of understanding religion, "a strange mix of tradition and modernity," disorderly proto-fascist scoundrels with no social status.

DISCIPLINES AND HERESY

From the contemporary sociological perspective, the Kanwar can only be a reactive assertion of ethnic, religious, or national (postcolonial) identity in a modernizing social context. Adopting a normative sociological language focused on *collectivities*, such a conclusion is unavoidable; if it is on the collective defined by solidarity or identity that the sociologist predicates her practice, this is what she will by definition collapse the phenomenon into. Yet both these figures are preconceived in abstract opposition to macrohistorical, teleological notions of secularist progress and civic liberalism. As the binary counterpart to this "collective" stands the notion of the "individual." Drawing from Cartesian metaphysics, this conception of the individual prioritizes a utilitarian cognitive interest in the world—the thing, the other, or indeed the self—and is predicated on a certain economy, whether of thinking, of volition, or of goods formulated in the idiom of mastery.[40]

One of the primary anchors, the conditions of possibility, of this story is a consistent refusal to consider religion as a *distinct* domain of social life but as always implicated in economic, political, psychological, or cultural concerns. After all, the person who suffers the excesses of the economy or the harshness of power and history, whose status and identity are ascribed in a global, near-incomprehensible network of social relations, is the same person who continues to walk—among millions—carrying the sacred water for Śiva's libations, even as his feet bleed and limbs refuse another step. Allied with such insistence on the necessary interconnectedness of life performances is the imperative not to closet them into a disciplinary or subdisciplinary enclosure such as "sociology of religion" or "anthropology of pilgrimage"—that is, an institutionally recognized social fact.

Such iconoclasm must begin with disciplinary boundaries themselves. The mandate of sociology, Durkheim (the father) had argued, scrupulously differentiating the subject matter of the discipline from biology and psychology, was to study "social facts," an objective entity—"a new species and *to them must be exclusively assigned the term social*."[41] And if sociology has developed and expanded various offshoots over its historical course, it finds itself nevertheless obligated to the promise, the assurance, and the apparent profundity of its paternal origins. The stigma faced by the heretic is a social fact: no *good* can come from violating the father's law. If Durkheim, however, would "exclusively" reserve the "social," as a property belonging to the family of sociologists, it is precisely the interests of the family (and a political economy, an ethics, an ontology predicated on it) that perhaps one must renounce to approach the condition of the human today—by definition, a "social" condition. Thus, I may be accused of violating the law of the father twice over. First, I will be approaching the very domain of the psychic from which Durkheim most struggled to break sociology free. Second, in appealing to psychoanalysis, I will be subjecting the "social" to an analytical tradition found to be in breach of the father's law and authority from the outset.

The trajectories and closures of academic disciplines are, however, no accidents. In this case, they are related to the historical dominance of functionalist and cognitivist orientations in the social sciences.[42] Thus, sociological narratives of contemporary religion are often defined by

grand abstract questions of the function and logical (im)possibility of religion in modernity, where both "religion" and the "modern" may be often
employed as monolithic terms with self-evident meanings.[43] Accordingly,
contemporary religiosity may be characterized as fundamentalist and
anachronistic, traced either to "postmodern" social processes or "primitive," "irrational" psychological processes.[44] Others would argue religious
behavior as a "rational choice," using the terms "reason" or "rationality" in a
manner that is both colloquial and characteristic of Chicago School neoliberalism.[45] The notion "rationality" may thus be used adroitly either to
positively assert the instrumental, self-centeredness of a Cartesian entity
in some places or to negatively exclude only the absurd in other cases.[46]

The growing interest in religious practices today is usually explained in
terms of the cognitive dissociations and cultural threats of globalization.[47]
Rarely are these formulations based on thick and considered ethnographic work on religious practices and the social and existential contexts
in which they are embedded. That "local" task is left to anthropologists—
who carry the extra methodological and historical burden of navigating
the wide chasm that separates the researcher from the object of research
on distant shores, in apparently "another" time—even as sociologists and
political scientists devise often sweeping, abstract statements on religious
practices across the globe.[48] Demonstrating the importance of a reflex-
ive sociological methodology that is alert to the continuities of religious,
moral, and economic practices and adopts an embedded analytical orientation that wards off reified subject and object divides is one of the objectives of this book. My primary goal, however, is to read, articulate, and
reflect on lived social experiences as they are performed in these religious
practices in contemporary India and, by extension, in the global South.
Accordingly, my choice of literature is eclectic and multidisciplinary.

A clear break with the contemporary sociology of religion aside, this
book is founded on the solid grounds of classical sociology, particularly the
sociology of Max Weber, which clearly rests on considering religion, economy, morality, and social conflict and recognition together as more or less
inseparable constituents of subjective integrity.[49] Speaking of "religion" in
the Kanwar outside its embeddedness in moral, economic, and sexual concerns would have been as meaningless as Weber describing the religious

beliefs of the Calvinists, or of soteriological religions in general, devoid of their moral, social, and economic significance.[50] While this departure may appear deceptively minor, following through with such an integral perspective in the context of the contemporary academic culture of expertise has been a challenging task, requiring something of a gestalt switch.[51]

The realization of this departure was conditional on another departure, the core of which is perhaps best illustrated by the Heideggerian movement from historical Time, an abstract collective temporality, to the temporality of *Dasein*; from considering people as things, present-at-hand to the anxieties of being human, from the individual contemplating the world detached and from a distance, to one anxiously embedded in social and material conditions and obligations and subject to all the risks and responsibilities thereof.[52] To understand the Kanwar performances, it was critical to shift from a hermeneutic that privileges abstract collectives and a teleological universal Good, which is deeply ingrained in sociological discourse and practice—although the Hegelian dialectic of the World Spirit is surely its most eloquent illustration—to instead center on the temporality of being-in-the-world.[53]

While Hegel's teleological universality is primarily a product of his immense interest in the progressive concretion or externalization of the Spirit and historical growth of self-consciousness as knowledge in a rather infinite progression of collective Time, Heidegger may be credited with bringing philosophical attention back to the finitude of human existence. He advocates looking first and foremost to the temporality of Dasein, being-in-the-world with one another in relations of care, concern, and solicitude. This conception is embedded in a fundamental critique of the Cartesian notion (followed through from Plato to Hegel) of the subject, which exists in the world in distance from other entities, including humans, and relates to them as but things, present-at-hand.[54] Instead, Dasein is always already affectively existent in the world with other entities, other human beings. From an analytical perspective, this time comes before any expectations of sacrifice for an abstract collective history—such as for political ideals of progress and emancipation— which itself can be a motif only in her own temporality. This conception of Dasein, which has been the bedrock of this study, also helps us recover another philosophical moment vital for any conception of agency—the Kantian critique of practical reason. Kant, Heidegger would assert, already had a more radical understanding of time than Hegel did.[55]

The autonomy of the moral imperative, Kant found, was indispensable for any conception of human freedom. The moral will alone, as "a transcendental predicate of the causality of a being that belongs to the world of sense," could provide a principle of freedom outside a fatalist empiricism in which time future would always have been determined by time past.[56] Whether an "*automaton materiale* when the mechanical being is moved by matter, or with Leibnitz *spirituale* when it is impelled by ideas," freedom then would be "nothing better than the freedom of a turnspit, which, when once it is wound up, accomplishes its motions of itself."[57]

To such moral quality of Dasein must we attribute both the social and moral obligations of everyday existence and the more generalized passion for historical emancipation on class, gender, and such grounds that drives critical politics and thought. Such moral obligation drives both social movements based, say, on class, gender, or environmental considerations and the multitude of resistances with their paradoxical expressions and necessary subterfuges that James Scott, for example, called "hidden transcripts." As Scott notes, "A cruel paradox of slavery, for example, is that it is in the interest of slave mothers, whose overriding wish is to keep their children safe and by their side, to train them in the routines of conformity."[58] A hermeneutic driven by this double movement—from a modernization or evolutionist paradigm with its conceptual antecedents in Hegelian teleology, Cartesian metaphysics, and Platonic forms, to Heidegger's existential phenomenology and simultaneously to the Kantian emphasis on the ethical—has been critical to the production of this book.

Additionally, Jacques Lacan's subversion of Hegelian teleology and a capitalist social structure in which its symbolic representations are embedded has been one of my primary anchors. For this recourse, as I have said earlier, I may be accused of disciplinary hereticism; after all, it is by differentiating the subject matter of the discipline from biology and psychology that Durkheim carved the institutional field of sociology as a robust and lasting field of inquiry—the study of "social facts," an objective entity.[59] Notwithstanding the institutional force of this separation, for my purposes, the distinction between the social and the psychic would have been fallacious. This opposition based in the knowledge formations of nineteenth-century Europe is altogether sublated in Freud, and surely in Lacan. While transcending this distinction, psychoanalysis—focused on understanding human experiences rather than a positive discipline of measuring them—also led into a more humane epistemology. It is therefore not surprising that psychoanalysis, unlike sociology that has progressively narrowed itself, has been a great factor in the development of twentieth-century thought, from cultural studies and critical theory to poststructuralist philosophy and feminist theory.

METHOD, TEXT, AND TERRAIN

Chapter 1 begins with a narrative of observations and impressions from the initial hours of my pilgrimage. Like the rest of the book, it brings together insights from conversations, interviews, and theoretical debates and interventions and picks up the thread of the journey at different points. Juxtaposing the empirical data with Weber's insights on the intersections between religion and economy, phenomenological theory, performance studies, and Indian metaphysical texts, the chapter demonstrates how religious practice is a means of performing and preparing for an informal economy. The narrative places participants' performances, artworks, ritual expressions, and the excessive labor of the journey in the context of participants' ordinary work (or lack thereof). In the context of the symbolic and structural violence of a hegemonic but exclusive neoliberal market economy—where about 90 percent of the workforce is informally employed, with few social, employment, or health safeguards—the religious field offers the possibility of an alternative sociality, as well as an opportunity for performative existence and for social recognition. It enables an "actual" identity that subverts the stigmatizing labels of "failure," "unemployed," and "outcast" by a dominant social order. It provides another textual medium, imagery (or mirror) for self-recognition to resist a dominant, appropriating ideology.

As part of a current habit of thought, scholars describe religious participation as a kind of market exchange. But in the Kanwar, participants express fears and anxieties regarding obligations for the life, health, well-being, and expectations of dear ones, expressly denying their interest in material gain. People feel justified to ask for a divine gift often only insofar as it can be seen as an obligation or gift to someone else. Chapter 2 analyzes such wishes and the speech acts of the religious vow in the context of highly precarious living conditions and widespread suffering. I look at the role that ego deferral plays. The chapter questions the functionalist idealism of some of the assumptions of sociological ideas of "uncertainty," as seen, for example, in Giddens's theory, to instead argue for a material, existential understanding. Engaging participants' concerns in reference to a customary ethic of care, and through conversations with Kant, Heidegger, Lacan, and Vedic texts, the chapter interrogates the dominant utilitarian notion of the "individual" to demonstrate a subjectivity that is from the outset relational and morally embedded.

Chapter 3 shows that these performances in a different, radical temporality generate hope and community—and therefore *work*—in an otherwise disillusioning and alienating, if not punitive, social order, which holds scarce promise. Analyzing the repetitive, obsessive, and mortifying character of the religious practices, it shows how they manifest the dread of everyday life. Using extensive ethnographic detail, the chapter shows how the deities and religious practices here mediate among the subjects and their temporal horizons, becoming the foci of a community among otherwise divided subjects. In conversations with psychoanalytic theory and critical phenomenology, the chapter demonstrates that there is a gaping lack in representation of some of the most overwhelming experiences, fears, and desires of social and psychic life in a dominant consciousness usually glutted by discourses of the nation, economy, work, daily bread, or the media. The mainstream world seems to have no time and means of accommodation for these concrete realities of life in the social margins, which therefore here are deferred, displaced to, and play out in religious practice. Narrative focus on personal historicity, the profound lived time of the subject, as opposed to historical Time with its focus on collectivities—both as events and factors—makes psychoanalytic themes such as the parallels with dream work, the simple economy of the pleasure principle, and repetition compulsion very important to the text. These emerge as powerful themes with a gestaltlike effect that makes coherent and legible the otherwise complexly coded and dissimulated effects and compositions of social and religious practices.

Chapter 4 continues with the ethnographic description of my journey in the Kanwar: corpses float in the Ganga Canal while police officers turn a blind eye, even amid reports of several participants drowning. Evoking the ubiquity of violence and apathy interspersed with moments from the exceptionally violent history of the region, I describe how although the Kanwar mobilizes millions of participants every year who walk across several hundred miles, through Hindu and Muslim habitations alike, it has not caused any major incident of the notorious Hindu-Muslim conflicts that have been a defining feature of India's late colonial and postcolonial history. Yet one can feel a palpable tension as the pilgrimage procession passes through Muslim neighborhoods. This chapter analyzes such tension in reference to the ubiquity of violence and state apathy, specific incidents of Hindu-Muslim violence in recent decades, and the exceptionally violent history of the region from a *longue durée* perspective. I argue that the conflict over religion is almost inevitably provoked by interests of power and politics. Differences in faith seem to take the form of actual violence only when stoked by statist actors seeking power. While notions such as "religious nationalism" or "fundamentalism" may direct attention to legitimate fears, based on real historical events and possibilities, they often facilitate misrecognitions of the social complexity of contemporary religion and systematically divert attention away from lived political and economic conditions.

The cognitive dissonances, and the religious overcomings, as Chapter 5 shows, also express deeply ingrained social hierarchies rearticulating themselves in the contemporary contexts of hegemonic nationalist and neoliberal ideologies. While the Kanwar obviously has a wide following, it is frowned on and reviled by a large section of society. Such disgust is most common in the English-language news media and among the urban middle classes. While the phenomenon is itself, I argue, a performative expression of the fears, desires, and aspirations of a majority living in India's challenging social conditions, resentment is provoked by its aesthetic transgressions. The indiscriminate, carnivalesque performances along with the lowbrow culture offend middle-class ideals. To these ideals and sections of the populace, this is a poor, botched, illegitimate version of religion that lacks the composure of "adult" religiosity. Such aversion is partly an effect of postcolonial anxieties. In the context of a project of national redemption conceived in reference to the projections, real or imaginary, of a violated, traumatic national history, there is a compulsion to project more or less good and beautiful images of an idealized, pure self to the world. Such a seemingly gross representation of religion therefore comes across as offensive and uncanny.

I argue that this aesthetic divide is an expression of India's vast economic inequalities, reflected in differences in habitus and cultural capital. While a liberal middle-class ideology and aesthetics dominate the society, the habitus and cultural performances of the vast majority come to be seen as gross and distasteful. The Kanwar then, I argue, enacts a conflict over habitus. Here, these sedimented hierarchies are overturned. The stigmatized popular habitus occupies the highways for several days and publicly performs itself as religious and sublime under the canopy of Śiva's bacchanal figure. The dialectical constitution of the pilgrimage is thus an enactment of political conflict. I also show how these conflicts are accentuated by and express the contemporary legacies of India's caste heritage.

Notwithstanding the complex social conflicts apparent here, such religious practices are rarely treated in sociological scholarship as forms of "resistance." Even in the subaltern studies literature, where such phenomena are prolific, they are usually seen as substitutions for other, explicit social and political causes and interests. Chapter 6 shows that the notion of "resistance" in the social sciences is normatively framed by sweeping abstract ideas of individual freedom and historical progression; religious actions then are more likely to be characterized as "fundamentalist" than seen as instances of social resistance. Anchored in an exegesis of rituals and enunciations in the Kanwar, this chapter advances an alternative understanding of resistance situated in a hermeneutic that interweaves the phenomenological critiques of Hegelian philosophy, Kantian ethics, and Lacanian psychoanalysis. I argue for a hermeneutical conception of resistance considerate of the temporality of being-in-the-world instead of an abstract teleological universal Good. Bringing psychoanalytic practice together with critical ethnography, the chapter reasons that such a notion of resistance is indispensable for a radical epistemology that can encounter the new, global infrastructures of repressive power and violence.

This work is informed by observations during three different pilgrimage seasons—2009, 2010, and 2011. On the first occasion, as a resident of this part of India and pulled by curiosity, I had short, informal conversations with participants taking a break from their journeys on the streets and waiting to perform the libations in Pura Mahadeva. It was, however, only in 2010 that I started doing systematic research on the subject. In 2010 and then again in 2011, I interacted with participants in Hardwar preparing for their journey on the banks of the Ganga or visiting the several shrines in Hardwar and the adjacent sacred town of Rishikesh. I lingered in these spots for about three weeks each time, informally conversing with the participants about their travel plans, religious interests, and personal life circumstances or motivations leading to their interest in the pilgrimage. I also keenly observed the life around me in these busy centers of religious activity. Finally, in 2011, I participated in the journey myself: first, doing the libations in the temple of Nilkantha, atop a mountain adjacent to Rishikesh, and then walking a distance of about a hundred miles between Hardwar and Pura Mahadeva, the site of an important Śiva temple in the state of Uttar Pradesh. In these pilgrimages, I was accompanied by a friend, a male about twenty years old whom I will call K in this narrative. We took turns carrying a single kānwaṛ and joined other groups at various points.

In addition to my observations and notes from the fieldwork and the many brief conversations, this work draws on sixty in-depth interviews during summer and winter of 2010 and 2011. I conducted some of these interviews in Hardwar, but the majority took place in two locations between Hardwar and Delhi. One is a town on the Grand Trunk road, which used to be a strong manufacturing center for textiles and other goods. Most of these factories shut down by the early 1990s, and the former workers and their families now usually depend on part-time employment in retail, casual labor, and an occasional job with the government or the organized private sector. The other location was a village on the banks of the Upper Ganga Canal. The interviewees were male and female, middle class and poor, rural and urban, with different levels of education, and belonged to a variety of castes. While some were seasoned veterans who had done the pilgrimage many times (with a few bringing the water from as far as Gaumukh, the source of the river in the upper Himalayas), others were relative novices still under tutelage. I interviewed people at different times—some had just returned, others had not been on the pilgrimage for a few years, yet others were preparing. In addition, I interviewed some participants in different stages of my own pilgrimage.

Settled on the banks of the Ganga, Hardwar is a buzzing center of religious activity and commerce. Beyond the priests officiating in various types of religious ceremonies, the teeming restaurants and sweet shops, stores selling a thousand varieties of religious symbols, statues, necklaces and many trinkets, it also has countless bookstalls selling religious books, booklets, and audio/video CDs. In addition to the sacred writings of Hinduism, such as the Vedas, the epics, Upanisads, and a variety of Puranas, these stores sell a lot of popular, inexpensive booklets with eulogies of various deities and shrines and rules for different types of rituals promising solace and assistance to the distressed. The number of written texts on the Kanwar are few, but there are scores of amateurish videos featuring dances, plays, and songs on the Kanwar—some earnestly devotional, others sensually provocative—that play nonstop in stores and booths throughout the route. I spent days and weeks looking for relevant bits in this heap of information and watching many such videos several times over. The following narrative veers between interview accounts, ethnographic observations, and interpretations of such content, interspersed with a discussion of scholarly, historical, political, and moral issues at stake.

CHAPTER 1

MASTERING UNCERTAINTY
Performance and Recognition in Religion

IT WAS SURPRISING how fast the glorious mountains with their great magnitude had receded in the horizon. The festive town of Hardwar, with its baffling mix of the evocative aura of a divine space at once ancient and timeless with a noisy, caveat emptor commercial culture, also retreated from the mind as we matched paces on the unpaved street several miles outside the town. We were part of a dense procession of participants in various shades of ochre carrying kānwaṛs, with branches of the procession extending hundreds of miles in every direction, and our thoughts frequently centered on the goal and the journey ahead. K, several years younger than I, yet a veteran who had made the journey many times, advised me on the choice of footwear, luggage, and clothing. "The journey would be formidable, and the most trivial-looking choices were critical," he had warned. I must acknowledge that I was perhaps in denial of the physical challenges—since, of course, millions were accomplishing it, and I also felt confident because of my regular jogging. Nonetheless, a premonition from losing marked contests in the past committed me to explicit determination. We walked with resolve, outpacing the flow of the procession and advancing toward a group of three ahead, among the fastest and most boisterous on the trail, who were continuously yelling slogans that were answered by the chorus of fellow travelers. "We must join them," K had said; "this will keep our spirits high and make the journey much easier."

In view of my research considerations, and to provide for contingencies (I was still convalescing after a prolonged fever), we had embarked on the expected four-day journey a day in advance, targeting the libations on the fourteenth of the month of *Śrāvaṇa*, that is, on *Śivarātri*, the day of the new moon (*Amāvasyā*). Our destination was Pura Mahadeva, about ninety-five miles away, a renowned Śiva temple on the banks of the Hindon River in Meerut. It was critical that we complete the journey and arrive at the shrine in time for the libations, while ensuring that the sacred kānwaṛ was not breached in any way. The ordeal would lose all merit if the kānwaṛ was breached—for example, if the containers were desecrated, fell to the ground, the water spilled, or if we failed to make it to the destination in time. Moreover, to ensure the integrity of the practice, we had to abide by a variety of stipulations regarding how the kānwaṛ was held, carried, rested, and worshipped.

For a veteran such as K, completing the journey was not much of a cause for concern as to accomplish it with élan. At times I thought it was almost an occasion for swagger, a sport to demonstrate his will and character in a more or less competitive sociality. At other times though K would become more solemn and reflective, haunted by his family's woes. This was not unusual. Although many would be making the journey bound by explicit vows, grateful for wishes that had been fulfilled or that they sought, the action devoted to Śiva was also simultaneously a sport, a recreational activity, and an engaged enactment of serious commitments, obligations, and overwhelming anguish. Lacking any formal education, K lived an almost nomadic life—a truck helper at times, living with family or relatives at other times, or occupied with odd errands in Delhi—with scarcely a source of income. In the sociality of the Kanwar, however, as normal conventions are disrupted and where the high of the sulfā and the arch renouncer Śiva (who, although the fierce Master of the world, lives in the wild in great destitution) were valorized, K held sway. K would mentor and assist me selflessly during the journey, going through it with exemplary certitude and affability.

If the pilgrimage was a chosen and familiar arena for K, for me it was novel. I was anxious about its protocols; what began as "objective" research soon took the form of a critical, in some sense inaugural, religious performance as it materialized through many conversations, rituals, and the expectations of my relatives. This added to my resolve as I matched paces with K, and we soon caught up with the group.

Ramlal was voicing the slogans, demonstrating an extraordinary aptitude for shooting out inventive, full-throated exhortations without interruption. For the most part, he sincerely hailed Śiva as Bholā (Simpleton or Fool); His wife, Pārvatī; Gaṇeśa, their child; the Ganga; or Hardwar. At other times, he would be more inventive and mischievously play on the sexual innuendos of the conjugal relations between Pārvatī and Śiva. We replied to his calls and marched ahead at a brisk pace on the banks of the Upper Ganga Canal. Carrying the kānwaṛ, we spoke of nothing else, maintaining an attitude of devotion and immersion in the sacred. Only during a break after several miles of walking, a couple of hours later, as we had some juice and everyone (but I) smoked sulfā would we briefly acquaint ourselves with secular concerns. The others seemed to know each other well; one was teased for already needing a muscle pain-relieving spray on his knees and ankles, even as Ramlal received accolades for his stamina and ingenuity despite his illness. He was suffering from stomachaches and loose bowels because of suspected food poisoning in Hardwar. Probably in their mid-twenties, all three were casually employed as construction laborers. Ramlal, who had been making the pilgrimage for seven or eight years, told us that he had almost forgone this year's pilgrimage for lack of money. He had asked his companions to forget about him and go on their own, but his wife would not suffer his gloom. "I was sitting at home dejected," he said, "as everyone was leaving. But suddenly my wife brought a loan of two thousand rupees [about forty dollars] and asked me to get ready immediately, because my companions were waiting outside."

This was a story I had heard very often. Every other participant had a tale to tell of leaving for the journey at the last minute after having lost all hope, against all intent and plans. It was usually because of the lack of finances or pragmatic consideration of the costs it would involve. Yet a last-minute swell would send one on the journey, an impulse that would break out of normative concerns—financial restraints, calm reasoning, the many expenditures of the adventure. Suddenly, in the manner of the immediacy of a call, desire proved irresistible, although of course in correspondence with the desires of so many others, as one saw a multitude, and many in one's circle, embark on the journey. The outcome is usually interpreted as a sign of the deity's will—unless the deity invites, the journey cannot materialize, by any means; but if He calls, it will take place despite any number of obstacles.

This refrain, echoed by almost every participant, even by those who have never been able to make the journey, succinctly expresses the peculiar dialogical character of the Kanwar. More than the obvious financial constraints, this demonstrates tensions of desire and responsibility, of faith and guilt, of religion and recreation, and of a shared temporality of *uncertainty* that bonds the actor with loved ones—here, the wife. This expression of a last-minute decision, a fortuitous event read as a sign of divine will, enacts and demonstrates many of the paradoxes of the participants' religious act and their social conditions.

OF PERFORMANCES AND INTERPRETATIONS

The Kanwar pilgrimage from Hardwar is today India's largest annual religious event, with an estimated twelve million participants in 2010 and 2011.[1] At its most basic, Kanwar refers to a genre of religious performances where participants ritually carry water from a holy source in containers suspended on either side of a pole. The pilgrimage derives its name from the device, called kānwaṛ, and the water is usually carried to distant temples for libations at a *śivalinga*.[2] The source of the water is often the Ganga or rivers considered its local equivalents, and the offering is dedicated to Śiva, addressed as Bholā or Bhole Bābā (Naïve Grandfather or Father).[3] The pilgrim, accordingly, is a *bholā* and in the vocative, *bhole*! Although there is little mention of the Kanwar as an organized festival in canonical texts, the phenomenon surely existed as early as the seventeenth and eighteenth centuries when the Jesuits and English travelers report seeing Kanwar pilgrims at many points during their journeys in the North Indian plains.[4]

This book focuses on a specific Kanwar phenomenon, in which Ganga water is collected from Hardwar, the renowned religious city at the site of the river's emergence into the great plains of North India. In a few cases the water is obtained at the glacial origins of the river at Gaumukh or Gangotri.[5] Although participants carry the sacred water to locations across northwestern India, a renowned Śiva temple at Pura Mahadeva in the Meerut district of Uttar Pradesh has been a key site historically. Colonial records from the late nineteenth century report two annual religious fairs at Pura, each involving several thousand participants. One of these was in February, on the occasion of Śivarātri, and the other in July/August during the lunar month of Śrāvaṇa.[6] The numbers remained in the thousands until about three decades ago. There is not much mention of the Kanwar in official records until the 1970s, beyond colonial accounts of the festival; according to my informants, only a select few undertook the pilgrimage following specific vows. Sometime in the late 1980s or early 1990s, however, the Hardwar pilgrimage in Śrāvaṇa started to expand. During his 1990 fieldwork in Hardwar, James Lochtefeld reports estimates of a quarter million pilgrims, a number that had tripled by his second visit in 1996.[7] In 2002, the number of pilgrims was estimated at four million, growing to six million in 2004, seven million in 2009, and above twelve million in 2010 and 2011.[8]

Young adult or adolescent males of mostly poor or lower-middle-class background, from both rural and urban parts of the contiguous states of Delhi, Uttar Pradesh, Haryana, Rajasthan, Madhya Pradesh, and Punjab, make up the majority of the participants, who often walk upward of a hundred miles—in some cases, several hundred miles—following extensive rituals. Most make the journey either in flip-flops or barefoot, and many aggravate their travail by various types of ritual rigors. For example, one version called the Khaṛi (Standing) Kanwar is defined by the commitment that the kānwaṛ will remain shoulder-borne throughout the journey. In another, the Daṇḍavata (Prostrate) Kanwar, participants advance by repeatedly stretching themselves on the ground, for a predetermined part of the journey. Some find the journey easier than others, but most people either take recourse to pain-reducing medicines or are high on cannabis. In addition to the pilgrims on foot, the phenomenon includes tableaux that illustrate mythic episodes in various art forms, such as sculpture, paintings, and live performances. Regular kānwaṛs are also often decorated with red polyester or georgette strips; garlands, pictures of deities, streamers, or tridents; and replicas of snakes, parrots, and so on.

FIGURE 1.1. *A young Kanwar pilgrim*

In *The Invention of Tradition*, Eric Hobsbawm and Terence Ranger called attention to the novelty, the modern and recent roots, of many a social phenomenon presented in the halo of "tradition" and invoked as an essential, timeless legacy of antiquity, a sacred sign of enduring national and ethnic integrity.[9] The old and timeless, these scholars showed, was often but a projection motivated by social and political imperatives in the present. Although the sacred characterization of the Ganga and pilgrimages to it are at least as old as the *Mahabharata*, and the custom of carrying its water over long distances is also possibly quite old, to appreciate the character, novelty, and meanings of the contemporary Kanwar, one must see it as a radical break from "invariance" and the past, as Hobsbawm and Ranger argued.[10] While the custom may be old and the track beaten, the social conditions and consequences of the Kanwar pilgrimages that have proliferated across northern and central India since the late 1980s and today involving tens of millions of participants are thoroughly contemporary, reenacted anew in the present. In its ritual, demographic, interactional, and contextual affects, the Kanwar may be read as a dramatized presentation, a performance that intricately narrates the pulse of social conditions in contemporary India. The past here is no demiurge but only another character or figure in a drama conjured in the immediacy of the present, the *hic et nunc*.

Few in the social sciences today would dispute this apparent shift of emphasis from "tradition" to "social construction." In understanding contemporary "religion" and its putative "worldwide resurgence," scholars have time and again brought attention to the political, social, and economic changes of the twentieth century as the "modern" form of social relations became ever more pervasive and increasingly penetrated every recess of social existence throughout the world. According to a wide consensus, as noted in the Introduction, the movement toward cultural and religious solidarity springs from reaction against social change and moral confusion, or anomie.[11] These prove to be ripe conditions for the politicization of religion and, consequently, for intergroup violence. "Ethnic violence in the era of globalization," "dead certainty"; thus Arjun Appadurai provocatively sums up the conclusions of a wide body of sociological, anthropological, and social psychological research that sees religious and ethnic conflict to be a consequence of contemporary uncertainties as long-held beliefs, worldviews, and practices are faced with the prodigious circulations of this epoch. Speaking of religion, this perspective arrives at a fundamentalist, fanatic side of religious communities resisting change, communities gathering against the flow of Time, often violently, but in the end, of course, in vain. There is some truth to this narrative that at once weaves the progressive, emancipatory epistemology of the World Spirit with a structuralist conception of identity and difference and the classical sociological figure of the "collective consciousness." No less significant in contemporary religion, however, is what this account, which must be regarded as a serious case of ecological fallacy, subdues, obfuscates, turns secondary and insignificant.[12]

Focused on the collective, the abstract, the historical and conceived from a distance at global levels, this perspective glosses over the actual, lived, finite existence of ordinary social actors. This is clearly not merely a sociological problem but one inherited from philosophy and epistemology in general. It is surely an ethical issue; more important, however, it pushes under the carpet—and thereby socially annuls—an entire world of lived existence, obligations, and issues and an epistemology that could relate them.

While interreligious conflicts and the identification of the Hindu and the nation may be important to the participants' identity conscious-

ness, they are by no means the immediate forces compelling their journeys. Beyond any discomfort with a changing world and its values or the
erosion of the naïve security of custom, these were participants (often
young) preparing for a life of material and social uncertainty, performatively mastering and enacting their anxieties and obligations at delicate
points, crossroads, of their lives. The religious setting was but an arena
to perform to the unique challenges of an economically destitute yet extremely hierarchical society, as well as to address their desires and immediate social responsibilities. This should be blatantly obvious to the most
casual observer of the phenomenological environment of these religious
practices, the participants' utterances and life circumstances, the composition of the rituals, each character in the scripts (or scriptures) that the
displacement of these realities by terms such as "nationalism," "fundamentalism," and "identity"—for all their truths—appears as an elaborate
ruse. As it so often happens, the self-evident truth is the least noticed. It
is social science trapped within a web of significations of its own making;
or perhaps "it too is profoundly enmeshed in social structures" and in the
circulation of truths as part of a "discursive regime," determined as much
by "relations of meaning" as by relations of war.[13] And has there been a
greater reason for war—the real war of bombs and drones and murderous
threats of making the sand "glow in the night," for example—in the last
few decades than the war of reason against the fanaticism of religion?[14]
But is not the search for deeper meanings, latent functions that are the
true motivations behind the smokescreen, the feints of manifest content,
the very raison d'être of the social sciences? Maybe so. Such functional-
ism, however, strays far from the principles and concerns of Freudian
psychoanalysis on which it may be modeled. For the last thing one may
accuse the "talking cure" of is ignoring the so many ways in which the
subject speaks.

Clearly, one objection that may be raised against my inferences is the
peculiar nature of pilgrimage as a religious phenomenon. However, as is
so often true, inverting the problem is more helpful. Why is pilgrimage so
marginal in the sociology of religion literature?[15] This literature has been
surprisingly aloof to the insightful observations on religion and social
issues in much of the excellent ethnographic work on pilgrimages world-

wide.[16] Perhaps an issue of scale is involved. Theoretical formulations on a global scale, on issues such as religion and globalization, have to focus on abstract formulations or on large global events, such as terrorism or ethnic violence. That, however, implies a selection bias. Division of labor and expertise among academic disciplines is another important factor. Whereas scholars in religious studies and anthropologists do detailed ethnographic work on popular religious practice, including pilgrimages in various societies, the broader discourse on religion and globalization is defined by political scientists and sociologists. More basically, however, I believe such neglect of pilgrimages reflects the continuing Kantian, Cartesian, cognitive biases of Western thought—embodied ritual practice has no place in theoretical discussions.[17] Human suffering, the pathos of common existence, is too base a subject to feature in "rational" analyses of religion and globalization. This is precisely my point of departure. Thus, I find that pilgrimage is an ideal site to deliberate on the social and subjective significance of contemporary religion. In India, of course, pilgrimage has long been a, if not *the*, predominant form of popular religious practice.[18] The Kanwar is then an exemplary case for studying the growing attraction of religious practices.

To better appreciate these findings, I suggest we begin by returning to Max Weber's profound observations on the relationship between moral existence, religion, and the economy.[19] Weber's *Religion of India* is a tour de force, awe inspiring for the insightful empathy with which it brings alive the social, economic, and moral paradoxes of different social groups thousands of years ago. Yet one cannot gloss over issues with some of Weber's more prominent comparative inferences. He not only sees Hinduism as an otherworldly religion that encourages a flight from the world, but for him mass religiosity anywhere could only be irrational and magically oriented.[20] From this perspective, only virtuoso religion can offer a rational ethic of social life. My findings suggest the contrary. As opposed to the ideologically charged harangue of institutional leaders representing "high" Hinduism, my research demonstrates a strong performative rationality to popular religious practice in the Kanwar. Religious practice critically mediates in the complex play of social relations here—on economic, political, moral, and sexual dimensions. Notwithstanding these issues, Weber's careful attention to the subjective import of interactions between religion and the economy has been instructive for this study. Instead of closeting these practices into a subdiscipline such as "pilgrimage studies" or "sociology of religion"—that is, an institutionally recognized "social fact"—one must assume the continuities of religion, morality, economy, social status, and politics. This much we owe to Weber's phenomenological sociology.

In presenting my ethnographic observations, I was faced with a number of alternatives. I have already mentioned that I found the "inner-worldly" and "other-worldly" distinction rather ineffective. Somewhat contradicting his multidimensional perspective, Weber also insists that religion be treated as a "distinct realm of social life," which countered my findings.[21] Continuing with classical sociology, some may be inclined to posit anomie as a natural explanation—particularly in view of the spate of social changes in India in recent decades. This may seem all the more pertinent since Émile Durkheim's ideas of collective representation and social structure have been central to some long and burning debates on Indian society and culture.[22] Moreover, as I mentioned earlier, associated notions of cultural and religious identity are frequently cited in the literature to explain the surge in religious practices, in India as well as globally.[23] In pilgrimage studies, Victor and Edith Turner's pioneering study of Christian pilgrimages saw pilgrimage as a departure from a differentiated, hierarchical social structure into a fluid, communitarian state. Withstanding many a critique, this exposition continues to be instructive.[24] However, there is also evidence to support John Eade and Michael Sallnow's contrasting thesis that emphasizes contestation in pilgrimages.[25]

Yet my findings were incongruous with many of these paradigms' propositions. My observations suggest that even though true, the lack of psychological or institutional integration into a changing, amorphous moral order, as implied by the notion of anomie, is an insufficient explanation. Social and moral obligations, lack of economic opportunities, anxieties about the future, sexual anxieties, and social hierarchy were far more important variables than cognitive discomfiture.[26] Moreover, this concept is somewhat of a dead end and does not facilitate ethnographic production. Likewise, my ethnographic data presented little evidence to call these actors "religious nationalists," "fundamentalists," or "reactionaries"; such categories scarcely speak to their concerns and the textual density of the narratives and practices here. And where the Turners provided an evocative, groundbreaking analysis of Christian pilgrimages, formal notions such as "communitas" and "anti-structure" did not offer sufficient analytical purchase. Instead, I found that the idiom of "performance," informed by a range of scholarly and cultural traditions—including, most certainly, Hinduism—allowed a much more culturally and personally meaningful, and I would argue, sociologically substantive representation. Of course, the theater analogy pervades social scientific fields. In sociology, dramaturgy has been the primary resource for the symbolic interactionist tradition. Thus, Erving Goffman's many studies of the staged quality of social interaction, preceded by the foundational studies on the social constitution of the self by Charles Cooley, George Herbert Mead, and Herbert Blumer, have had a defining influence on the evolution of the discipline.[27] Judith Butler's celebrated characterization of gender as a stylized repetition of bodily gestures and actions gave this formulation yet another critical edge.[28] On other shores, anthropologists such as Victor Turner and Clifford Geertz were attracted to the symbolic significance of rituals and the dramatic manner in which they played out structural facets of non-Western societies, their cultural beliefs and social divisions.[29] All these studies are informed by enduring literary, cultural, and metaphysical traditions and developments in twentieth-century philosophical and psychological theories. If anything, this scholarship has systematized dramaturgical vocabulary and observations to produce formal tools for social scientific analysis.

Such systematization of dramaturgical analogy has contributed substantially to the advancement and expansion of modern social scientific research. However, my findings called for a return to the primary metaphor. I found it necessary to directly call on the ambivalence, play, and existential resonances of "performance." More specifically, the participants are self-conscious of their actions, and existence, as a game, a drama, *līlā* (play). This is conditioned by the extraordinary status of this notion in Indian texts and popular culture. Thus, for example, one participant accompanying us to Nilkantha, a temple complex at the top of a mountain close to Rishikesh, remarks wondrously on the ritual austerities of hordes of fellow pilgrims: "All this is *māyā* of the Ganga!" The notion of *māyā*, at once phenomenon, play, effect, creation, gift, wonder, and illusion, figures very commonly in everyday discourse in India.[30] This highly ambivalent notion conceptualizes existence as play, where boundaries separating the real and illusory, truth and falsehood, are continuously shifting and altogether permeable. This understanding of life and social obligations as transitory, "a game, a dream, a sport, a drama," commonly mediates encounters with everyday social reality.[31] Thus, the great Vedantic philosopher Śaṃkara reasons in his commentary on the *Māndukya Upaniṣad*: "For, evolution in any sense (other than illusion) is not known to us, and is superfluous even if demonstrated."[32] At the same time, however, one must not regard Indian popular culture as exceptional. Performance, and therefore its apperception, is a transhistorical and transcultural fact of human life and consciousness.

In the following ethnography, the word "performance" is used more to express participants' own existential relation with the transience and arbitrariness of their life and social circumstances than to draw objective and critical attention to the dramatic or the institutionalized quality of their social interactions. I speak of performance not in a cognitive frame to emphasize the staged nature of human action but in an existential and materialist register, as the fact, the struggle, and lived anxiety of being-in-the-world. Moreover, "performance" here is paired with "recognition." On this point, I think it is important to evoke some of the philosophical issues involved.

The term "recognition" has appropriately been central to modern philosophy. Thus, in Georg Wilhelm Friedrich Hegel's seminal illustrations in the *Phenomenology of Spirit*, it is the dynamics of the encounter with the other, the battle for recognition, that leads to the development of self-consciousness.[33] This dialectic of recognition simultaneously shapes consciousness and constructs the human as a working and therefore historical being. However, if in the Hegelian project, recognition is conceived in the idiom of mastery—whether over the object or the other consciousness—and work is recognized only for its historical value in a kind of universal, endless temporality, I would like to draw attention here to a

different temporality—one that Martin Heidegger illustrated: The finite temporality of being-in-the-world, of concerned human existence
alongside others.[34] Instead of conceiving time as infinite in the form of
world history, this perspective emphasizes the finite life of human beings
who witness death all around and are conscious that one's time and the
other's time—insofar as it may be distinguishable—is always at risk. "As
soon as . . . [one] comes to life . . . [one] is at once old enough to die."[35]
Heidegger's radical intervention (following from Friedrich Nietzsche and
Søren Kierkegaard), which relied as much on Eastern philosophies as
on ancient Greek society, foregrounded the lived paradoxes of ordinary
human existence, perhaps for the first time in Western philosophy.[36] Self-
consciousness here is social and existential; being-in-the-world is also
being-with-one-another. Sociological theory and anthropological studies
have further demonstrated the many dimensions of social recognition.

It is this phenomenology of being-in-the-world and being with and
responding to one another, and to social expectations, that my use of
the terms "performance" and "recognition" should evoke. I believe such
a phenomenological orientation also integrates Weber's primary interest
in *verstehen*, participants' own perception of the significance of their actions; after all, in the form of Nietzsche, a great factor connects Weber
with Heidegger.

Of course, "performance" as a figure of achievement and ability, de-
serving of appropriate rewards and recognition, is a dominant theme in
competitive economic life. In recent decades, this liberal capitalist ideology has been indeed imposing itself and increasingly setting the terms
for social relations in India, much as it has been doing throughout the
world.[37] The disembedded market economy increasingly clothed in neoliberal ideological constructs of human capital and the finality of market-
based discursive constructs today asserts itself as the dominant power and
idiom governing social relations and our economic, cultural, and political
futures.[38] The market economy imposes itself with near absolute power
over the whole gamut of social relations, even as *exclusivity* is the primary
mechanism of incorporation. Yet the structure of the economy remains
primarily informal, with widespread poverty and more than 90 percent of
workers employed informally.[39] In India's deeply hierarchical and oppres-

sive society, such experience of economic, and thereby social, exclusion one cannot fail to register, and yet as thoroughly deny insofar as one must keep working with it (for there is no exit).

This motivates an exploration of alternative fields to express one's desires, talents, and obligations; to perform social existence; and to be recognized as a self. In the achievements of the Kanwar, despite the pain and hardships, in the common competitive banter and wagers, in the anxious expressions of self-worth, the ethnographer finds a repetition of messages exchanged with a dominant neoliberal ethos. It is a repetition of the subject of the economy, its expectations and directives, in an alternative and definite field. For adolescents and young adults set to encounter the full might and overbearing structure of the "real field" of the exclusive economy, these are obviously anxious steps that call for compulsive practice, "working through," or perhaps "walking through."[40] Religious practice: a special arena with conditions conducive to repeating, performing, and expressing the concerns, associations, and anxieties repressed by the dominant collective conscience.[41]

This book demonstrates that the Kanwar performances enact the concerns as much as the dearth of work; they provide alternative works and other means of recognition. Much as social existence in general requires performance, whether to obtain rewards, meet social roles, enact relations, or to merely survive, religious practice here is a continuation of performances that simultaneously complement, compensate for, challenge, and play with mundane social life. To draw again on a popular cultural idiom, religious practice here operates as another *karma-bhūmi* (field of action or performance).[42] One is as likely to see a repetition of the imperatives of the social order as its disavowal; as often the continuities of normal social cleavages as the production of new communities; as clearly the subject's sufferance of the symbolic order as a subject finding her *jouissance* in the belly of this order. In short, the social conditions and existential struggles of the participants play out radically in these performances before (of/after) the deities. Moving conceptual concerns aside, I now move on to the ethnography. The following narrative begins with events and observations during the journey and progressively interweaves reports from the interviews. K is my companion and guide.

A STEADY PERFORMANCE

It is the morning of the third day of our journey. We spent the night on the median of a highway, the kānwaṛ hanging by a signboard next to us. I had kept waking up to ensure the kānwaṛ was safe; I also knew K went to sleep very late. But I thought he had been uncharacteristically lethargic this morning. By the time we started, it was already past ten o'clock. At this time, most pilgrims would have covered a significant leg of their journey for the day and would be preparing to rest before it got too hot. I realized that K had been consciously procrastinating so that a group of his friends, several miles behind, could catch up with us. I acquiesced to waiting; however, after two hours, when I realized they were making a stopover much before they reached us, I could see the whole day vanishing and reasoned with K that we leave, especially since they were to head on a separate route from the very junction where we waited. K had been adamant, an attitude I found surprising at that time. Only later would it occur to me that those seasoned pilgrims were well equipped with cannabis, which K had been starved for in my company. Submitting to my perseverance, however, K lifted the kānwaṛ and commented in obvious annoyance, "Let us see, brother, how much you will walk!" I felt the slight but was relieved to be back on track.

With his brisk pace, K soon disappeared with the kānwaṛ as I trudged in the background carrying our belongings. From the town of Muzaffarnagar, the route merged into the wide national highway, which had been cleared for the pilgrims, save some local traffic on one side of the median. Although a sizable portion of pilgrims had separated from Muzaffarnagar, we were with the main stream headed toward Delhi. Giant blisters covered the sole of my left foot—watery pockets underneath the skin squished and squashed at every step. Besides, my ankles were swollen, knees almost locked, with intermittent shooting pain. Surviving on ibuprofen, I trudged along while keeping an eye out for K and our kānwaṛ. The afternoon sun was at its worst, burning as much through the sky as off the tarred surface beneath. Few pilgrims remained on the road; most had found shelter, whether in the many makeshift roadside restaurants, in the transit camps, or under the trees. "Bhole, where will you be doing the libations?" I asked a group of young men. "In Delhi," they replied. Walking on, I joined a middle-aged man, a skilled construction worker (*mistri*) by profession. I inquired how long he had been on the road. "I left Hardwar on the afternoon of the twenty-fourth," he replied (the same day we did). The conversation continued:

> There were several younger people with me; they left the day after. They were curious why I was leaving so early. I told them, "You will all be on sulfā . . . you will take long breaks, and then you will gallop like horses. I don't do that; I prefer going at a steady pace." These people bring the kānwaṛ, and then they limp around for weeks in all kinds of gait. I am back to work the next day, without a sign. Then they are shocked at my endurance. I walk at a steady pace—neither too slow, nor fast!

Responding to another of my queries about his wishes from the pilgrimage, he said, "No, I didn't ask for anything . . . except for peace and happiness in the family." He reminded me of another man of the same age group I had known last year—also a skilled construction worker. I had hired him from the bus stand in the town for a renovation job at my parents' house. The bus stand was a central place where workers gathered every morning. Small construction work generally involves a mistri and one or two unskilled or semiskilled assistants (*beldār*, or shoveler); the going rate for the mistri was four to five dollars per day, and for the beldār, two to three dollars per day. A client proceeding to the station would inevitably be surrounded, hustled by workers speaking over one another, offering their services. Exhorting and occasionally pulling the person in their direction, they point to one or the other of the mistris sitting on a roadside prop—a bicycle and a small tool bag beside him— to supervise the work. The mistri, usually an older person, may accost the client, but more often, protective of his status, he looks with hope but waits patiently to be approached. The crowd usually thins out before noon, and those unable to find a job begin to return home disappointed, hoping for better luck the next day. A desperate few linger around in the afternoon hoping for a stray opportunity.

An amiable, even-tempered man and able and trustworthy worker, the mistri worked with us for several days before informing us one evening that he would be leaving for the Kanwar. "I will stop by after the Kanwar [in a week's time]," he told me. "I will complete the job, if you should still need me." We had about a fortnight's work left, but he was aware that since I was rapidly running out of vacation time, I could not wait for his return. If there was any minor loss of opportunity here, he portrayed being unaffected by it; like all the previous years he had been bringing the kānwar, this was a preordained choice. Although without the opportunity of an extended interview I knew little of the personal histories of either worker, the Kanwar here offered a mandatory departure from the chores, struggles, banality, temptations, and humiliations of everyday life. It was a sovereign time in the unmediated proximity of the Absolute.[43] One of my older respondents expressed this imperative explicitly. A frail but sprightly man in his sixties, he was part of a large, joint family (which included his children and grandchildren) and worked as a security guard at a hostel in a nearby town, about six miles from his residence, to and from which he cycled in perilous highway traffic every day. "I tell them in no uncertain words," he said, referring to his family, "I will bring you every penny from eleven months of earnings, but one month, ah! will always belong to Bhole Nāth."

In such cases, the pilgrimage may be seen partly as a time—a place, occasion, and medium—to delimit, and to rejuvenate from, an existentially overwhelming, distressing, almost inhuman (or, perhaps, all too human) life of labor and suffering. For these men of a mature age, it helped reaffirm faith in long-held values and, in the context of a phenomenal surfeit of commodities, images, and expectations, in the goodness of a temperate life. Traces of the paradoxical social significance of the pilgrimage of these veterans may be found in its resonances, at an earlier life stage, in the religiosity of Kamarpal—where the contradictions are less reconciled or more animated.

ŚIVA AND THE HIERARCHICAL SOCIETY

We met Kamarpal late in the journey at our final overnight stopover, a few miles from Pura Mahadeva. The next day, the thirteenth of the lunar month of Śrāvaṇa, would be the first day of libations, when the water would be ceremonially poured over the śivalinga—a cylindrical rock as phallic symbol, emblematic of Śiva. We had decided to do the libations in

Pura on the thirteenth, since we were already close. Besides, the prospect of libations in the Pura temple on the fourteenth was daunting. There would be enormous crowds with multiple queues extending over a mile, and stampedelike situations had been frequent in the past, despite hundreds of police officers engaged in crowd control and management. Following a common practice, we would do the libations of the fourteenth at a neighborhood temple in our town.

For the overnight layover, we laid our plastic sheets in the open inside the compound of a local power station, which was relatively secluded from the turmoil and loud music on the street. In addition to the block of electricity pillars and the office building, the compound included dozens of deserted houses with cracked roofs and shrubs sprouting out of their splintered walls. This was a fate that these houses, constructed for government employees, shared with many public housing projects throughout the countryside. Although the small inhabited pocket of the compound had been cleaned, the wild growth in the vast deserted stretch seemed to have proliferated in the monsoons. As we eased onto the ground, frogs started to leap over us. K did not like the sign: "Next, it will be a snake," he said. He climbed onto one of the dilapidated houses to check the terrace but did not find it encouraging. Instead, we decided to eventually move to a couple of raised concrete platforms nearby. I was still lying on the ground when a group of pilgrims spread their plastic sheets next to us. "These people call me their guru," Kamarpal, a medium-built, personable man in his early thirties introduced himself.

There were four or five other men in the group, all much younger than Kamarpal. "If I am to be the guru, I tell them," he said, "there will be no bhāng or sulfā on the way. . . . We will do the libations at Pura on the thirteenth, followed by the village temple on the fourteenth." As the conversation continued, Kamarpal would tell me, "I have always been a devotee of Bhole Nath. I am a mistri . . . married, have two children—a girl and a boy. God has gifted my hands with a skill; with these hands I can support my family," he said, trying to communicate an element of labor's pride. Kamarpal's account showed an effort at self-motivation and a desire to maintain moral courage and personal integrity amid unfavorable conditions. "One of my brothers is a police inspector; another is an insurance officer. My father was also a government servant. I am the youngest—the only black sheep in the family!" he said, with a smile in expectation of my solidarity. "I tried everywhere but have not been able to find a proper job. I will get one though; my *guruji* says, 'You will have success eventually; only it will be late coming—there is a lot of struggle to your life.'" Kamarpal's guru is a retired bank manager in Delhi who was recommended to him several years ago.

> I had told the referee, the guru must be a devotee of Bhole Nath. Initially, I was wary, since the guruji worshipped Gorakhnath. But he pacified my doubts by informing me that Gorakhnath was Śiva's avatar. He is a very accomplished person; he has made a temple in Delhi . . . and has supernatural powers. It was only last year that my brother was hospitalized for a long time because of a serious issue. . . . We were all very worried. I went to my guruji in Delhi to seek his help. He said, "Don't worry! He will be well by tomorrow." My brother recovered miraculously over the next few days.

Kamarpal's family members do not take kindly to his faith. "My brothers and father are inimical to my faith in Bhole Bābā. They rebuke me for it regularly: 'So, the Bābā will deliver you?' they say [derisively]." Conscious of the paradoxes here, Kamarpal continued, with an ironic smile, "Even this time, when I was leaving for the Kanwar, my father stepped up to me, ready to hit—he hurled the choicest abuses. He abused Bhole Bābā too."

Kamarpal's story demonstrates the struggles of existence in a poor, deeply hierarchical society. On one side is a hegemonic social order defined by an accumulative, this-worldly rationality, evident in the dominant bureaucratic or capitalist ethic in the secular sphere as well as in the nineteenth-century Hindu reformist movement, the Arya Samaj. Aimed at a revival of a "rational" and "authentic" ancient Vedic Hinduism in light of the colonial encounters with European monotheism, this movement has left a particularly strong impression in this region.[44] Although I did not find an opportunity to verify it with Kamarpal, it was quite likely that his family was influenced by Arya Samaj.[45] On the other side is the case of a person injured by this dominant ethic and his recourse to Bhole Bābā, the generous One, and the pilgrimage to seek assistance in the dominant order and find a different, absolute imaginary order as well as a social niche. Even as he struggles against the symbolic violence of a dominant social ethic, Kamarpal continues to perform and aspire to roles in the dominant order. Here, he seems to be in line with a precept commonly reiterated in North India: "You must not relinquish your own responsibility; God will help only those who are willing to help themselves."

Kamarpal's predicament exemplifies Jacques Lacan's brilliant figuration of the manner in which the symbolic, the imaginary, and the Real constitute, and are involved in, one another—like a Borromean knot. "The trinity . . . —one and three in a single stroke."[46] If the symbolic here is the dominant ideological order (a rationality represented through the father, the brothers, and the market), and the imaginary is the character and mythology of Śiva as well as the ego-ideal, the guru (the bank manager, a person accomplished both in the symbolic and the imaginary order, an aspect that also translates into Kamarpal's own ideal ego as a guru to others), the Real is the traumatic, perhaps incessant encounter of these forces in Kamarpal's particular historicity, which has been motivating the more than a dozen pilgrimages he has made as well as the everyday experience of living. In the Lacanian schema, the moments of the pilgrimage, the investment in Bhole Bābā and the pilgrimage rituals, have a partly hysterical structure.[47] It is the split, barred subject ($) impelled by a traumatic core, the *objet a* approaching the subject's signifier (S1) in the symbolic system, by trying to expel dominant ideological formations (S2) as far as possible, for a brief yet compulsive period of time, perhaps for the time of the pilgrimage or the time when he looked at his skilled hands with apparent pride.[48]

$$\frac{\$}{a} \longrightarrow \frac{S_1}{S_2}$$

FIGURE 1.2. *The hysteric's discourse*

CONCERNS WORLDLY AND OTHER-WORLDLY

While Weberian ideal types have habituated many of us to think in stereotypical ways, especially concerning the putative "flight from the world"
character of Eastern religions—Hinduism being often cited—it would
be a misperception to think of the Kanwar pilgrim's departure in such a
manner. This is not a flight from the world; rather, it addresses the world.
It engages the world, gets a purchase on it, precisely by transcending it.
The pilgrimage is a social intervention. It is an alternative medium of existence, a possibility or search for sovereign subsistence.[49] It operated as another field for enacting one's being human, being alive, or being someone
in the context of an alienating, dehumanizing symbolic order. The pilgrimage, I found, intervenes in the social order through the very figures
and moments of transcendence. It provides a field for the participants
to address their desires and immediate social responsibilities and rise to
the unique challenges of an economically destitute yet very hierarchical
society increasingly dominated by a liberal capitalist social logic. This is
an open field, one without any gated entries or institutional constraints,
yet a challenging and productive site to practice and prove one's resolve,
talents, and good faith.

In his study of Protestantism, Weber found that the Protestant religious ethic and practice conditioned the subjective orientation to work.
It was in work and through evaluating each other in terms of capital accumulation and behavioral propriety that the Protestants morally and socially engaged themselves in the world. Today, the ethic and accumulation
of capital are, of course, the only game in town. In a global social order
increasingly governed by neoliberal ideology, capitalist economic institutions have become the only regular, legitimate option for "work" and practically the only socially legible text to demonstrate one's ability and moral
sincerity. As Pierre Bourdieu pointed out in a compelling analogy with
the imposing power of the psychiatric discourse in the mental asylum, the
neoliberal discourse has all the features of Goffman's "strong discourse."
This is "a type [of discourse] which is almost impossible to combat and
whose 'realism' is difficult to question because . . . it represents the coor-
dinated actions of all the forces which count, all forces which combine in
giving reality the shape it has."[50] In addition to its imposing presence and

authority, this remains an exclusive game, with only a selected, disciplined few allowed in. If in the previous interaction with Kamarpal, one witnesses a relatively tense relationship between the field of the pilgrimage and the social order, in other cases—despite the differences—this interaction may be far more complementary.

"It was more than twenty years ago, still a teenager, that I first went for the pilgrimage. Ever since, I eagerly wait for this time of the year. . . . I anyway like walking. I walk a lot. . . . That is how I spend my time. I can walk the whole day." Shyam thus narrated his fondness for the Kanwar. "I had been worshipping Bhole Bābā since childhood and then happened to go for the Kanwar. . . . I entered the game early," he concluded with a flourish. After all these years of Kanwars from Hardwar, the previous year he found a companion to go up to Gaumukh, the glacial source of the river 160 miles upstream from Hardwar, at the roof of the Himalayas. "The harder you work, the more you have to gain. . . . I can't think of a pilgrimage merely from Hardwar anymore; it has to be Gaumukh." Repetitively and delightfully describing the astonishing experience of an avalanche that almost wiped them out at the river source, he continued:

> The revered Ganga showed us her terrific form. . . . Huge boulders and massive snow surged out of nowhere at an unimaginable speed. The river took away one of our bags; we barely escaped. . . . When we told others of this near-death experience, they would say, "But you went there to see the Ganga's true form, didn't you? That's what She showed you then." . . . They were right!

Shyam has a job that pays for his labor, a paltry one hundred dollars a month. For Shyam, who comes from a Brahmin family, the priestly caste, religious practice is a normative activity. Although members of his family insist that he limit his religious observances to home, the pilgrimage is far too tempting for him to follow their advice. In the labor and rewards of the pilgrimage, the phenomenal excesses of this journey, its repetitions and terrific aspects alike of Śiva and the Ganga, Shyam seems to find his jouissance. It is as much a negation of the flatness of everyday life as it is a continuation, accentuation of the symptom, the walking, which is his peculiar way of traversing the world. What remains a symptom yearlong transforms into the central performance during the pilgrimage.

If for Shyam, however, part of the power and effect of the Kanwar has been its recurring quality, for his partner in this audacious journey involving 260 miles of walking, a majority of it in the mountains, it was a first pilgrimage. Yaspal had been a volunteer caretaker of the small village temple for many years before he quit after "some resentful villagers" cast aspersions on his integrity. The responsibility of receiving returning pilgrims at the temple and attending to their ritual and commensal requirements had prevented Yaspal from going on the pilgrimage all these years. On this inaugural journey, he collaborated with Shyam—a veteran, earnest pilgrim—on a demanding encounter with the great goddess at the source. "The Ganga has always held a special attraction for me; after all, in our lands, She alone is manifest." But there was a pensive touch to Yaspal's description of his religious attitude: "The temple duties meant a lot to me. I was not pleased with this loss of responsibility. That was how I contemplated spending my life . . . in the service of the temple and its deities. I had refused marriage and family life as well; however, when my married, younger brother died a few years ago, my parents coerced me into marriage."

Only in passing would Yaspal mention the avalanche in Gaumukh, although he had lost his bag and money to it. Instead, the protracted time with the goddess and its mighty phenomenal presence were an avenue for solace after the long association with the small, peaceable village temple. A person with a conspicuously contemplative aspect, Yaspal told me several stories of his experiences tending to the temple idols and the visitations of the deities in his dreams. "Only the saints," he continued, "can experience the spirituality of the world, the true phenomenal effect of existence, in their daily living; most of us only get glimpses of it in our sleep."[51]

OF STAKES

Not all participants, however, subsist in the modesty we find in the cases just described. In other instances, the correspondence between the normative attitudes of the pilgrimage and the dominant social order can be much more abrupt and their differences, even when they supplement one another, much more explicit. A majority of Kanwar pilgrims are young men taking their first steps into adulthood. In highly challenging and uncertain economic conditions, amid a mad rush of young men likewise vying, where the prospects of stable and respectable employment or life course are faint and illusive, these are daunting steps. This anxiety-laden experience is further intensified by expectations and desires provoked by the continuous spectral presence of a global array of aspirations and commodities, which are expertly coded to tantalize and provoke.[52]

For many then, the demands and joys of the pilgrimage provide a voluntary and accessible field of performance. At the same time, it is the field of the Absolute, and although families like Kamarpal's are not uncommon, the pilgrims are usually assured that their labor and good faith will be recognized by their dear ones. Here, recognition from the family is particularly crucial, since it is from the claims and expectations of the family that the most emotionally swaying and insistent—at times, nagging—demands emerge.

A couple of miles before the power station, we decided to take a break at a tube well in the middle of sugarcane and paddy fields. Taking my blistered, swollen feet out of ill-fitting shoes and saggy socks, I limped into the water pool. After a day of drudgery in muggy weather, the pleasure of sinking into a stream of refreshing water rivaled, and multiplied, the relief of being close to the end of the journey. I had been relishing the water for a while, with K taking time off in the sugarcane fields, when a group of slender young men—the oldest of them perhaps no more than eighteen or nineteen—arrived at our station. Drinking off the water spout, they wished to enter the pool. The eldest got into a brief conversation with me, as another group of adult men sat down on a log lying by the adjacent room. He continued the conversation, telling me how today they had walked from the highway junction, about twenty-five miles away, with barely a break. In the flow of this moment of pride he could not resist a wager: "No offense to the Bābā's grace, bhole, but I am ready to bet that none in this procession of pilgrims could beat us. I believe we could outpace anyone to the temple." Acknowledging my own battered condition—which may have partly provoked the hubris—I nevertheless enjoyed persisting with the game. "But," I said, "my brother might be willing to take a dare." As he inquired of his whereabouts, I pointed to K, who was just stepping out of the sugarcane bushes and must have appeared a worthy rival.

When K drew close, I informed him of the wager. "What is at stake?" K asked him with a straight face. Now dismissive of the challenge, he replied, "Nothing, bhole . . . only, may whoever makes it first also offer their libations first." K was unimpressed. The situation turned normal; after a brief lapse into mirth, the solemnness of the occasion dawned. One of the pilgrims who had joined later had overheard the claim. Nursing two large blisters on one of his toes, he remarked to his colleagues, "The bholās there claim none can beat them to the temple." The others nodded somewhat unapprovingly but seemed to take it in good humor. "This is my third pilgrimage," he continued; "I always get these blisters. . . . They are always at the same spot." Later, K would boast to me privately regarding the wager, "I'd have turned him into a whirling gig, but what is the point of damaging one's body."

Referring to their own behavioral lapses, two brothers I interviewed— young men working in the liquor business—said, "Sometimes, you have a dream or an event that reminds you of an oversight, of a misconduct. . . . You fold your hands and ask for Bhole's forgiveness and try to be careful thereafter." The competitive pulse and an anxiety of social performance in the middle of uncertain and arbitrary conditions registered in their religious experiences as well. With an uncle, whom they idolized as a brilliant and astute person, who had successfully negotiated the challenges of liquor retail despite being barely literate, the two brothers had become part of a real estate and liquor retail enterprise. Both were very religious; they had both made the pilgrimage multiple times and were ardent devotees of Sāi Bābā. This renowned mystic of the nineteenth century with his shrine in Shirdi (Maharashtra) has an extensive following throughout the country. The two brothers thus described their faith in Śiva and Sāi Bābā and their religious experiences:

> The pilgrimage is a lot of joy. It is much fun and pleasure. . . . One gets immersed in the flavor of Bhole. We never had bhāng ourselves, though some of our friends did. . . . No alcohol, of course, but bhāng is Bhole's ritual gift. [One recites: bhāng and datura on his body; his neck adorned with snakes; day in and day out; Bholā drinks cups of bhāng.] . . . Bhole Bābā has always granted us everything we asked. . . . If you ask with true faith, Bābā will

certainly grant it. . . . Of course, God will not come to you to claim that He fulfilled your desire. It is for man to understand that.

For much of our conversation, the brothers spoke in tandem, in a rapid, agitated tempo projecting on the deities an often impetuous, transferential relationship. On one occasion, for example, the younger one had a dream:

> It was about eight o'clock in the evening, and I had slipped into slumber, when I had a dream. . . . I saw Sāi Bābā standing there, he as if shook my legs to wake me up. "You had promised to visit Shirdi, after the contract was announced . . . but you did not come." [now speaking over one another] We had promised to visit Shirdi, after the contract . . . once we were free. The very next day, immediately, we took the train to Shirdi. . . . No seats were available . . . but we sat on the floor and later paid the ticket collector five times the fare to procure seats.

Sāi Bābā is well known for the miraculous assistance he provides to his devotees. For the brothers craving success in social conditions where much is left to chance and at an age with a lot at stake, where the gap between success and failure is as yawning as it is fickle and arbitrary, and where everything depends on a little luck, a little help—a hardly recognizable divine hand, so to speak—this reflected a kind of anxious resort to supernatural assistance. And although the brothers appeared to be workaholics, single-mindedly pursuing success under anomic circumstances, they seemed to transfer their anxieties to the deities.

During the pilgrimage, in general, I found that a competitive banter was common when the pilgrims rested, after hanging their kānwaṛs aside, a conversation I could not conceive taking place when they were carrying the kānwaṛ on their shoulders. Thus, on the first day when a pilgrim we met en route said he would be doing the libations two hundred miles away in Vrindavan, my colleagues—who were proud of their strides—later privately expressed their incredulity, questioning how he could possibly make it with his "sluggish pace." In fact, many of my respondents portrayed a sense of achievement in their ability to make the journey in a short time. Amma, an elderly woman I interviewed, a veteran who had mentored several younger women on the pilgrimage, took pride in her claims of making the journey in a short time but for the encumbrance of the novices. She rarely shied of boasting of her leadership skills, for example, in breaking through police cordons to facilitate shorter and preferred routes for pilgrims—who followed her cheering—or her ascetic faith and endurance in avoiding any indulgence during the pilgrimage and living merely on chai and homemade sweets she would carry. But Amma too had her rivals.

"That woman had a rough time this year; she was bedridden for almost two weeks," Shamli told us dismissively. Shamli was a young and vivacious married woman who lived close to the one-bedroom worker's quarter in which Amma lived with her son's family. Shamli herself lived with her family in a tiny shack, badly flooded by rainwater this monsoon, in a slum called the Harijan Basti, where most residents belonged to the "untouchable" community, traditionally and metonymically identified with sanitation work. Shamli's family, as she told us, was a Brahmin family. She worked as a full-time maid at a middle-class house, while her husband—an alcoholic whom she had finally been able to persuade into abstinence after many years of effort—usually scoured for casual, unskilled work. Shamli had been going for the pilgrimage for eight or nine years with her friends; this year, however, she undertook the Khaṛi Kanwar, a demanding version of the pilgrimage, defined by the rule that the kānwaṛ will not rest; the person carrying the kānwaṛ must remain upright through the length of the journey. Thus, the brief relief the pilgrim could obtain would be from companions willing to stand with the kānwaṛ while she rested.

> Several years ago, my daughter's leg was struck by polio. She had a prolonged fever, and she came out of it with one of her legs become thin as a twig. I kept her in the private hospital for fifteen days, but to no advantage. The doctors were helpless. I beseeched Bābā to heal my daughter . . . promising she will bring him a Khaṛi Kanwar. We made the journey this year; this is the first time I was confident she would be able to pull it off. . . . She is, of course, very young, so I carried the kānwaṛ most of the way. Her brother helped me a lot; he would stand with the kānwaṛ for hours, allowing me a nap. The father, however, did not; . . . he never missed his sleep. He had tried hard to dissuade me, saying it would be too strenuous, but I remained firm and told

him, "I will do it; why are you bothered?" I was back to work the day after the pilgrimage. I will be doing another pilgrimage next year to make a pair.

In addition to the annual Kanwar pilgrimages, Shamli regularly visits a famous temple of Bābā Mohan Ram in Bhiwadi (Rajasthan), about seventy-five miles from her town. She lights an oil lamp there on the second day of every lunar month as part of the rituals. ("The journey is inexpensive; to and fro, it only costs two dollars by train.") One of the major references of Shamli's religious practice—one she shares with several of her friends and perhaps a certain social class in general—is a delinquent, alcoholic partner. This situation not only leaves the burden of family maintenance completely on the woman but also suppresses any hope of a better future. Yet, amid the pain and drudgery of life, the promise of the future is the primary (perhaps the only) viable source of inspiration. "I have been praying to Mohan Bābā for a better house and requesting that the kids' father abstain from alcohol and be more responsible. He used to be an alcoholic . . . but is now reformed." The future here is the solace of the present.

   The priority of the future in this experience of time is in concert with existentialist phenomenology, where temporality is figured in the unity of a future that constitutes the present in reference to a having-been.[53] As the becoming of the future, the present is the active shaping of the world in the form of work. A temporality that renounces this anticipatory character, this care for the future, usually has little patience with work. "My husband was a complete alcoholic; he would rarely work and give us any money—now, however, he has quit drinking, and he turns every penny in." "Yes, every penny," reiterated the kids, laughing. "I give him the pocket money from my own hands. . . . He went to Mohan Bābā twice with me and took an oath not to drink again. . . . He cannot drink anymore. . . . If he does, he throws up," she said.

   The deity here mediates among the subjects and their temporal horizons; the work of the deity articulates the foci of a community among otherwise divided subjects. One may think of the "throwing up" either as possession by the deity, as Shamli seems to imply, or as a sign of alienation from the ethical subject of the word addressed to the deity and to the cherished dreams and hopes of one's loved ones. Shamli's paradoxes echo in her description of her friend who lives close by and works in a factory in another town: "We have been going together for the pilgrimage all these years. The poor fellow leaves at six in the morning after preparing meals for everyone and returns at eight in the evening to more drudgery. Her husband is an alcoholic . . . but he has quit now. 'We will not take you for the pilgrimage with us, if you drink,'" we have warned him." These performances belonging to a different temporality generate hope and community—and therefore work—in an otherwise disillusioning and alienating, punitive social order that holds scarce promise. "Their father rested for a day, but when I have no rest myself, how could I allow him to rest any longer?" Shamli continued, underlining her motivation to improve her situation. Beyond the push on the family, her excellence during the pilgrimage was, of course, for Shamli, evidence or assertion of her own performance. It was a means of self-encouragement; excellence here was an indication, a continuation of her excellence in daily life—which likewise echoed from the unusual fortitude of her friend.

Although women feature in the pilgrimage, a majority of the participants are young men, and many of the common motifs reflect this social characteristic. Pilgrimages often begin at a very young age and are, for many, the first steps into maturity on the road away from home, and these expectations seem to carry over the solicitude of the family, particularly of doting parents. They vindicate the proof of a home and the promise of security. If the pilgrimage is where one sets out to perform—and, short of many alternative avenues, will continue to perform both the drive and dejection for years to come—proving one's sincerity, good faith, and apparent competence in meeting one's promise and the family's expectations, such expected sacrifices may be seen as demands or demonstrations for recognition. In the field of the pilgrimage, in this chosen and open site of action, the pilgrim will likewise showcase and be recognized for many of his niche talents.

THE QUINTESSENTIAL KANWARIA

During the last several days before we picked our Kanwar, the *ghats* (riverbanks) had been jam-packed as participants timed their departure from Hardwar to reach the destination by the appointed occasion of Śivarātri. The buzz and clamor were daunting—it was a crowded place, much of it occupied with sacred objects and activity, which one inadvertent step could potentially defile and lead to disaster. Crossing over to the central ghat, I felt so overawed I kept standing on the bridge for what appeared like a long time. I had been indisposed from fever for a few days, which seemed to have affected my nerves; but that takes nothing out of the deterring quality of a geography marked by such concentration of extreme moral and emotional investment of this vast a body of people. Once I was actually on the ghat though, the surroundings seemed much more friendly, familiar, and personal, the place navigable.

Two days before the journey, K led our shopping trip in the crowded streets of Hardwar. "We will carry pitchers," he said to me. "Wait, you will marvel at how I decorate our kānwaṛ!" We purchased a solid cane; two steel pitchers with a capacity of about 1.5 liters each along with cord nets to hold them; and smaller items, including a few ribbons, a pair each of spoons, and little bells and tridents. K then worked diligently for several hours, only occasionally accepting my assistance. After skillfully wrapping the cane in ribbon, he tied a pair of knots on each side. The outer knots were tied around spoons to be used as vessels for the incense lighted at the time of prayers, while the tridents and bells were tied at the inner knots; the space carved between the two knots was used to secure the cords holding the pitchers. K was emphatic that the firmness of the structure was vital; in this long and critical journey, any structural flaws in the kānwaṛ would be unpardonable. K had a flair for precision in his craftsmanship, which reflected the pride he took in his own lean and muscular—that is, efficient—physique.[54] "He is a quintessential Kanwaria [Kanwar pilgrim]," one of our young female relatives had described K to me.

The ghats had been much less crowded the week before. Although there was still a lot of activity, particularly morning and evening, and one could see Kanwarias everywhere in their distinct ochre, bathing, decorating, and lifting their kānwaṛs, the numbers were fewer. Most of the pilgrims at this time were from distant locations in Punjab, Rajasthan, Madhya Pradesh, or central and eastern Uttar Pradesh, a good number of them, in fact, on their way back from Gangotri or Gaumukh. Among them were pilgrims carrying large amounts of water, up to ten to fifteen gallons, often in the form of multiple pitchers on either side. With their belongings and the padded carrying pole, the weight could easily be more than a hundred pounds. In view of the heavier burden, these pilgrims began earlier. The onerousness of this exercise greatly impressed me; I often looked at them and their ware closely, amazed by the willpower and devotion. I think I shared this feeling of wonder with most of the others; as one of these pilgrims would prepare to lift his kānwaṛ, or happened to pass by, he would often be greeted by a buzz among captivated onlookers impressed by such formidable labor and devotion.

On one such occasion, K and I joined some other curious passersby watching a pilgrim perform the preparatory rituals before lifting the kānwaṛ. Karam was a wiry man, unusually adorned for the occasion—below a white T-shirt was a shining, silken dhoti tied with a waistband of the same material. Wearing little earrings and around his neck the common *gamcha*, a thin cotton towel in ochre most Kanwarias carry, he appeared a stranger (perhaps a Bengali) since men from this part of the country rarely cared to dress as ceremonially as in eastern India, where goddess worship is more common. The kānwaṛ had three pitchers of water on either side; the two at the base were large, probably with about three gallons of water each, and the others must have contained at least two gallons each. A craftsperson had finished weaving a net of ropes around the pitchers to hold them firmly. A perfect, professionally made net was vital to the journey; and despite all the chances Hardwar presented of deceit, no laxity could be expected on this front. As a shopkeeper assured us definitively in response to my concerns days later when we bargained for the same service for our kānwaṛ, "Bhole, this is serious; there can be no latitude for error in this service!"

The pilgrim was bound for Delhi and had already made the pilgrimage more than a dozen times, although this was only the fourth time he was taking the *jal*, as the water in the containers alone (without the decorations) was called. With Śivarātri still two weeks away, he was allowing sufficient lead time to cover the 130-mile distance unhurried. "How heavy is this, bhole?" I had asked him reluctantly. "I don't know, bhole!" he replied with a smile, discounting the materiality of the burden; "there it is, for you to see." I could not help expressing my wonder: "It must be a heavy task, bhole [carrying the weight over such a long distance]?" Looking at the heavens and then around at the others seeking their affirmation, he waved his hands to indicate the indeterminacy of the issue and to dismiss my query. "Where is the burden, bhole? It is not mine to bear; Bābā is the one who will be carrying." The people around nodded in approval.

Such denial of the pilgrim's agency is a universal facet of the Kanwar. Almost every pilgrim will deny his own role in carrying the kānwaṛ; there is an unequivocal deference of agency to the great Lord who is the gravitational center of the pilgrimage. This implies a dissipation of the ego, a renouncing of the self, of one's individuality in resigning oneself to the deity—a reverential disintegration of the subject and the submergence of her act in favor of the absolute Act, Māyā (creative performance), of the Universal Master. If the subject implies a libidinal centripetality—from a linguistic perspective, she who can say "I" in an intersubjective field—it is precisely a denial of the subject we see in this aversion to saying "I."[55] Such denial of the ego is perfectly consistent with the transformation of every individual, every interlocutor into a bholā. Thus, it is indeed Bhole Bābā who has the responsibility for the burden. The Bābā's responsibility for the burden, even as the pilgrim is its medium, corresponds with the transfer of one's personal worries and concerns onto Bhole Bābā; trust them to the final, omniscient will of the Innocent One—Aśutoṣa, He who is easily pleased and is kind and generous.

FIGURE 1.3. *Making kānwaṛs*

Watching on the ghats of Hardwar as scores of pilgrims diligently decorate their kānwaṛs during the festival is a captivating sight. In a majority of cases, the participants purchase a partly decorated or bare frame from the market—this includes two small baskets attached to a bamboo stick with an arch made of split bamboo at the top. Then they decorate the frame with ribbons, streamers, garlands, and pictures and insignia of deities. At times, plastic replicas of snakes and parrots—the former a sign of Śiva, the latter regarded a pleasant creature, also a sign of felicity—are tied to the ends of the stick. Although one may be critical of the cheap, even tasteless quality of some of the generic decorative items—"Yes, one has to put on all this trivia!" one remarked—pilgrims prepare their kānwaṛs with delicate care. The baskets are laid with kusha (halfa) grass in which the Gangajal (Ganga water) is kept, either in many tiny bottles or a couple of bottles, containing about a liter of water each, on either side.

Those more certain of their skills go to great lengths to craft special kānwaṛs; many such veterans lead groups of pilgrims as mentors or gurus. They often bring the basic frame of the kānwaṛ with them, prepared at home, leaving all decoration to the time of the pilgrimage. A particularly popular structure this year was of a śivalinga seated on a large platform, with a snake's hood shading it and surrounded by pillars—all made with

FIGURE 1.4. *Kānwaṛ with a replica of a śivalinga*

colorful, embroidered silky cloths stretched around frames. Usually, pictures of Śiva, Pārvatī, or Gaṇeśa would be mounted in front, with a vessel for lighting incense, and the whole structure would rest in the middle of two solid poles, which required four to carry. In some cases, a small water pump and battery would be hidden below the structure to artfully provide a continuous trickle of Gangajal on the śivalinga and to illuminate the kānwaṛ with string lights at night. I could not find an opportunity to interview a guru working on the decorations—it would have been imprudent, and impossible, to interrupt their intense absorption in the work. But I watched closely on several occasions as one of these veterans brought up a fine piece of work out of a bare structure, minutely attending to every detail, the pride in his work resonating in the pride and admiration of other group members attending to the master's craft and helping as apprentices. More than once, we were informed by an apprentice, "The guru is a master at his work; he has been doing this for more than a decade—he likes to do every bit of it with his own hands." Although conscious of the strangers' attention, the guru would keep attending to his craft.

RECOGNIZING WORK

"Today, once established, capitalism is able to recruit the workers it needs relatively easily in all industrialized countries and in every industrial region within individual countries. In the past, it was an extremely difficult problem in each single case. And even today, it cannot always achieve its aim without powerful resistance."[56] In Weber's insightful observation, we see that the dialectic of the desire to not work and of being forced to work is surely as old as life itself.[57] As Weber demonstrated in his analysis of the Protestant ethic and its transformation into modern capitalism, this normative structure simultaneously implicates moral and theological estimation, economic condition, and social worth.

This becomes particularly unequivocal in conditions of global neoliberalism in which the market logic becomes a universal grid of intelligibility for any kind of social practice, from individual action and motives, to the family, and to the state executive.[58] In this paradigm, which has been a powerful force across the globe since the 1980s, there is no division of rationalities, no reason that the human be pulled in different directions—

everyone is (assumed to be) a calculating actor placed in a consistent and determinate field. There is no room for any alternative horizons of morality, existence, or history; the world is unipolar.

The dialectic of such social construction of the subject is well represented by Jock Young's formulation of the "exclusive society."[59] As Young showed, this is a society that first appropriates the subject through an unprecedented commodity culture programmed to inject market indicators into social relations, and seduce as consumers, while rejecting an ever-larger number of people as workers. It is thus an economy and social structure that produces "rejects," an operation possible only after it has first appropriated them in practice and as knowledge objects.

The religious setting was an alternative field for participants to prepare and to work, to be socially recognized, and to effect and recognize themselves as subjects with social and moral worth. Thus, for example, Kamarpal's case clearly demonstrates that religious symbolism, ethic, and belonging provide another horizon in the context of an alienating and stigmatizing social order. The religious practice provides an "actual" identity out of terms with ascriptions of "failure," "unemployed," and "outcast" by a dominant social order. It provides another textual medium, imagery (or mirror) for self-recognition to resist a dominant, appropriating ideology. At the same time, it is important to note that (much in the manner of Lacan's illustration of the intricate ties between the symbolic, the real, and the imaginary) this alternative field is not other-worldly; rather, it is a time and space engaged in the world.

These performances demonstrate simultaneously the features of social existence that find wide expression in the contemporary economy and others it barely acknowledges. For example, the competitive banter, Amma's self-praise of her leadership, the exchanges by the tube well, the frequent wagers, and the careerist motivations of the brothers in the liquor business all show the competitive dimension of social relations. At some level, these performances reiterate the economy and its expectations. They often do so in anxious anticipation or preparation since many of the participants are at the threshold of adulthood, a life stage where "serious" performance must soon be delivered. Conscious of the heavy odds stacked against a predictable career in the organized economy, this sociality is practice for the unpredictable expectations, the scarcity, and life consequences of the informal economy.[60]

Not everyone, however, is young or male, nor is competitiveness the primary attitude. The labor, the pain, the resolve, and the moral fortitude demonstrated here are also a performance of the suffering of everyday life, a demonstration of one's unrecognized excellence and of the will to persist and deliver on responsibilities to one's loved ones. While the economy is obviously a dominant force in participants' lives and, consequently, has been a recurring figure in the previous narrative, by no means does it exhaust one's life orientations. The artistic works; the labors of the journey; the identification with Śiva; the phenomenal appeal of the river goddess; the many opportunities for showing one's tastes, talents, and predilections; and the communitarian sociality address timeless concerns of human existence. The iron cage has scarcely any patience or place for such desires and imperatives.

The religious performances simultaneously prepare for, challenge, and cavort with this totalizing social and economic order. In view of these observations, I find it very surprising that contemporary scholars should be so unanimous in seeing the contemporary global popularity of religion as a reactionary assertion of cultural identity in the face of social change and modernization. Such a proposition implicitly assumes liberal capitalism as a final, universal, and, in the end, justified game. It advances a normative, uncritical understanding of capitalism, putting the focus on cultural issues without attending properly to social and existential suffering. In the Kanwar, however, we can see it is hard to miss the deep significance of religious practices in allowing ordinary subjects to face and live meaningful social lives amid an imposing global capitalist order. This also asks for renewed attention to the many literary and philosophical connotations of the terms "performance" and "recognition." As Śaṃkara in his *Bhāṣya* (Commentary) on Gauḍapāda's *Kārikā* notes: "It may be urged in this connection, that when choice has to be made between the metaphorical and actual sense of words, the latter ought to prevail. We say—no."[61]

CHAPTER 2

"EVERYTHING IS A GIFT, BHOLE"
Custom and the Ethics of Care

WE FOLLOWED KARAM for some distance from the ghats. By the first stop less than a mile away, I had pumped up the courage for the indiscretion to inquire if his journey was motivated by a wish. "Everything is a wish, bhole! Everything is a gift from Him!" he replied. Wishes are an important facet of Hardwar's religious life as of the Kanwar. Situated atop a hill close to Har-ki-Pairī is the extremely popular temple of Mansa Devi, the goddess of wishes—where almost every visitor to Hardwar pays obeisance. In the temple compound is a ficus tree around which pilgrims tie an ochre thread as they mutter their wish. Once the wish is fulfilled, they make another visit to the temple to untie a thread. The trunk and branches of the tree are inundated by a mass of threads, although the temple administration must clear the tree from time to time. Even though Mansa Devi is the premier site of this practice, such wish-seeking threads and trees are quite common in other temples as well, including the important Śiva temple at Nilkantha above Rishikesh. The vow, usually centered on a wish, is often the organizing force behind the Kanwar.

There is a secretive, at some level, sacred dimension to wishes. Engaging the subject's most pressing needs, desires, or fears—as would send one on an ordeal such as the Kanwar—they belong to a subjective order of temporality radically different from that of regular commerce. To mingle the objects of such anxious concerns—a sacred field—with the platitudes of normal conversation and expose them to trivial social judgments is to jinx them. "Whatever you ask for, never tell anyone!" Amma had strictly advised me. The secretiveness, of course, can also serve pragmatic considerations of avoiding domestic conflicts. Since desires can indeed be scandalous, one person's dearest wish may be an abomination to another. Thus, when this participant on his onerous mission evaded my query, it was a polite response to an intimate demand, unbecoming of a stranger.

Yet his response was quite authentic. Since a wish is only relatively discrete, it usually emanates from a broader field of concerns and obligations and involves, minimally, a note of thankfulness and a prayer for the continued well-being of one's loved ones—as well as for a more general peace and goodwill. Having expressed their disinterest in material gain from devotional activity, or at times after describing specific wishes, my respondents would usually add, almost as an aside, either a supplement to more specific wishes or self-evident fact: "A request for the safety and well-being of your near ones of course goes without saying."

Some would explicitly acknowledge an exchange dimension, but generally not without a second thought. Thus, "not for wishes . . . [after a moment] . . . yes . . . we are confident of Bhole Bābā's generosity; after all, you may ask as much as you want of God; the more you ask, the less." The elder brother sitting next to him nods in agreement: "Yes, Bhole Bābā! He is very generous. Actually, my younger brother had a chronic ear ailment in his childhood. And Mother had prayed to Bhole Bābā, saying that her son would bring Bābā's kānwaṛ once his ear heals." Others are more circumspect, anxiously dissociating from connotations of profit to their pilgrimage. Of the seven times he has been there, Shailesh avers he has never asked Bholenath for a reward:

> But for one exception, I sought Bhole's blessings for passing class X exams, promising that I will bring his kānwaṛ the following year. . . . I was going through a very hard time; I would work night shifts in the factory and take exams in the morning, without a wink of sleep. But I passed the exam; it was Bābā's miracle.

Another participant denies any motives to his pilgrimage: "No, I never went for the pilgrimage in pursuit of a wish." Yet others may quite matter-of-factly, and in the assurance of custom, attribute their pilgrimage to a wish: "I brought kānwaṛs imploring Bhole Bābā, first, to help me find a job and, later, since we had three daughters and no son, to gift us with a son."

On the whole, while an expectation of restitution seems an important aspect of the offering, there is a reluctance, a denial in identifying or being identified with the idea of exchange. A certain register of forgetting is involved, a distaste for "exchange with the deity."[1] Such hesitation needs to be considered in reference to the hegemonic insistence of market rationality, its overdetermined quality, the free hermeneutic license it enjoys in our time. The element of remuneration in the pilgrim's act—whether a silent expectation, a demurral, or (rather ironically) even an assertive demand—guards against appropriation by the widespread order of economic reason. It recoils against such an allusion, insists on a difference for which, outside the references of a particular, and in some ways closed, reserved discourse (custom, *śraddhā* [faith], *dharma* [duty], and so on), it has difficulty finding words for precisely, one may say, because of the power, the pervasiveness of this market rationality.[2]

Instead, it is possible to hear echoes of a similar insistence on difference in the departure from the laws of market exchange that Marcel Mauss described through the notion of the gift.[3] The gift, Mauss found, much like the items of exchange, circulates often as an obligation, an imperative—though not countersigned by positive law—but never without an excess, an exaggeration, immoderation, a certain operation of time that keeps it incommensurate with the economic system of measured exchange.[4] Manuel Moreno Arcas notes that "the immediate repayment of a debt to the god is equally considered to be distasteful and ungrateful. A suitable period of time must pass."[5] According to Mauss, the gift "by definition . . . cannot be reciprocated immediately. *Time* is needed to perform any counter-service."[6] And what is Time here but nothing, a pure difference, a departure that inserts into the form of this circulation a decisive indeterminacy, a foreign element that confounds this circle of exchange even if, as Mauss finds, it were the very reason, the originary force driving exchange.[7] Before venturing into what the pilgrim "takes," what he wants, however, we have to recollect what he has to "give," since his desire to give is significant. After all, the frequent refrain, "Bhole Bābā, I will bring your

Kanwar," addresses the deity's desire. This complexity is perhaps best illustrated in the composition of the religious vow.

BEFORE THE DEITY: TAKING A VOW

As in most pilgrimages, a primary facet of the Kanwar is the vow, a solemn statement performed either as the promise of an anticipated offering of the Kanwar after a wish is granted or simply as the declaration of an offering. The vow is the inaugural act, a sacred commitment well in advance, even years ahead, of the actual pilgrimage.[8] The vow: a discursive event at the threshold of intention, simultaneously partaking of the world and transcending it, encapsulating both the moment of desire and its sublimation, so much so that it is metonymically extended to a vast body of Hindu household rituals, the *vratas*, or votive rites.[9] Not surprisingly, Émile Benveniste finds in the "oath" the principle of subjectivity itself: "the instance of discourse that contains the verb ["swear," "promise," etc.] establishes the act at the same time that it sets up the subject."[10]

From passing an exam to the health of a child, the wish for an offspring, a daughter's marriage or for a job, the content of the vows in the Kanwar is as varied as are human desires and fears. Commonly and minimally, the pilgrimage involves a note of thankfulness and a prayer for continued well-being of one's loved ones. Implicit here is faith or, as the pilgrims frequently aver, śraddhā in the deity (Śiva) and his power. The term "śraddhā" is everywhere in these narratives. It stands for one's unwavering faith in (or regard for) the deity, the practice such that this quality of the performative act becomes almost synonymous with the person. It is the pilgrim's drive, the talisman necessary for a successful pilgrimage, as my respondents declared at different points: "those unable to walk a mile, in śraddhā they do a hundred"; "our śraddhā in Bhole Bābā"; "without śraddhā, the pilgrimage is destined to be abortive"; "these days only a fraction truly goes out of śraddhā; the rest are there only to have a good time"; "how does one explain pilgrims going a hundred miles in a wheelchair, if not for their śraddhā"; and so on.

Etymologically a Sanskrit word, "śraddhā" is closely connected to the "vow." According to Monier Monier-Williams, śraddhā is "faith, trust, confidence, belief in"; depending on the context, it can also be "desire, longing, wish."[11] The correspondences of this word in the Indo-European group of languages have provoked abundant linguistic attention. One certainty is its relation to the Latin *crēdō*. As Benveniste notes, "The exact formal correspondence between Latin *crēdō* and Sanskrit *śraddhā* is a guarantee of ancient heritage."[12] In the Vedic sacrifice, *śrad* (trust) frequently appears in relation to Indra, the heroic, warrior god. The context is often of Indra's exploits and the patron's (of the sacrifice) bestowal of faith or trust in Indra's victory, for instance:

śráddhitaṃ te mahatá indriyáya
ádhā manye srát te asmá adhāyi
vŕṣā codasva mahaté dhánāya

"We have trust in your great Indrian might, and it is for this reason that I have thought [*manye*]: trust has been put in you; rush forward like a bull to win the great prize of combat."[13] The śrad was an offering granted to the deity based on his proven record, premised on the understanding that the deity would return the favor in the sacrificer's own earthly struggles. The confidence placed in the deity includes the assurance of being restituted; faith itself is the surety of the return. It amounts to making an obligation. To cite Benveniste once more, "The act of faith always implies the certainty of remuneration. . . . There is some sort of *do ut des* [I give that you may give] between men and gods."[14] Likewise, articulating the logic of the "Brahminical sacrifice," the philosopher Jean-Luc Nancy quips, "Here is the butter? Where are the gifts?"[15]

The assumptions of reward may be as important to the contemporary idea of śraddhā as they perhaps were for the ancients. Thus, several scholars have emphasized an instrumentality to the vow, a quid pro quo, frequently using the language of a financial transaction, debt and repayment, whereas some of the more pragmatic ones may "pay only for divine services rendered, and after they are rendered."[16] Furthermore, these observations appear discursively consistent with the axioms of exchange and compensation in the rational choice tradition of the contemporary sociology of religion.[17]

Yet such a conclusion remains hasty; much of this reasoning, questionable. Although these readings make tangible observations, their import is overdetermined by the predominance of the market idiom in our times. This also shows the limitations of a text-centric approach to analyzing social relations—the general tendency to identify antiquity with origin, the risk of essentializing the past and canonizing yesterday's possibly contested and socially discriminating, power-determined rituals and interpretations as universal truths. An economistic abstraction completely skirts the subjective anxieties that support the performance and may amount to a cavalier neglect of the social relations and obligations among which such promises operate. Located in its customary social and performative significations, and in relation to powerful surrounding discourses, the vow is a complex, highly ambivalent performance. If this fundamentally asymmetric practice, outside the circuits of knowledge and exchange, closer to the paradoxes of desire than the positivity of contract, is equivalent to an exchange transaction with the gods, it is by the same measure a denial and refusal of such equivalence.

THE GIFT IN THE VOW

The pilgrimage offers to the śivalinga water par excellence brought through labor and hardship from the Ganga, from a particularly sacred spot in the river. This is an offering to Śiva's liking; after all, it was Śiva who in his matted hair had received the celestial Ganga on earth. The pilgrimage repeats, commemorates this act of divine union, this instance that manifests the pinnacle of Śiva's glory. It pleases Śiva, for "without the Ganges, Śiva would remain the scorching brilliant *linga* of fire."[18] Thus, it is a ritual fact, the śivalinga *requires* oblations of milk or water, preferably Ganga water. In some of the great temples of Banaras, Śiva's renowned abode, the pouring of Ganga water "goes on from dawn to dusk." Hordes of men "hoisting huge brass pots of Ganges water on their shoulders ... mount the steps, shouting Śiva's name—*Hara Hara Mahadeva* and entering the sanctuary to pour their lavish offerings on the linga."[19]

The water of the Ganga is essentially sacred; nevertheless, through the laborious transportation of the water in the Kanwar, according to a series of injunctions that accentuate and maintain its sanctity, the pilgrim reconstructs this sacredness and enacts a formidable testimony to its value. Albeit the offering of Ganga water is a generic ritual, the pilgrim makes it

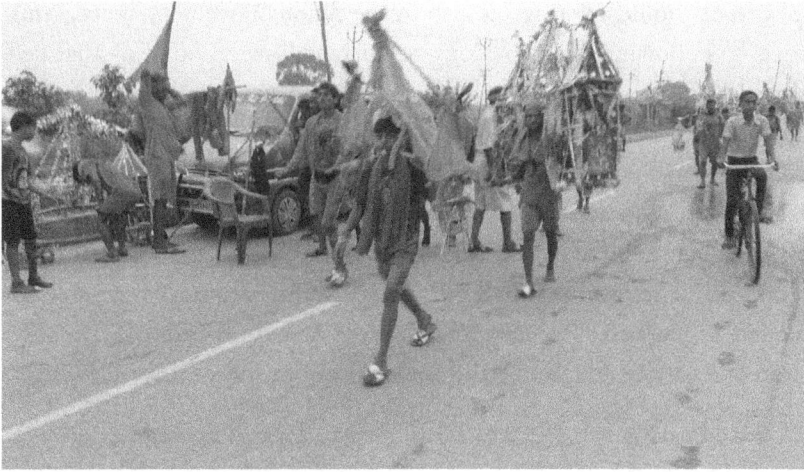

FIGURE 2.1. *Pain and the gift*

an exceptional act, a sacrifice, performatively recollecting its sacredness. The sacrifice is in the renunciation, in the performed intensity of this giving.

This is an abundant giving, not simply for the exertion of the pilgrim, the pain he goes through, the water that is heartily poured over the śivalinga, but also and just as important, by the effervescence of the collective, the excesses of the festival: the feasts, art performances, commotion, intoxicated bodies, pain and suffering, and vigorous participation of the spectators.[20] The lavish offering correlates with another figure of giving—giving one's word. As noted previously, the vow involving the promise of a Kanwar offering inaugurates the pilgrimage. There is a symbolic connection between the vow and the libation, the act of pouring liquid offerings over the deity. In the everyday ritual practice of linga worship, one enunciates the wish while pouring milk or water over the śivalinga. Linguistic connections between these figures extend into the archaic, where the archaic is not necessarily only a figure of historical time but perhaps also of what Julia Kristeva has called, following Freud and Heidegger, the "timeless atemporality" of the unconscious.[21]

While tracing the linguistic relation between "libation" and "security" in *Indo-European Language and Society*, Benveniste observes that whereas the Greek *spéndō* is "to make a liquid offering," its nominal derivative *spondē*, or "liquid offering," is also in the plural "agreement, truce, armistice."[22] Following the genealogy to ancient Greece, he finds that ceremonial liquid offerings were made to the gods while seeking security, a guarantee of safety. By the time of the Attic orators, the term had developed a distinct political dimension, referring to a pact or pledge of mutual security between contracting parties. In the Latin, *spondeo*, the offering as the mediating factor was thereafter obliterated, "though its function remained"; the term retained only the juridical meaning of a surety or pledge, a guarantee or "insurance against risk."[23] A promise, spondeo, from one party is followed by *re-spondeo* from the other. Thus,

> this dialogue is constructed on a legal formula: a *sponsio* by one party and a *re-sponsio* by the other, forms of a guarantee which is henceforward mutual. . . . "*Respondeo, responsum* are used with reference to interpreters of the gods, priests, specially the haruspices, when in return for the offering a promise is given and security in return for a gift; this is the "response" of an oracle and a priest. . . . We may adduce a parallel expression from Germanic: OE [Old English] *andswaru* "answer" with which we may compare Gothic *swaran* "to swear, pronounce a solemn formula"; the Old English (and modern English) word is almost literally *re-spondere*.[24]

Lexical correspondence in the Indo-European group of languages is extensive. While this genealogical event may be at a remove from the ritual composition of the Kanwar, it nevertheless reaffirms the dimension of surety and confidence to the offering. The vow that accompanies or anticipates the offering is commitment of the greatest rigor. It is binding. It demands absolute integrity, consciousness, and responsibility from the subject—in this instance, as if subjectivity itself becomes lucid.[25] In the Kanwar, the inviolability of this pact goes without saying.[26] Because the vow is so intricately interwoven with the subject's desires, concerns, and sense of ethics, it can be safely assumed that one will be only too eager to conform.[27] Such assured proclamation by the subject invites and anticipates a fitting response from the deity. The vow thus is its own guarantee. The specific enactment of guarantee or reassurance in the form of the offering is transposed to the event itself as an affirmation of, or desire for, a more generic sense of security.

Having mentioned his disinterest in material gain from the pilgrimage, Shailesh added, "A request for the safety and well-being of your near ones of course goes without saying; everyone makes it." In my observations during the pilgrimage, I found a palpable anxiety regarding familial well-being and security inevitably mentioned as an aside, either as a supplement to more specific wishes or self-evident fact dismissed even as it is pronounced, to be a common denominator. If people disengage from connotations of profit from the deity, the desire for familial well-being is deemed too minimal or fundamental to qualify as commerce—it is a nondemand that does not fall into the circuit of measured exchanges. To appreciate such anxiety, it is important to take a close look at the pilgrims' existential circumstances.

As I describe in greater detail in the next chapter, in northern India, everyday life continuously wades through stark impressions of injury, disease, and death, "a vast sea of poverty and the visible added evidence of human degradation":[28] public spaces and hospitals crowded with poorly attended ailing bodies; chaotic traffic with an accident frequency more than ten times that of the West where every second step could possibly be a near miss; and the frightening incidence of violent crimes such as murder and kidnapping for ransom. Shailesh was scarcely in his teens when his father's mutilated corpse was recovered from a railway track; a cousin who mentored him for his first Kanwar was crushed by a truck; a brother-in-law died in an accident with a tractor; and Shailesh himself survived a serious head injury in another traffic accident. For the past several years, he and his wife had spent a major part of their earnings on expensive allopathic treatment for her blocked fallopian tubes, after having tried every other medical alternative, from community healers to Ayurveda and homeopathy. Omkar, a regular bholā, lost his eye in an accident a few years ago but refused to abstain from the pilgrimage that year: "I have lost an eye and the medical expenses have turned me bankrupt, but I can't miss the pilgrimage; if not for Bhole Bābā the accident would have been fatal. My body was ruined, but His blessings have helped me recover." Disease and impaired body parts were equally integral to other respondents' narratives.

Ramsharan walked his first Kanwar with a high fever; Rajesh's pilgrimage was in fulfillment of a parent's vow for healing his ear when he was a child; Munna went on the pilgrimage imploring Bhole Bābā to heal his son's congenitally infirm leg. Likewise, polio-afflicted Sudhir continues to wait for an able-bodied friend to help him bring his Kanwar on a wheelchair. The extreme precariousness of health, life, and livelihood means a continuous and high-stakes financial struggle for Bhimkumar and his brother, who were tenuously employed at a retail shop to carry small cargo in cycle rickshaws; Shailesh, who recounts an endless struggle of making ends meet and marrying off his sisters ever since his father died; Munna, who runs a small grocery store; Ishwar, who grew up in a family of agricultural laborers and desperately wanted a job; and Kapil, who left his destitute family and lives virtually on the street shifting from one form of casual employment to another.

Dreadful uncertainty hovers over everyday life, from the health of loved ones to the family's livelihood, to the ability to meet compulsory social obligations. The registering of these concerns is signaled by an expression common not only in the Kanwar but also in religious visits across North India: "Bābā has called (or invited)." If the deity is the goddess, "Mother has called" or "There is an invitation from the mother." The call here is a sign of parental love, of being the object of the deity's desire. Where the figure of love is present, the relationship is unique, unmediated. The deity's concern here is with the subject in the singular, in the particularity of the subject's condition as it factors into or contributes to the subject's symptoms ("Bhole Bābā understands your concerns deeper than you can yourself"). The expectation of the invitation, deemed the paramount condition for the materialization of the pilgrimage, is also the hope that the circumstances will remain auspicious. In a milieu where hardly a day goes by without word of a death, a major accident, a surgical mistake, or a close encounter with debilitating deprivation, it invites the assurance that no misfortune meanwhile will obstruct the anticipated pilgrimage.

There is a wish there that the subject would be able to satisfactorily negotiate expected obstacles, which are formidable yet routine. "Every time I had no clue where the money would come from, but Bhole Bābā took care of everything in the end," says another of my respondents. The miracle here is reminiscent of one of his experiences of the pilgrimage itself: "My foot was badly injured, with about ten stitches, but I requested

Bhole Bābā to help me complete the pilgrimage. I then walked for three days and was able to pull off the *yatra* [journey] without any hindrance, though I was bedridden for several days thereafter." The Bābā inexplicably helps navigate these insurmountable and routine odds; what happens to be objectively formidable and uncertain becomes subjectively negotiable. As though it were a temporal arc anxiously anchored in the future, the vow beckons propitious circumstances to warrant another pilgrimage or another journey to a religious shrine.[29]

Under such precariousness of life and livelihood, the constant threat of, and exposure to, accidents, disease, and debilitating poverty—in a word, suffering—that marks social life for an overwhelming majority of people, it is hard to imagine a desire more significant and pervasive than the well-being of one's dear ones.[30] Therefore, Mary McGee can note that "many rites observed for the good health of a child are not performed when a child is sick, but rather are observed on a punctual and regular basis for the purpose of maintaining good health."[31] The absolute pact and desire of the vow correlates with, reenacts, as Lacan observes for the Sadean fantasy, suffering as the "indestructible support" of the "play of pain."[32] The resolute pain the Kanwar pilgrim demonstrates, whether by playing up or otherwise, may be seen as an account of the faith and suffering that supports it. Thus, a reassurance of security comes across as a return, a gift in return of the sacrifice, of faith, śraddhā, which have been our concerns in this chapter—reassurance, a surety, a response as it were to the resolve and anxiety that invoke the spondé, the sacrifice from the subject.

CONTEMPORARY SOCIOLOGY:
THE CASE OF THE MISSING SUBJECT

In *Globalization and Religious Nationalism in India*, Katrina Kinnvall extensively treats these issues of anxiety, security, and religion in relation to globalization in contemporary India. Following the formulations of the sociologist Anthony Giddens, Kinnvall argues that by "challenging simple definitions of who we are and where we come from," globalization invokes feelings of insecurity and existential anxiety that make individuals seek security through alternative affirmations of self-identity. The author then reasons, in a familiar structuralist vein, that potential sources of

security are arbitrary—"any collective identity that can provide such security is a potential pole of attraction."[33] In this discourse, religion's compelling appeal lies in its firmness as an "identity-signifier." How does the
construct of identity that social scientific studies seem so often to stress
capture the performed concerns of the subjects here: concerns about the
well-being of their loved ones, the lived reality of harsh material circumstances, the agonies of fulfilling social and customary obligations?[34]

A closer look at the psychological assumptions of theories of identity
indicates several key problems. To explore these, I suggest a short detour
into Anthony Giddens's understanding of identity, since he explicitly addresses the psychological aspects. Moreover, Giddens formulates a theory
of identity in tandem with the notions of "anxiety" and "insecurity" that,
as I have described previously, are significantly at play in the Kanwar
performances. That these motifs of Giddens's theory have been recently
mobilized to explain contemporary religion in North India gives us more
reason to reflect on his formulations.

It is surprising that Giddens upholds conventional liberal assumptions about the self, relying on psychoanalytic and phenomenological
traditions that actually offer radically social and relational constructions
of the self. Giddens's account of identity builds on the child psychology of
Erik Erikson, whom Lawrence Friedman aptly described as "identity-
architect."[35] Briefly, Erikson has reasoned that healthy childhood experiences that demonstrate the reliability and trustworthiness of the caretaker
help the child develop a sense of self-identity and a feeling of basic trust
in the external world. Giddens extrapolates this logic to argue that basic
trust so developed gives the child a sense of identity or self that, over time,
is transformed into the adult's trust in routine practices and into a consistent narrative of self-identity.[36]

But in instances where such basic trust does not develop, the sense of
identity remains deficient, which results in an eruption of existential anxiety. This is manifested in neurotic behavior and the inability to lead a "normal" life.[37] Thus, the formation of self-identity depends on trust in given
social practices. Anxiety, on the contrary, is explained as a consequence of
unhealthy parenting, lack of confidence in the caretaker's return. Notable
here is the emphasis on consistency between the self's identity narrative

and given social practices; that is, on the cultivation of an ego that would be at home in prevalent social practices.[38] A glaring problem with such a formulation of the ego is its uncritical stance on reality.

The upshot of Giddens's theory is that the affective must submit to the cognitively deciphered rationality underlying social practices.[39] The subject must conform to the given reality; the ideal is a disciplinary equilibrium. Disequilibrium is tantamount to failure of the project of self, a "false self," an inability to be "normal."[40] Such constructions are premised on the reified idea of a Cartesian self, which seeks its "own" preservation and interests. This construct of the individual is not only unacceptable to Freudian or Lacanian psychoanalysis, which dwell on the multiple, inconsistent agencies in the subject; it has also been persistently questioned in philosophy at least since Nietzsche and Heidegger and in the complex understanding of subjectivity in poststructuralist and postmodern theory. As Mervyn Bendle points out in a compelling critique, this emphasis "on the ego's adaptive function overlooks the ego's own state of alienation and also relies on the assumption that reality itself is an unproblematic realm to which adaptation can be made."[41] Thus, in Lacan, for example, (whom Giddens happens to dismiss rather hurriedly), reality is conceived as substantively an effect of the symbolic order in which the ego finds itself implicated by virtue of its misrecognitions. There is no given substrate that may be defined as "reality" to which the subject may securely adapt.

If we are to confront the notion of "reality" as problematic at all, it is impossible to dispute Lacan's stark rebuttal of Erikson's theory of ego development:

> If this point of view [Erikson's] is true, we will have to abandon the notion I tell you to be the essence of the Freudian discovery, the decentering of the subject in relation to the ego, and to return to the notion that everything centers on the standard development of the ego. That is an alternative without mediation—if that is true, everything I say is false. Except, if what I say is false, it becomes extremely difficult to read the slightest of Freud's texts and understand anything in it.[42]

Heidegger likewise extensively questions the Cartesian notion of the individual as an entity relating to the world as extended substance (*res extensa*) outside itself to show that Dasein is always already being-in-the-world and exists phenomenally in relations of care and concern. In stark contrast to the negative appraisal of anxiety in the previous formulations, in Heidegger (along with other insightful commentators on the human condition, such as Kierkegaard and Sartre), anxiety is a fundamental mode of being human. Social practices may be reassuring, but they are no less alienating by the privation, the nullity that peeps deep out of them. This manner of everyday being-in-the-world, Dasein fleeing in the face of the uncanniness of its potentiality-of-Being, is "not only tempting and tranquilizing; it is at the same time alienating."[43] Anxiety interrupts this mode of being, thus putting Dasein in the face of the fundamental nothingness of the world. Whereas "for Heidegger, anxiety is constitutive in its uncanny [*unheimlich*] influence, such that homelessness [*unheim-leichkeit*] is our primary condition; for Giddens the self-representation of anxiety is a secondary phenomenon, in so far as we are first of all 'at home' [*zu Hause*] in the world."[44] Instead of being part of a logic of individual self-survival, anxiety is an existential effect—a concernful openness in temporality—that puts the human into a primordial attitude of care and responsibility. This relational quality of the self is altogether missed in identity-focused explanations of contemporary religion.[45]

If the mother's absence affects the infant—and anxiety, psychoanalysis tells us, is an affect[46]—how appropriate is it to interpret it, as Giddens's conception of identity leads him to presume, as a "need" for "security," a logical predicate of the child fearing for its "self"?[47] To Giddens, anxiety is fear of a danger, though diffused and without a definite object.[48] However, is this not rather an anticipatory imposition of a discourse of self-interest, a biological discourse of survivalism on the affects and affections of a self, particularly in a case where our inability to give signification to this term "self" is most evident? After all, strictly speaking, there is little meaning to the "self" here (or anywhere) outside its involvement, say, with the one who takes care of it or the "here" and "there" of some object—a cotton reel, for example, in Freud's *Beyond the Pleasure Principle*—in which it finds itself spatialized, temporalized?[49]

That the caretaker should return is something, but as significant for the child—and the signification of the child's crying should not be taken as nonambivalent or always already without a history, a phenomenology—is that the caretaker go away. It is such a structure of the mother coming-and-going we find repeated in Freud's observations of his grandchild playing with the cotton reel, where the seminal concepts of the death drive and repetition automatism would first appear.[50] Seeing the mother leave, the child went on to play a game, alternately throwing the reel he holds by a thread under the bed and pulling it back, roughly exclaiming in the process, "Fort!" (away) and "Da!" (here). Thus is enacted the paradox of the child's desire and the pathos of human existence through being with and dividing into the object and precisely, Lacan remarks, as he, eighteen months old, steps into (the binary form of) language, becoming "engaged in the system of the concrete discourses of his surroundings."[51] Not only is the joyful greeting (Da!) of the affirmative or unifying moment, of presence, strictly of a pair with the banishment of the object (Fort!), but, as Hyppolite's sublime commentary on Freud's *Verneinung* vouches, insofar as it is a symbolized affair, the game is itself the work of the instinct of destruction—of negation—operative in the second order as a negation of negation.[52] The child's game, this proper demonstration of the subject's entry into the social world—the world of the symbol—shows that "a fundamental attitude" of negation, of destruction, of being-toward-death attends on the positivism of what Giddens would call "basic trust."[53]

Perhaps the more cogent expression of the infant's condition may be the fact that it misses the mother, her company of love, an affective relationship in which contact is primary.[54] Already in the introductory lectures, Freud says, "A child is frightened of a strange face because he is adjusted to the sight of a familiar and beloved figure—ultimately of his mother."[55] Moreover, Freud's voluminous literature on the Oedipal clearly suggests that the child's anxiety belongs not to the register of the restricted economy of "need" but is characterized by the infinitude of desire. Its reference is an excess, the voluptuosity of time with the mother.[56]

ANXIETY, RESPONSIBILITY, AND THE PILGRIM'S SELF
In the Kanwar, in its exorbitant gifts and desires amid figures of self-denial and the spectacular celebration of the deities, in these excessive

performances that implicate custom, family, gods, and social circumstances, it is hard to imagine the economy of a self barely hanging on to routine practices and living in minimal trust ever being haunted by risk. The concern about familial well-being in the pilgrims' narratives as well as a consideration of the pilgrimage rituals shows the relevance of the figure of "anxiety" in the pilgrims' performances. However, such anxiety or insecurity, an inevitable effect of lived material conditions, of the continuous foreboding exposure to poverty, disease, and death, is hardly explicable as a cognitive phenomenon. The existential immediacy of these circumstances is clearly *a world apart* from the figures of "risk" and cognitive "uncertainty" in contemporary sociology. Whether in relation to general circumstances or a more specific concern—a child's health, a sister's marriage, a desired job—such anxiety is almost always articulated in relation to others.

After their father's murder, Bhimkumar's mother left their home in a village several hundred miles away and moved to a town near Delhi. Over the years, along with her two sons who worked as rickshaw pullers, they saved money and dreamed of returning to their village. When cousins schemed to confiscate their small landholding, the mother moved back to the village to reclaim their land, and the two brothers' families took turns staying with her. Bhimkumar vows that he gives all of his savings to his mother so that they may together rebuild their lost world. A similar imperative of responsibility haunts Munna, who is worried about his child's leg: "Every parent worries about his child's health and future."

"Bhole Shankar," he continues, "is very simple and kind. He is able to deeply comprehend and care for your problems." Perhaps the same trait of comprehending through kindness or empathy for the particular pulls Shailesh to Bhole Bābā. Having worked since he was thirteen in a factory as replacement for his murdered father, Shailesh has been the only wage earner in a family that included his mother, three unmarried sisters, and an infant brother. He worked full-time during the day, preparing for the exam only at night. "My life has been an endless struggle, but thanks to Bhole Bābā, we have been able to keep up." He recounted several tales of adversity, particularly the ordeals he and his mother went through arranging dowries for the sisters' marriages, yet taking pride in how they had come off with heads high. To Shailesh, who still broods about his father's violent murder, the laborious ritual walks seemed to have the significance of a rite of passage, one more circumstantial than prescriptive. They were tests of his resolve and fortitude, repetitions of a traversal of adversity in its intense physicality on that most responsible of grounds, faith or śraddhā.[57] Ishwar's request for a job is likewise inseparable from the financial conditions of a landless rural family; his desire for a male child is driven partly by familial expectations and the intense dynamics of a network of social relations. Manoj's pilgrimage in fulfillment of his parents' vow, and Kapil, who, as we will see, cannot resist wallowing in his family's misfortunes, are no less relational.

The pervasive anxiety about familial well-being is similarly structured. Much as a necessary difference of time—form, occasion, and such—intervenes between the gift and its return, so in the Kanwar there is an irreducible difference of identity between the pilgrim or the vower and the subject of the wish. It is a difference that insists, even where the self is seemingly at the center, whether through an imaginary of one's dues, a symbolic responsibility, or a deferral of the desire to another.[58] The request from the deity thus operates in the register of a gift; the subject finds itself obligated to ask for a gift but only insofar as it is a gift to someone else. The exorbitance of the sponsio or the libations gifted to the gods anticipates a similar exorbitance of the gift in return, re-sponsio. The conviction of this demand is assured by the fact that the expected gift is not as such for the "self"; it is meant to *re-sponde*. It is a responsibility, to a *sponde* from someone else, to all those, indeed a sociality and all that may be called transcendental, one is obligated to for the countless gifts, the giving beyond measure that has given one one's being.[59]

We have seen that the vows and the painstaking rituals of the Kanwar reflect the subjects' deep concerns about the well-being of their loved ones. This customary ethic, however, is not discrete. Performatively articulated, the responsibility for the family here implicates the subjects' desires and a sense of responsibility to tradition itself, which, after all, is the support of the deities. The following case illustrates how a customary ethic is involved in the responsibility to family or the notion of family itself. Now nineteen years old, Kapil has gone on the pilgrimage regularly for the last seven years. Most recently (in 2010), as he was living penniless in a new place, he found it difficult to go on the pilgrimage. Fortuitously, however, at the eleventh hour a friend approached him for company on a motorcycle ride to Hardwar.

Though rather unconventionally, Kapil was able to present Bhole his Kanwar. Pleased, he reverts to the common refrain: "If Bhole Bābā wants you to come, He will find you a way around all obstacles." Kapil was particularly preoccupied with an account from his childhood days:

> We used to have cows. My mother took great care of them. She had a reputa-
> tion of being very kind; she would never refuse anyone milk. Then there was
> a fire in our barn one night. I was very young. The three cows there turned to
> ash. People say they howled to their death. Our house was at a distance, but
> none of the neighbors helped or came to tell us. Our family has since been
> on a curse.

Kapil's interpretation may not be far off the mark. Soon after the incident, finally breaking under the torture of domestic violence, Kapil's mother left the family to live with a man from a rival community. In the closely knit Jat community of rural North India, where even formal divorces are rare, this became the subject of great opprobrium and dealt a strong blow to the lives of the family members. Kapil was forced into accepting that his mother was dead and, to this day, continues to talk of her as dead.[60] His elder brother became a pathological alcoholic; Kapil never went to school, became addicted to chewing tobacco and smoking before he was ten, and early in his teens began to work as a helper on trucks. "I do not like going to my village," he says. "I don't like meeting my brother, or father. My brother is a scoundrel; my father, however, is too innocent, a fool." He adds, "Our family is living a curse because of those poor cows. I have been unfailingly bringing Bābā's Kanwar, only begging that we should be relieved of this curse."

The subject here is implicated in the fate of the family. Much as Kapil tries to sunder a relationship that seems to have brought him only misfortune by denying it and by moving away (or moving endlessly if the trucking is a sign), he finds himself obligated to it. Wherever he may be, Kapil says that he returns to his village at the time of the pilgrimage.

The force of this obligation is customarily articulated by reference to the tragic fate of the cows, these beings much loved and revered in this partly pastoral community. In a rational frame, Kapil can hardly be blamed for either the cows or the fate of his family, but such a calculation would be foreign to the register of such accountability.

It is hard to find a more lucid illustration of such customary responsibility than the instance of Antigone, who forsakes the promising prospects of her youthful life, going against the law to perform the death rites for her brother and thereby to fatally plunge into, share in, her family's *até* or misfortune (insofar as it does not absolve the subject of responsibility).[61] Antigone's responsibility is beyond the law, it is an unwritten responsibility, yet it is a product of language and therefore of the law.[62] "Involved is an horizon determined by a structural relation; it only exists on the basis of language of words, but it reveals their unsurpassable consequence . . . for from my point of view my brother is my brother."[63] And whereas Antigone's tragic situation may be exceptional, such acceptance of something in the register of a family's misfortune, with a temporality that "began to be articulated in previous generations," is, and Lacan's word is quite instructive here, the base relative to which in transference the subject counts the analyst's vote.[64]

The self that participates in the gifting ritual is always an ambivalent, dispersed self. This should not surprise us, since the notion of the individualized self itself has historically been the corollary of the advent of a certain kind of economy.[65] Insofar as the gift exceeds this particular economic idiom, it also indicates and constructs a self that is not a derivative of this order. But is the mode of giving that subtends these performances restricted to the "family"? What defines the limits of love and responsibility? I have argued that the notion of the individual is insufficient, if not counterproductive, in understanding the subject of contemporary religious performances. Instead, I have tried to show how religion here is performed by subjects embedded in their relations and in a customary idiom of ethics. The "family" in this context may be defined only as a customarily demarcated intimate circle of relations and responsibilities that radically involve the subject. Its members may frequently involve parents, kin, spouse, and children, but any such demarcation may be referred as much to the charters of the Enlightenment that restrain love—a "feeling, that is to say, the ethical in the form of the natural," this "most tremendous contradiction"—to the privacy of the family, to thereby make it disappear in the exteriority of civil society and the state, as it may have a history outside or in contravention to it.[66] Likewise, one may as easily associate this institution with a certain orthodoxy or treat it as a potent ethical reserve, as Partha Chatterjee does in his exhortation that Hegel's eloquence on the family be reimagined in the context of the community or in Gerd Meyer's recent proposition that the care received in families may be a "useful metaphor or narrative" for an imaginative construction of ethics.[67]

Engaging with these concerns thus requires a reconsideration of the notion of the "subject" in contemporary sociological understanding. This liberal conception of the subject, as I have argued, reduces being to a utilitarian interest in the world and a certain economy of thought, will, or goods interpreted in the idiom of mastery. In the previous accounts, we see that the radically relational and ethical performances evidenced in the pilgrimage are incompatible with this liberal idea of the subject and that the performed subjectivities of the pilgrimage indeed emerge in difference from these hegemonic assumptions.

CHAPTER 3

OMINOUS SIGNS

Of Dread, Desires, and Determination

IT WAS A SMALL BRICK HOUSE with a courtyard in the front, which also housed a tiny kitchen; inside, there were two rooms, one after the other. The *devatās* (divinities) were lined against the kitchen wall, six little concrete, houselike structures with tapering roofs set on walls about a foot high. Devatās are usually placed in the fields, so we were surprised to see them inside the house. "We have our devatās here, by us. Our village is far from here," the woman explained. "They chose the place, wanted to be here. That's fine, I said. 'You should be happy'. . . . They would appear in my dreams." The devatās were her children who had died either in infancy (two boys and a girl) or did not see light. They were good spirits, dear to the family, the mother, who remained with the family in their afterlife.

Usually the devatās are *pitrs* (ancestral spirits). During hard times, when things are frequently going wrong—the crops have been failing, marriages have been canceled at the last minute, someone has had an accident, too many people are falling sick—the affiliated Brahmin family would be consulted to organize a *havana*, a ritual offering of purified butter and other ingredients at a fire altar. The officiating *pandit* (priest) may divine that a particular ancestor is unappeased and recommend that the spirit be set up as a devatā. The devatā would then be made and ceremonially installed at an auspicious time, attended by another havana, which would include, after food offerings to the devatā, a religious feast for Brahmins and the distribution of small gifts.

Here, it did not need a Brahmin to divine. The mother herself dreamed frequently of her little loved ones whom she had failed to protect and sorely missed. The love and responsibility, the memory, the company could be sustained by having them beside her as part of her daily life. As devatās, they continued to live and participate in the family's life not only by their regular presence—they stayed close—but also through venerations on festive occasions. At such times, a *divā* (a wick in clarified butter) would be lit in their honor, and they would be the first to be served food. At other times, special occasions and feasts would be arranged for their worship. And after the nominal serving, the food would be served to Brahmins. Intermediary to the spiritual world, Brahmins are held in high esteem; this regard, however, is no less based on their own supreme giving status—as receivers of the gift, of consecrated leftovers.[1]

The love is not without dread of these spirits, who suffered an untimely death and were entitled to and quite likely harbored grudges. It was important to appease and be kind to them, as much in love as out of fear. Keeping them alive in one's memories and life was important to keep them benevolently disposed. Such benevolence of the spirits would be propitious. In addition to appeasing the spirits, the bereaved mother, when pregnant again, also secretly asked for the blessings of Śiva, the generous Lord of the world of spirits: "Bhole Nāth, I will bring your Kanwar. . . . May my child be born healthy and survive!" Her husband, who had been bringing kānwaṛs for some years, did not know this when she announced she would be accompanying him that year. She had had two children since, the elder now about twelve years old. "But you never told me," he had said. "What is the point of telling till things have actually turned right?" she responded. The traumatized mother was wary of revealing her secret—lest she jinx its fortuitous effect—till she was certain that things had actually, and rather unbelievably, turned out right. The possibility of something going awfully wrong, of tragic accidents, she both dreaded and knew too well, was never remote.

In recent years, thanks to the ethnographic work of scholars such as Nancy Scheper-Hughes, Loic Wacquant, Veena Das, and Javier Auyero, there is a growing sociological discourse on the phenomenal excess of violence in the everyday life of marginalized subjects.[2] These ethnographies show subjects trapped in the double bind of neoliberal structures that simultaneously overwhelm the collective with their undisputed, final, *winning* ideological representations and exclude a growing proportion of the people as economically and culturally incompetent and dangerous outcasts. "*Even the dead*," Benjamin would say, "will not be safe from the enemy if he wins. And this enemy has not ceased to be victorious."[3] This chapter speaks of the representations of the phenomenal dread of everyday life in religious practice in contemporary India. I argue that the dread of everyday existence, which is as salient in a biographical temporality as it pervades the phenomenal environment, connects and transfers between religious practices and everyday life in India for the marginalized masses. For such dread, dominant liberal discourses, such as of the nation, economy, or egocentric performance, have neither the time nor the forms to represent, perform, and abreact.

Economic marginalization goes hand in hand with discursive or symbolic domination, not only expressly by a statist order or a global network of neoliberal structures but also through the normative insinuations of academic representations exhibiting the certitude of objective knowledge, which champion supposedly "progressive" and "universal" standards and historical goals.[4] Narrating the influence of macroeconomic structures and policies in the everyday labors, traumas, and performances of the marginalized, in confined life courses and dead-end futures, is a novel and crucial sociological contribution of contemporary urban ethnography.[5] However, given the rather hermetic character of academic disciplines and subdisciplines, few of these critical scholarly discourses have percolated into the sociology of religion.

The following narrative focuses on the reflection of the dread of everyday existence and the precarious performances of social roles and obligations in religious practice. Religious practice here, I show, expresses, performs, and represents concerns, anxieties, fears, and images that are repressed in the dominant consciousness occupied by, say, discourses of the nation, economy, work, or the media. For some of the most overwhelming experiences, fears, and desires of social and psychic life in dystopian conditions, the mainstream world seems to have no time, no means of accommodation, no sites for registration, no performances. These realities are often deferred and displaced to, and play out in, religious practice. As these motifs of "repression," "displacement," and "repetition" would indicate, this analysis is significantly informed by psychoanalytic theory.[6] The subject here is a phenomenological entity, as situated in a personal historicity with its memories, anticipations, and significant others, as it is a relatively open site perceiving, registering, and responding to a charged sensory environment.[7]

DREAD AND MORTIFICATION

"'I will have to do it, Mother. . . . If I don't, who else will? . . . Otherwise, He [Śiva] will keep on breaking [*khandita*] our lives,' said my younger son,'" the elderly woman recollected. It had been more than a decade since his elder brother, sitting beside his four-year-old almost fully paralyzed child in the hospital, had pleaded for the recovery of his child.

> He could not speak; could not lift his hands, nor legs, nothing was left, had even gone blind. . . . "Hey Śivaji, [said the father,] I will bring your kānwar on my shoulders and offer you jal [holy water] not from Hardwar but from Gaumukh itself . . . but at least improve him such that he can talk to us, that he can drink and eat on his own.

Her grandchild was now eighteen; "so intelligent," continued the woman, now full of pride. "One of his legs is sure affected, but he runs a shop and is very smart in his studies." A Kanwar from Hardwar, however, was one thing; from Gaumukh, another 170 miles, at the roof of the Himalayas, quite another. Before he could find a companion to accompany him on the journey, the father himself died, from "paralysis and heart attack." The onus shifted to the younger brother, who also, despite some pilgrimages from Hardwar, found it hard to gather the courage and find a companion for the trip from Gaumukh. "Some time ago," she continued, "three of my buffaloes, all of them very vigorous and healthy, died within a year. . . . We could not believe it. . . . I had not been for the pilgrimage for some years. 'Bhole Nath,' I pleaded [in grief], 'don't test me so much! I have not forgotten you.'"

They stopped rearing cattle after that, and over the next two years the younger brother—the boy's uncle—brought the Kanwar from Gaumukh twice to deliver on his expired elder brother's promise. The possibility of God's displeasure was too much to take for a family that counted on His beneficent disposition. "We cannot even live without Him," she said, her voice turning soft and heavy. Most years she had undertaken the Kanwar as well as pilgrimages to other religious centers with only the wish of the well-being of her loved ones and seeking peace and welfare in general. If it is out of dread that the actor seems to frequently seek the assistance of Bhole Bābā, the demands of the Bābā are to be feared no less. As we sat on a parapet by the canal, we decided to suspend the kānwaṛs by the parapet itself, seeing no other place. In the process, several caveats were exchanged. "The two sides of the kānwaṛ are not balanced," one observed. Another said, "Make sure that the kānwaṛ [any part of it] does not pass over someone else's . . . that they are all evenly set." Yet another advised, with fear of a part of the kānwaṛ touching the ground: "Your kānwaṛ hangs low. Why not try the tree there?" At every step, there was an obsessive anxiety to abide by every requirement, to repetitively ensure the ritual appropriateness of every action, the symmetry of every alignment. The violation or failure of every stricture carried the final threat of the fragmentation, the failure (*khaṇḍita*) of the pilgrimage, the offering itself. When lifted, the kānwaṛ had to be borne on the right shoulder and could be moved to the other shoulder only around the back, never in front or above the head, and, as far as possible, with the containers evenly balanced. No animal or person could be allowed to pass under it.

The ritual cleanliness of the bearers was equally significant. The pilgrims had to wash themselves in their clothes, not only in the morning and after defecation but after every meal in which solid food had been consumed. A compulsive quality may also be seen in the necessity of immersing the whole kānwaṛ in the river, after the vessels are filled; or in the pilgrims who traverse the distance to the shrines, repetitively measuring their bodies' length on the ground. Likewise, it is critical that the pilgrimage is repeated; the pilgrimage is made in pairs or in groups of five or seven if avowed in such a form. And although not all stick to this imperative, all pilgrimages constituting one vow (or intention) should be repeated using the same pole. The series of abstinences, behavioral and dietary, to be repeated by the family at home, further emphasizes the compulsive quality of the ritual.

The word *khaṇḍita*—breaking down, fragmentation, disintegration— invoked in reference to existence earlier is also precisely the word used for the Kanwar if it cannot be completed, if it is breached. It disintegrates. The precarious carrying of the water is the precarious carrying on of life itself, its breaking down, a sign of impending disaster. The obsessional character is toned by one's abject conditions. The desperate expectations from the symbolic order are correlatives of precarious social conditions. The expectation of demand from the symbolic order (in conditions of mass unemployment or underemployment), the anxiety that attends, anticipates every demand that the subject promises to unconditionally meet—for the seemingly most trivial of them may potentially, like a hidden trick, like an omen, make or ruin everything—constitutes itself in reference to the precariousness of circumstances. That is, in reference to a phenomenology saturated with daily, foreboding exposure to disease, poverty, misfortune, death, humiliation: a neighbor consumed by tuberculosis; a gruesome accident on the road yesterday; a child who barely escaped being run over by a speeding motorcycle; the friend complaining her kidney was removed by the doctor, a crook, on the basis of a false diagnosis; the crowded clinics filled with rude staff and authoritarian physicians; word of a young relative who burned himself to death; the anxiety over a child who is frequently sick and does not seem to be growing; a drunken man drowned in the open sewage line in the neighborhood this evening; the agonizing humiliation of someone (or oneself) pulling a rickshaw being slapped by a policeman. "If the obsessional mortifies himself," says Lacan with characteristic insightfulness, "it is because . . . he binds himself to his ego, which bears within itself dispossession and imaginary death."[8] Butler in her paraphrasis of Hegel is equally to the point: "Although devotion appears to be a form of self immersion, it is also a continuation of self-beratement as self-mortification. . . . The sanctification of abjection takes place through rituals of fasting and mortification."[9]

VISITATION

The anxiety of following every diktat, almost to the extent of inventing new ones—since there are scarcely any canonical texts—is part of the performative construction of the pilgrimage. And insofar as the performances, the desires, are tied to one's performances in the world, it reflects a compulsive anxiety to ward off every possibility of infringement, every untoward event, every threat to fortuitous possibilities, to the desired objective—often just for life to keep to its ordinary course. Bimala, one of my respondents, tied her recent misfortunes with the consequences of not meeting a promise, when a deity warned her in her dream, days before people were leaving for the pilgrimage:

> It is a man; he comes from the direction of the pond to stop at the doorway, next to my cot. "People make pronouncements and then don't fulfill them," he says. "What did we commit?" I ask him. "Didn't he vow a Kanwar?" he answers back, referring to my husband. "Did you bring it? Did you have it brought? Isn't that why your home is in ruins?" "I will have it brought," I say, "this time . . . will that be okay?" "It is up to you," he replies; "bring it if you wish; forget it if you don't want to." I do not know who he was . . . must have been one of our devatās warning us.

Others sitting with us concurred: "It is a devatā's call; some devatā warned you." Bimala's family had been forced to move from Delhi to this small town in Uttar Pradesh after her husband died a year ago. He died from a wound on a foot struck by a brick during construction work. The wound had festered when he kept working in a paddy field despite the injury and, "according to the doctor," because of his heavy drinking, which undercut the effect of the medicines. "I am willing to die," he is said to have insisted, "but I won't abstain from liquor." Earlier, the elder son had absconded after a tiff in the family (probably over the father's drinking), after which the father had vowed he would have him bring a Khaṛi Kanwar on his return. The young man did return for a while but left again, and when his wife asked him to bring the Kanwar in lieu of the son, the man was evasive.

The rebuke in the dream alarmed Bimala, who immediately began consultations the next morning. "You will have to bring the Kanwar in his

place," people said. "Take the younger son with you and have him lift the
kānwaṛ in his brother's name." Without a penny at home, she nevertheless quickly arranged a loan and made the necessary arrangements. And
although she faced many problems during the journey because of intense
chafing between her thighs, together the two successfully brought the
Khaṛi Kanwar in the others' names. The pair would be completed next
year. "But whenever the elder one returns," Bimala insists, "I will have
him do a pair too . . . even if I have to pay the expenses myself."

We can see here that the pilgrimage has to be completed, whether the
wish is fulfilled or only partially or nominally fulfilled, and whether it is
completed by the vower or a subject assigned through a series of substitutions: the parent calling in the child's name, the wife replacing the husband, one sibling filling in for another. One felt the compulsion to keep
the faintest word to the deity, the smallest hint of a pact. Although some
may categorically say, "I will make the pilgrimage when X happens," in
most cases, the anxiety is such that the pilgrimage needs to be completed
in any case. The smallest trace of fulfillment has to be seen as a sign of
his beneficence, beneficence one feels compelled to construct or decipher
rather than deny. But coupled with that, one also sees the play of desire.
There is an attraction to the pilgrimage, as the occasion, the season arrives.
As one of my respondents put it, "There is a joy that takes over my heart at
the time, making my hair stand on end and tears well up in the eyes." The
dream here thus also manifests a desire to go on the pilgrimage, merged
with the desire for the vow to actually come true, for felicitous conditions
at home. As the head of the family, Bimala was now making her own deci-
sions and also assuming expanded responsibilities for mentoring her wards.

DESIRE AND THE DREADFUL GOD

The desires, whether for the many joys and pains of the pilgrimage or domestic felicity, the company of an absconding child or general peace and
well-being ("Bābā, grace everyone with your benevolence"), are merged
with dread and a premonition of misfortune. Such collapse of desire
and dread into a singularity, two sides of the same phenomenon, finds
a perfect adumbration in Śiva, in his complex character and the bountiful, timeless mythology surrounding him along with Satī/Pārvatī, and the

Ganga.[10] On the one hand, Śiva is the destructive principle itself, gar-
landed with bones and skulls, smeared in ash from funeral pyres, drinking
bhāng from skulls with rotting flesh, his dreadlocks filled with snakes,
throat blue from deadly venom, and in the middle of his forehead, the all-
consuming, grotesque third eye, which once burned Kāma, the god of desire, to ashes.[11] Thus, for example, once "Brahma said to Rudra, 'Śiva, lord
of Satī , perform creation,'" but Rudra said, "'I will not perform creation.
Do it yourself, and let me destroy. I will become Sthanu [the pillar, an
ascetic].'"[12] Surrounded by ghosts and goblins, this drunken, necrophiliac
ascetic is, in his own words meant to dissuade Satī , an "ugly naked beggar
who makes his home in the burning ground, who smears his body with
ashes taken from burned corpses."[13]

On the other hand, this Kāpālika (skull bearer), Bhasmabhūta (made
of ashes), Vāmadeva (the crooked god), Bhikṣāṭana (wandering about for
alms) is also Bholā, the Simple One or the Fool, and Āśutoṣa, who is
easily pleased; he is the most generous and the greatest renouncer. Śiva
fulfills everyone's wishes. Such descriptions of Bholā—and, by extension,
of the devotee, the bholā—are very frequently cited, as for example, in the
following excerpts from popular material on the pilgrimage:

1.   Lord of the three realms . . .
     Yourself a seeker of alms . . .
     Settler of the universe . . .
     You live in the wilderness . . .[14]

2.   To Indra you gave all wealth . . .
     Nectar you gave to the gods, keeping the poison to yourself . . .
     To Bhagiratha you gave the Ganga, for everyone to bathe . . .
     Lanka you gave to Ravana . . .
     To Rama you gave the bow and arrows, to Hanumāna, the Lord . . .
     Yourself you remain in drunken ecstasy, drinking bhāng from a skull.[15]

And at the same time, Śiva—the phallic god usually worshipped in his
iconic form with the lingam placed in the yoni—is Desire, Kāma itself; his
dreadful countenance also makes him most desirable to Satī as well as to
countless other women.[16] And in later Tantric editions, Śiva as Bhairava

is but the lesser deity, the consort who resides by Śakti at every Pīṭha (Seat).[17] In a widespread practice, young unmarried women worship the Śivalinga every Monday with offerings of milk and often request desired characteristics in their future husbands. Generous as he is, Śiva—who is also Ardhanārīśvara, God who is half woman—understands and disposes desire. He is simultaneously the supreme ascetic and a householder; the power of his *tapas* (meditative heat) is such that even marriage and cohabitation cannot affect his ascetic potency, and Śiva remains a *brahmacārin* (celibate) despite marriage. Śiva is the greatest of yogis (ascetics) and an equally great *bhogin* (hedonist), and the two affects are often merged in the existential aesthetic, the ethic he epitomizes.[18]

In one respect, however, phenomenal representation is not tied to affect; a level of arbitrariness or play is involved. If Śiva's frightful and disgusting aspect arouses dread, in other cases, for example, in the worship of Laddu Gopāla (the adoption of the infant Kṛṣṇa in a form of Vaiśnavite worship), the purity attributed to the deity may be even more mortifying. The worship demands meticulous rituals, attention, and discipline, and the smallest violation of the deity is fraught with the greatest danger. On the other hand, Śiva's aspect with its manifest forms, in its appropriation of the phenomenal forms of death and destruction—ashes, snakes, poison, fire, sex, nakedness, monstrosity—seems to be more "liberating." It perhaps provides greater abreacting efficacy and, thereby, the abandon of Śaivite religion, the merger of opposites. Thus, Bhavan, one of my respondents, described an uncle who had been on several Kanwar pilgrimages and who used to regularly smoke sulfā; however, once he "adopted" Laddu Gopāla, "he renounced everything, not just sulfā and liquor but even onions and garlic." The idol is kept in a separate room that is cleaned every day and can be entered only after bathing. The idol is worshipped and offered milk twice a day. Moreover, a house in which the deity has been installed cannot ever be locked; a family member has to be at home all the time. While the deity's presence is very auspicious, violation of his purity portends grievous consequences.

"It is like bringing Bālājī home," continued Bhavan, a college-educated, unmarried man in his mid-twenties, "but the Bālājī rites are of course much more difficult." Much like the purity of the infant Kṛṣṇa, the celibacy of Bālājī—the infant Hanumāna—requires stringent behavioral regulations. The ritual adoption of a Bālājī idol, according to this respondent, requires forty-one weeks of *vrats* (fasting rituals), including dietary regulations as well as sexual abstinence. "It is extremely difficult to pull it off; the Lord will put numerous obstacles in your way . . . and if you fail, the consequences are very bad; therefore, few people take the challenge; but if you can make it, you will see the Lord himself, manifest." The dread that binds the subject to the security promised by Hanumāna or Bālājī, powerful like the wind, or the domestic bliss promised by the adorable playfulness of the infant Kṛṣṇa, or the generosity of Śiva repeats itself in the religious performance. Since the deities are powerful and to be feared, as much by the self as by others, it is precisely their power that assures their influence on the forces of the world as well as on the spiritual alignments that may bring bad fortune.[19]

The dread that binds the subject to the security promised by the deity also repeats itself in the religious performance: the sudden invitation, the case for visiting the god, "You cannot go on the pilgrimage unless He calls you." This refrain, as I have noted previously, is common to most North Indian pilgrimages, although particularly salient in the context of the Himalayan goddess Vaisno Devi. In one popular, and widely filmed, rendition—"Chalo bulāvā āyā hai; Mātā ne bulāyā hai" (Let us go; an invitation has arrived; the Mother has called)—the expression reckons a return to the mother, now the divine Mother, the time of her authority, and the care, protection, and endearment her presence promises.[20] She would both listen to one's agony and grant wishes. The figure of "invitation" is often characterized by specific existential references, shared by both the goddess pilgrimages and the Kanwar. The invitation, as I have noted earlier, is the paramount condition for the pilgrimage—"unless He invites, the journey cannot materialize, by any means; but if He calls, it will take place despite any number of obstacles." "No one can go just like that, whatever offering you may announce, but when He calls," said Amma, one of my elderly respondents, forcefully emphasizing, "you go automatically. . . . Only then will you raise a step."

And it was in reference to the same force of the call that Bimala had recounted the dream that had sent her on the pilgrimage. "We simply did not have the wherewithal for the journey till the last minute; it was totally out of question; and then I had this dream." The "invitation" has the added resonance of its specificity, of being God's elect, the recipient of divine grace and therefore felicitous, blessed—"Everything is fine; God has been generous."[21] The call has to be followed, literally, by a visit.

And almost every visit, whether to the goddess or in the Kanwar, expresses the desire to come yet again—if the deity wishes and times are propitious. In addition to the absolute agency of the deity, since the pilgrimage depends on circumstances being propitious, on events being favorable, or perhaps a wish being fulfilled—since it depends on desire—it asks to be assured that everything will be fine and no untoward incident meanwhile will preclude the anticipated journey. It seeks the assurance of security amid the dread, the ravages of time, of *Kāla*, which is as much Death as Duration.

But, of course, circumstances are not always felicitous. One must acknowledge the blessings of Bhole Bābā and not appear ungrateful, for things could always be far worse and life itself is a gift; still, there are instances where His injustices are hard to condone. Thus, Kshetrapal, who has made more than a dozen pilgrimages, several of them Khaṛi, questions the Lord's justice:

> Bhole Bābā does not fulfill anyone's wishes. . . . He doesn't do anything. It is just that we bring the kānwaṛ out of our own desire. . . . My wife's pair of Khaṛi Kanwars remained incomplete. She did the libations in this very temple. . . . Where was Bhole Bābā? . . . She died [the same year] before she could complete the pair . . . leaving three children behind her.

"Leaving me alone to look after them," he continued poignantly. Kshetrapal nevertheless continues to go on the journey, every year. The journey continues despite His injustices—"I will keep going as long as I can still walk, as long as there is some desire left. The suffering He inflicts, one will have to endure." And the wife's pilgrimage itself would be completed at some point, "by her child," says Kshetrapal. In the completion of that particular journey, the Khaṛi Kanwar, by the child who would have come of age, Kshetrapal would also have completed a critical component of his own journey or performance in the world: fulfilling a primary responsibility to the departed companion. But if fate continued to be defiant, the vow would still be completed. "Why not you?" asked someone in the background yet again. "It is better the child does it," he replied, after having avoided the question, the unfortunate contingency, for a while, "but if it falls on me, I will have to endure that as well."

Bhavan, who comes from a family with several members invested in religious activities and who had himself made six pilgrimages, likewise acknowledged the difficulty of the times and expressed misgivings about divine help. Two years ago, a taxi he used to drive was stolen from the street in broad daylight, "at two p.m., within a span of fifteen minutes. . . . The owner filed a police report against me; I had to recompense the cost of the car. . . . What other option does a worker have?" This development made him disillusioned with the job, although he continues to drive rental cars that can be returned to the owner every evening. "I have not progressed since finishing my studies . . . on top of that, this loss."[22] If there is little that is certain here, he nevertheless keeps feeling for certainty in Bābā. "When here, I am more disturbed . . . but in Hardwar, my mind is set on Him. I don't go after sightseeing, et cetera. . . . I just look for where He might be, where I might have His *darśana* [sight/encounter]. . . . I will climb a hill, a rock, and look around." In some of Bhavan's expressions, the pilgrimage was truly complete only if one was able to touch or embrace the lingam or at least have a clear, satisfying darśana. Here, the sensuous perception of the lingam—in those days of the pilgrimage—seems to carry the effect of the actual manifestation, darśana of the deity, an exalted motif of Hindu religious belief or tradition.[23] Bhavan's desires correspond with the experiences of his father, an ardent devotee of Hanumāna. "Although he will rarely talk about it, on days when he is very tense . . . Hanumāna manifests himself to him . . . and then he is at peace."

And if it is in the power of the mighty Hanumāna, who conquers all fear, that his father finds solace, for Bhavan, Śiva is the great source of energy and inspiration. "The slogans hailing Him give me so much peace. My body feels suddenly animated, energized. . . . Even if you don't say them yourself, just hearing those inspires you." Nevertheless, Bhavan continues to wait for some wish to be fulfilled, for a whiff of divine assistance. The obsessive adherence to the protocols of this Master, Śiva, continues the anxiety in relation to the arbitrary whims and demands of that other master, the diviners of the symbolic order. It weaves in the anxiety attending and anticipating every demand—demands one hopes for, awaits—from the equally elusive worldly masters, chances that one is well aware make or break lives. There is a transfer, a communion of affects between the different orders. While the pilgrimage is often a merry, carnivalesque occasion, on the other side of its spirited merriment one also finds the compulsions of a desire to follow, to serve much-anticipated commands of the symbolic order that, however, never seem to come. In other cases, even when the wish fulfilled may be so grave, the gratitude so binding that the subjects feel compelled to perform the journey year after year, the dread may nevertheless continue to haunt.

THE GREATER SUFFERING AND
THE CASE FOR RENUNCIATION

Unlike the commotion at the many temples and ghats of Hardwar, the temple of Bilvakesvara, located under a hill about a mile southwest of Har-ki-Pairī (God's steps; the primary ghat of the town), has a rare, quiet, verdant ambience. Here, Pārvatī, in one of her avatars, is said to have meditated on Śiva, following which the Lord appeared to grant her a boon. The place where Śiva manifested himself hosts the central temple complex, while the site of Pārvatī's meditation, deeper in a hill recess beside a stream, has another temple with a small well, the Gauri-Kunda. By the *kunda* (a natural pool) on that day sat a man dressed impeccably in trousers and a shirt, perhaps a local, chanting hymns. Outside, two middle-aged couples who had just finished bathing in the celebrated waters of the stream packed their bags.

The Kanwar couples had been in Hardwar for a few days, and there was some confusion over whether they would begin the journey that day or the next. "We come for the pilgrimage every year," said one of the women. "My only child was brought dead from the hospital. . . . The doctors had given up and had let him go. There was no hope. 'Śivaji,' I had then cried in front of Bhole Bābā, 'I will not ask you for anything else ever again in my life, grant me the life of my child!'" Her husband stood by, nodding somberly. The child, they said, revived miraculously. "His debt on us is infinite. We will keep coming as long as we are alive, as long as these limbs will still carry us." We lingered for a while and, on the way back, again came across the two couples. The women had sought shade under a tree, while a heated argument was going on between the two men sitting by the curb of the narrow paved pathway. The man we had conversed with was frantically challenging the claims of the other, who spoke in a more subdued manner. The other person had apparently suggested self-reflectively that the fact he looked old beyond his age was the result of a lifetime of hardships. "I am scarcely forty," he repeated for us, "but already look older than a fifty-year-old. This is because of a life of endless hardships. . . . I began working when I was not yet twelve."

Our previous interlocutor, a few years older than this man, sensed a negation, an underestimation of his own suffering. "I began to work at twenty, but I have been through so much pain . . . through one ordeal after another." If the latter was provoked by an apparent discounting of his suffering and ordeals, the former recognized in these signs of early aging the ravages of time—life's tribulations, as if one could not help losing against them; even when one had conquered them, one after another, with the greatest heroism and courage, they would have the last laugh in the ruins they left behind. For the man, who indeed looked much older than his age, a weary countenance seemed to be as much the repetition of a lifetime of suffering as its confirmation—if not for recognition by likewise competing others, perhaps in the face of the absolute Other.

The endless tribulations of life in one place seem to correspond with the endless iterations and excesses of the journey in another. In phenomenological terms, the individual is but one boundary for such experiences and their affects and resonances, which determine the social field for a vast majority. "I just keep repeating Bhole Bābā's name as I walk, and as long as you are doing so, everything remains fine," said Basant, a man in his mid-fifties who has been on the pilgrimage almost every year since the late 1970s. "Earlier, I used to take the Kanwar to my native village in Haryana," continued Basant, recounting a time when the rivers were crossed by ferries, the roads were infested with robbers, and the pilgrimage was rather obscure and had many fewer participants. "People would occasionally mistake us for snake charmers."

It has been a long time since then. Following the many pilgrimages from Hardwar (several of them Khaṛi), for the last two decades he has been bringing kānwaṛs from Gaumukh; in addition, Basant has made pilgrimages within the Himalayas, taking the sacred water from Gaumukh to the upper Himalayan shrine of Kedarnath. A widely traveled person, he has many tales to tell: of deep valleys and gorges; perilous tracks to Kedarnath, where one would not come across a human being for hours on end; of a boulder hurtling down a mountain he barely escaped; of exhaustion and indefinite periods of hunger and thirst; of walking in the night while in fear of robbers and wild animals; of villages that live off water from the streams; of landslides and a cloudburst when the paths were flooded with four feet of water; of dangerous mountain roads. Once, as he was coming down from Gaumukh with the jal, he ran across fellow villagers who had traveled uphill by carpooling. Visibly shocked, they said to him, "Basant, disaster struck!" "I had my heart in my mouth," said Basant; "I feared the worst. I thought the vehicle had fallen into the valley." However, they had been saved; their car slid backward toward the deep river valley, about to topple in, but had been saved at the edge by a god-sent rock that stuck into the underside.

Basant's expression of his desire for the pilgrimage is evocative. "As soon as the month of Sāvana [Śrāvaṇa] sets in, I have the compulsive feeling to leave. Every morning, after prayers, I will reach for the calendar . . . check the various dates. . . . I feel restless." Some of his enthusiasm for the journey has perhaps been inherited from a family with an extensive tradition of Śiva worship, especially on his mother's side, where his uncle and grandfather had both made several pilgrimages. "My grandfather [and later, mother] would make little Śivalingas and statues of Śiva, Pārvatī, or Gaṇeśa from clay . . . say, 11 or 101, or 1,001 [an auspicious number] of these." The idols would be worshipped ritually, using milk, rice, bael leaves, and bananas. The sacred objects would be made in the morning and dispersed in the canal or the pond after prayers in the evening. At times, when the practice would become associated with a particularly strong wish or concern, it could include resignation, the offering or promise of as many as 125,001 Śivalingas. If the labor of the offering manifested the force of the desire, if it was meant to convince the deity of the artist's, the devotee's compulsion and gratitude, the dispersal of the works in the waters every evening also had the effect of renunciation. It is precisely the mood, the existential attitude, of the renouncer that seems to appeal to Basant. "Now, where I am concerned," he continued,

> I don't have any wish in mind. . . . Otherwise, there is no limit to human wishes. . . . About Śivaji, you see, what people aspire for, He rejects. The world likes dresses, ornaments. . . . Śiva stays away from them. The world likes palaces; He looks for crematoriums. . . . It is the same for the Kanwar . . . just need to have five to ten days' worth of bare necessities, like the ascetics, that's all.

In his highly controversial studies, the French sociologist Louis Dumont argued that in the history of India, a society structured on the principle of hierarchy, the renouncer has been the only creative figure. In Dumont's portrait of the fundamental code of Indian society, the Indian is *homo hierarchicus*; the renouncer alone breaks from the vise grip of the caste society to be an individual-outside-the-world.[24] Setting aside Dumont's essentialist propositions, it is important to note that the oppressive concerns of regular social existence are clearly a key impetus to renounce social roles. The desire to leave the householder's conundrum and become a renouncer is expressed quite commonly in Indian homes, usually as a threat, a last resort in times of conflict or excessive anxiety. By its definitiveness, other-worldly character, resignation, and the loss and difficulties it represents both for the subject and the addressees, the declaration verges on that of suicide—a symbolic death. In the pilgrimage as well as the other votive rites, the desires and agonies of everyday life are expressed as much as they are renounced or transcended; they represent as much involvement as detachment. The pilgrimage is itself as much a departure from the ordinary social world as a return to it. The tension expressed in the structure of the pilgrimage—the going and the returning—is close to that which is afforded by the phenomenological edge of the suicide threat—a will that verges on action, a departure that may or may not actualize.

The play of this duality perhaps finds its best analytical illustration in Freud's astute observations in *Beyond the Pleasure Principle*. Particularly pertinent here are Freud's reflections on the peculiar game (discussed in

Chapter 2) he saw his grandchild play to master the mortifying experiences of the departure of the mother to whom he was greatly attached. "The only use he made of any of his toys," Freud says, "was to play 'gone' with them": a habit of throwing the toys in a corner under the bed, giving in the process "vent to a loud, long drawn out 'o-o-o-o' . . . [which] was not a mere interjection but represented the German word 'fort' [gone]; and in a more complete version, pulling the object back, hailing the reappearance with a joyful 'da' [there]." Realizing that these observations were incompatible with the pleasure principle, which had been at the center of his theories to this point, Freud finds himself forced to recognize a drive of which the pleasure principle would be but one component. Beyond the pleasure principle, he sees in this compulsion to repeat—which may often dawn on people as an obscure fear of "some 'daemonic' force at work"—an impulse more primitive: the death drive.[25] Likewise, in the case of a person in analysis, Freud says, the compulsion to repeat childhood events in transference "disregards the pleasure principle in every way."[26] The child's game here demonstrates a rejection, a renunciation of the object of one's interest, the mother, in view of her inevitable departures, the phenomenological complications of being with her. This was followed by an expression of the pleasure in her consequent return. The compulsion to repeat the dreaded moment and the pleasurable feeling of the mother's return "converge here into an intimate partnership."[27]

In both its joy and self-inflicted violence, this "peculiar tension" closely represents the performative intensity of the pilgrimage. First, there is the worldly experience of dread (a relentless exposure to pain, suffering, and social demands, as biographical as it is phenomenologically pervasive) that forces the subject to repeatedly depart from the world, to renounce it again and again. This is followed by a return, in peace, carrying the sacred water, yet also in a painful, mortifying manner and often with an element of fractiousness. In this repeated practice, now in control and in a field of one's choice, an absolute field, one also sees an element of mastering over otherwise repressed affects. As Freud meticulously describes in his "Remembering, Repeating and Working-Through," the best way to negotiate the repressed impulses was to repeat them in the "definite field" of the analytical setting, "a playground in which . . . [they are] allowed to expand in almost complete freedom." The transference allowed by the religious field and phenomenon "is a piece of real experience, but one which has been made possible by especially favorable conditions."[28] At this point, one must radically if cautiously consider the transferences between psychic and social dimensions of repression. In view of the large-scale, manifestly social nature of the phenomenon we are considering—a social issue instead of a personal trouble, as Mills may have differentiated—"repression" is another word for the lack of satisfactory discursive and moral (self) recognition by the subject as much as by the social or institutional actors in reference to which she addresses herself. The pilgrimage becomes an alternative field of performance, simultaneously repeating the traumas of daily life and transferring, transforming, binding them to a sacred occasion and performance. For the subject, here an adult, it will also be a site to practice her resolve.

AGENCY: BETWEEN PAIN AND DREAD

"Once it so happened," said Basant, "my brother while bringing the Kanwar from Hardwar tripped on a speed breaker—the kind they make in the villages, with wood stumps covered by soil—and badly sprained his ankle." Among his siblings, Basant's expired brother was the only other person who used to bring kānwaṛs. However, since he had lived an urban life, suggested Basant, he was not as versed in walking in this manner. The injury delayed him, and he sent word home that he would be late. When Basant, who had brought the Kanwar from Gaumukh, reached home, the sister-in-law reprimanded him for not getting his brother along. "But I never met him," he had to reply. The next day, he went back to his brother in a neighboring village. Seeing him barely able to stand, Basant offered to carry the kānwaṛ for him. The brother, however, was firm: "The kānwaṛ I will carry myself, even if the legs are to be amputated." Continued Basant, "Slowly, we made it to the temple; he carried the kānwaṛ himself although I walked with him. He fell very ill at home thereafter and was on intravenous fluids for several days."

Although people frequently carry each other's kānwaṛs, bring joint kānwaṛs, and helping one another is considered meritorious, here the suggestion, the context of failure, the hint of an inability to complete the sacred, all-important journey made the subject refuse the assistance, perhaps especially when he was so close. Evidence of a lack on this chosen ground would imply a deep, essential lack that threatens to repeat in every other sphere, in every other responsibility, and most immediately in the object of one's wish or vow. This is a widely shared view, perhaps the defining feature of the event: the compulsion to complete the journey despite all obstacles and physical excesses. Failure in this religious, chosen task—although surely not unknown—most regard as disastrous, a fundamental failure. It would be inauspicious. Thus, while many may seemingly pull off the journey without grave difficulties, a good number labor to the end with evident pain and suffering. The tracks are often blue from feet soaked in a blue solution supposed to prevent blisters; although it is regarded as ineffective by many, trays filled with the solution are ubiquitous. Numerous participants toil in heavily bandaged, bleeding feet, after the skin from the blistered soles of the feet is removed by medical personnel. And the frequent medical stalls on the way, either selling or freely distributing antibiotics and basic medicines for pain relief, fever, muscle strain, diarrhea, and other common ailments, are crowded with clients.

"I was vomiting on the way back from Gangotri this year. The air pressure on the mountains creates a problem. My body has started developing fever from cold these days. . . . Bathing in the freezing water gives shivers." Basant kept speaking of his own problems in bringing the water from Gaumukh after describing his brother's ordeal. Despite precautions and extensive guidance, pain and suffering in the pilgrimage are as common as the resolve they provoke. This is evident in the experiences and narratives of many of my respondents. "I had a high fever on the way," one said, describing the experience of his first pilgrimage, "but I was determined to complete the journey even if I were to die." In other cases, where participants may not be as vocal about their resolve, their ritual completion of the journey, despite intense pain and struggle, speaks for itself. In another discussion, Amma had been critical of a woman in her group for dithering while taking the frequent showers:

> "My thighs will chafe," she said, and did not bathe properly. On the other
> hand, I immerse myself in the shower without hesitation and nothing happens

to me. . . . In Bābā's journey you have to do everything with a pure heart. Her
thighs got stuck onto one another from chafing, giving her a very hard time.

Because the pilgrims took frequent ritual baths in the open while fully
clothed and were unable to bring spare clothing in their minimal bag-
gage, they would often continue to walk in their wet clothes. The dilemma
is worse for women; younger women in particular rarely change clothes
after baths because of privacy considerations. The wet clothes rubbing between the thighs on skin tender from the bath can cause intense chafing
and bleeding, making every step of the journey an ordeal. When later
Amma introduced Bimala as the person who had the difficulty, the latter acknowledged that it had been a painful trip. Bimala's ordeal as she
carried out a Khaṛi Kanwar (covering the distance with very little rest or
sleep), despite pain and anxiety, in a time of grave difficulties in her family
and in apparently not very sympathetic company, can only be imagined.
About another woman who went with her last year, Amma would say,
spreading her hands indicating a tree trunk, "her legs were this swollen."
A man speaking of his own first journey likewise pointed to his knees:
"My legs were draped this high in bandages. . . . The toes were completely
ulcerated; I walked on my heels." Amma herself had a goiter and had
gone on the pilgrimage without a break for many years—although often
deciding at the last moment—even when battling fever and injuries.

Yet in certain instances it becomes just too difficult to complete the
project—almost arbitrarily as the obstacles add up. In the middle of the
journey where every step may be painful and the destination inconceiv-
ably distant; or a possibly feverish, enfeebled body is no longer able to
orient itself to the project; or perhaps just the circumstances are not right
or the company is unsupportive, the journey may have to be aborted. The
woman showing us Rati's place was perplexed and somewhat dismissive:
"What could you want to know from her? Her pilgrimage remained in-
complete." Rati's house was next to a small temple where a soothsayer,
a devotee of Sāi Bābā, sat for a few hours every evening attending to
people's everyday anxieties and concerns about the future. A composed,
middle-aged woman in a sari, dressed and looking like any ordinary, married Hindu woman, she would listen to people, answering their questions

and offering advice and comfort, while meditating before a picture of Sāi Bābā. As I sat in the temple later that day after my conversation with Rati, a woman asked her, "My parents are both old, and my brother's family does not care for them. Can you tell me, which of them would be the first to die?" "You, a daughter, why would you ask such a question?" she asked in turn. "They are concerned and want me to inquire," she said. Nodding understandingly, the seer closed her eyes while gazing at Sāi Bābā's picture and made a few observations about the poor treatment of the parents and the current goings-on and continued: "I see both your parents; your mother will still be healthy . . . your father I see in a wheelchair. I see him leaving earlier." When the petitioner repeated to confirm, the seer only nodded subtly, as though hesitant in intruding over fate and such final matters. Just then, a man circumambulating the Śivalinga at the center remarked, "There is relief in my stomach pain since yesterday, after several months." "Keep to the regimen I gave you; it will go away completely," she responded.

Rati, a young woman who had been married for several years, had not gone for the Kanwar with any new wish; rather, the pilgrimage, her first, was in thanksgiving for the child who had survived after several of her children had died in infancy or sooner. "My pilgrimage would have been completed, if only our companions had been supportive. . . . They would not stop and kept pushing. I came crying till Roorkee," she observed regretfully. Rati's feet developed giant blisters, which made it difficult for her to walk. And halfway through the journey her companions saw her off by train, along with a young nephew accompanying her, and an older woman in similar agony. The other woman had a previous injury, which was aggravated during the journey, and a hairline fracture was diagnosed later. "But I only had blisters and could have completed the journey. They could have sent the other woman on her own. . . . At least my pilgrimage would not have been cut short," Rati had continued pensively.

RESOLVE, SIGNS, AND DELUSIONS

The first time I can remember having been hit by bhāng, a paste made from the buds and leaves of cannabis, was in 2001 at an outlet outside the renowned Mahakalesvara temple in Ujjain. There are a limited number of such outlets, three or four in selected towns, where the drug can be legally sold—although irregular stalls abound on festive occasions—usually in the form of *thandai*, a sweetened cold drink of diluted milk or water to which crushed leaves and flowers of the cannabis plant are added. Initially, the effect would be a mild elation, a slightly buoyant feel of reality. Soon, however, time consciousness would change radically. A most vivid experience one instant would recede at an alarming speed into distant, spectacular imaginaries; spoken words faded into the distance even as they were uttered, thus washing away the coherence of every sentence. Every return to the present, at the blink of an eye as it were, would have the same consequence. "It fragments the consciousness; bhāng comes from the Sanskrit bhāng [to break, to rupture]," explained the eminent Hindi literary critic Madan Soni, during one friendly interaction. One would be thereby occupied by a spate of transitory imaginary experiences, each more vivid and forceful than the other; the subject here, like a leaf, being blown in the wind in different directions. "An absolutely blizzard-like production of images . . . so extraordinary, so fleeting, and so rapidly generated that we can do nothing but gaze at them simply because of their beauty and singularity," Walter Benjamin noted of his experience of hashish.[29] Walking in unfamiliar streets and riding pillion on a motorbike with this loss of sensory grip on reality had been exhilarating and mildly anxiety provoking.

During the pilgrimage trip I first had bhāng, with K, while climbing the mountain to Nilkantha. It was a good trip, a climb of about six miles from Rishikesh. Situated immediately at the point where the Ganga exits the Himalayan mountain range to enter the great North Indian plains, Rishikesh, about twenty miles upstream from Hardwar, is the other major center in this sacred geography. The town is host to a number of religious institutions, āśramas, and temples. It also features in the Indian itinerary of most Western tourists attracted by a heady mix of religion, the natural magnificence of the Himalayas, and, equally important, relatively cheap and easily available marijuana. Between the tourists and the *sadhus* (sages) who abound here, money is perhaps exchanged as much for religious experiences as for marijuana supplies. One of the twin sacred towns, Rishikesh is likewise a part of the common itinerary of the Kanwaria. As important for the Kanwaria, however, is that the town is a transit point for the Nilkantha temple in the mountains immediately above.

After bathing in the river, we had collected, like other pilgrims, a small quantity of water for libations in the temple. It was early in the pilgrimage—in fact, it was only the first day of Sāvana—yet an already impressive crowd was climbing on the paved pathway. Intermittently in the crowd, one would come across a person advancing in a much more demanding manner, measuring the length of his body on the ground. In this form, called the Daṇḍavata Kanwar, at every step the pilgrim would stretch himself on his belly, and the tip of the stretched arm would be marked on the ground by a companion; the next step would repeat the action, beginning at the mark. It would be an extraordinary and painful journey of about six to eight hours for these pilgrims; many end up with their palms, bellies, and knees chafed, swollen, and bleeding.

For us, however, it had turned out to be a relaxed journey in fine weather; a light drizzle earlier had cooled the air, and the abundant foliage on the mountains seemed to have come out fresh from the shower.

FIGURE 3.1. *Daṇḍavata Kanwar to Nilkantha*

The bhāng we obtained at a wayside stall had at most a faint euphoric effect, and we gaily climbed the mountain before being pulled, immediately outside the temple, into long queues progressing at a snail's pace alongside a rocky wall infested by monitor lizards. The lizards played in the crevices immediately above, looking us in the eye, while we cringed away amid the hectic pushing and shoving in the queues. Not surprisingly, the lizards attracted much attention; some travelers were issuing warnings against provoking them; others curiously followed their movements, attracting attention to new ones peeping between the rocks; and yet others saw in this another confirmation of Śiva's presence—"They will not harm anyone here; this is their place, beside Bhole Bābā." The threat passed without incident.

The next and last occasion I had bhāng, only half-knowingly this time and with very different consequences, was on the first evening of our main pilgrimage. Despite the harshness of the sun, the journey to Roorkee had been smooth; we had covered the twenty-mile stretch in about six hours, including a few breaks. We stopped for lunch at a *dhābā*, a wayside restaurant with the barest furnishings in which a number of Kanwarias were sprawled on dusty carpets. As I looked around for an opening to suspend the kānwaṛ on frames that had been set up for the purpose, K took the kānwaṛ from me to ensure there was no ritual violation and that it was securely placed. "No part of the kānwaṛ should pass below or above anyone else's kānwaṛ," he advised me at the time, "and one always has to be on guard; keep the kānwaṛ close, within sight, lest a stray dog or another animal pass under it or someone violate it." Locating a space, K tied the kānwaṛ to the frame with the strings we were carrying for the purpose. Even as I waited on K, observing the lesson, I could feel the fatigue in my legs and a painful stiffness in the joints, which, I feared, did not augur well for the journey. I hoped the pain would subside after the rest, but after the break when I had to limp my way to the obligatory shower at a nearby water outlet, the worst fears seemed to be coming true. For a body unaccustomed to walking such distances, and in flip-flops, the rest had had the opposite effect; my ankles and knees were hurting badly, and the soles of my feet were sore from my body weight—a stage indicating the impending abscesses. The open bathing place, set up by an adjacent rest camp, had multiple showers at which several people—women, men, and children alike—pressed to soak themselves. After managing to get a few seconds under the shower, I walked back, trying to ensure the sandy soil did not fill up my slippers. I had been advised that grains of sand would scrape the skin between the toes, especially if it rained.

Other members of the group—all of them of a working-class background and habituated to manual labor and walking in bare feet—looked in relatively much better shape, although, as mentioned previously, one had been liberally spraying a pain reliever on his joints and another was suffering from loose bowels, a particularly nagging concern since he would need to bathe every time. I lifted the kānwaṛ with the hope—better, the wish—that once we set out on the march and my body warmed, the pain could be suppressed. That, however, was not to be. No sooner had we started than I found myself falling behind the group, seemingly one of the fastest on the route. I would accelerate to catch up with them, but with frequent twitches from the ankles and fear of aggravating the injury to the increasingly tender soles, I kept falling back. The mood of confident resolve I had previously followed was gradually giving way to anxiety. This was only the first leg of the journey, and Pura Mahadeva appeared hopelessly distant—the future course seemed hazy and unpredictable.

Seeing my deteriorating condition, K offered to carry the kānwaṛ and I took instead the bag with our belongings. We had covered about four miles and took another break during which the others rubbed and smoked sulfā (cigarettes filled with cannabis powder) in a nook in the fields—apprehensive of being seen by a group of following acquaintances—while I sprayed my ankles and knees with borrowed pain reliever. But rest, at least in short periods, was no answer to my condition, and when we got up again, with every step I felt a squish in my soles—watery pockets had developed between the skin and the flesh. Another mile, and as a gap built up between us, I purchased a thandai from a peddler, a boy ten to twelve years old, only half aware of the possibility of bhāng in it but also partly I think with the hope of emulating K and the others who had been smoking, expecting some magical relief for my legs. However, if it was some assistance for the journey I sought, this adventure surely had the reverse effect. The young man seemed to have added a liberal dose of the plant, and soon I was finding it hard to keep myself steady. At this point, although we had planned to stay the night at Mangalore, another two miles, when I saw a large camp on the way, I was able to convince K to break the day's journey, and we parted company with the group.

While K tied the kānwaṛ at a frame, I spread myself on the dusty carpet in the tent, close to a fan, and closed my eyes—the bag under my head, slippers under my feet. And I soon descended into a half sleep, my eyes now open, now closed, the mind seamlessly flipping between transmogrified perceptions of the surroundings and dream states. With the complete loss of control over my body and mind, out of grip with sensory reality, and sensing a fever, I had a feeling of complete vulner- ability—deserted and alone in an unfamiliar place and at a critical time. Fearing a protracted fever and the endlessness of this delusionary state, I felt the complete hopelessness of my ability to complete the pilgrimage and ritually, safely deliver the sacred object to its destination. The dread of the embarrassing failure of the pilgrimage loomed in front of me in the form of so many fantastic visions of past failures. In these visions—amid a cacophony of surrounding voices and interspersed with a phone call from my father, who I knew had no faith in my physical prowess, and K's brief visits—the looming failure of this trip turned into both a confirma- tion of past failures and a prognosis of impending ones. They created the frightening impression of a doomed life, the inability to meet any prom- ise, any responsibility, deserting others in my own utter inability to cover the journey. Therefore, when in the morning I woke up in a sensible state and without fever, it was great relief. Although still apprehensive over the reliability of my limbs, I was bent on completing the pilgrimage. I would also religiously stay off bhāng hereafter.

THE MISSING DREAD

In one of the essays on his hashish experiences, Walter Benjamin notes the continuity between the mind's normal trails and the spectacle it gen- erates under the influence of the drug. Whereas in the normal state, he notes, free-floating images heedlessly fly by the mind, under the influence of hashish these images—now in extraordinary shapes—present them- selves to us without requiring any attention.[30] Thus, fleeting images that otherwise "simply remain in the unconscious" in this case present themselves vividly without any effort. Since these images are of course not mechanically optical, one may add that such experiences also rejuvenate affects, memories, desires, which otherwise find no room or expression in conscious life. Without overdetermining the drug high, let us note that this has Freudian parallels in the return of repressed associations and affects. Furtive emotions, fears, desires that go almost unknown or unrecognized return in the form of a slip of the tongue, a symptom, a dream image, a pattern of forgetting—a whole different realm of being whose patterns Freud will delineate, interpret, and illustrate through a lifetime of work as the "unconscious." This would echo in Nietzsche's observation that "the great principal activity of the organism is unconscious."[31]

The performances in the pilgrimage indicate a parallel phenomenon. They demonstrate the powerful presence of a nether zone left unrecognized or repressed in normal public practices or the dominant modes of the consciousness: a nether zone that yet unfolds explosively in these religious practices and in a mythical vocabulary, a world of gods, devatās, rituals, repetitions, phrases, exhortations, fears, vows, resolutions, desires, desires of the other—a world of apparently timeless, collective performances congealing at a large scale in the form of an alternative text, a text of unbelievable appeal that sends millions marching. Yet one cannot think of this "zone" as an island, an identifiable thing present elsewhere; it is the effect of continuities, of differences.[32] It is a sequential efflorescence in touch with exclusions, refusals, a shortage of signifying and thereby practical possibilities. It shows the limits, the shortages of the consciousness—or what we may have to here qualify as a certain "dominant consciousness"—the limitations of ideological force, of networks, cartels of signs that exclude in power-oriented processes, historical as well as geopolitical, and as active in a certain sphere marked as "religion" as anywhere else.[33]

In its treatment of this "other" realm, where psychoanalysis seemingly retreats into the individual, a kind of personal historicity—which, as the previous narrative should show, is no less important here—the performances in the pilgrimage also show an agglomeration of affects in which the individual is but one border. These affects are as embedded in personal histories as they are relational or free flowing—friends, relatives, self, deities, cows, streets, all feature in a phenomenological continuum. Thus, Benjamin's emphasis on the sensory is important; it underscores the phenomenological aspect of these affects or impressions that seem to pass by the consciousness without being acknowledged or recognized— or indeed are denied and yet may register deep, precisely by virtue of this negation, as "repressed" or "the unconscious."

I have suggested earlier that in a context marked by continuous and foreboding exposure to poverty, disease, and death and to the violence and humiliations of everyday life, life's excesses that may feature as much in personal history as in the encounter with the other's suffering, the experience of dread is part of the tonality of everyday life. All one finds oneself seeking is peace and well-being as much in reference to the self or immediate relations with their longer temporal involvements as, say, on the street or in the past, which nevertheless keep repeating in dreams. "Hey Bābā, do good to everybody. . . . Let your grace be on everyone," Amma would interject multiple times in our discussions, almost arbitrarily, out of context. This experience of dread also drives desire—the desire to escape it, conquer it, forget it, or as much the desire to suffer, repeat it, to practice, master the falling,[34] and thereby, also the resolve to persist.

In one respect, then, we find in these religious practices dread, anxieties, desires, concerns, and images that go unrecognized, unaddressed— mockingly, cynically suppressed even—in the dominant collective consciousness, which is usually the discourse of the nation, the economy, work, egocentric achievement, or mediated spectacles. For such desires, fears, and their psychic life, the world otherwise has little patience or means for registering or performing—except perhaps for drinking, squabbling in personal relations, or a general brusqueness in social conduct.[35] One hears a new intimate, heartrending account of death, suicide every day—of a relative, an acquaintance, a family member. In distant parts of the country and nearby villages, women and men commit suicide using pesticides, a violence that threatens to get personal anytime. This dread and the desires that are its corollaries for which there is no time or place in everyday reality are deferred to these religious practices.

CHAPTER 4

DAMNING CORPSES
Violence, Religious or Secular?

WALKING TOWARD the ghats of the Ganga in Hardwar, one usually passes through a maze of narrow streets lined with small shops dealing in religious fare and situated so densely that they appear to run into one another. With awnings and raised floors extending halfway into the middle of already narrow streets, the shops playing devotional songs and music sparkle with the golden hues of necklaces, bracelets, and other ornamentations; pictures and statues of deities; and *rudrākṣa* beads, sandalwood slabs, religious apparel, and sacred threads. Some also sell *prasāda*, food offerings to the deities, usually including rice puffs, sugar balls, and a hint of dry fruits, along with fresh bael leaves, flowers, and incense.[1] Passing through this threshold, one gets glimpses of the waters of the great river goddess, whose timeless legends, miracles, and felicity are etched in the memory of the visitor, who rushes incredulously through these streets, longing for a sight (*darśana*) of the manifest, the river goddess. As a *bhakta* (devotee) solemnly said to me, "In our lands, the honorable Ganga is the only one manifest" (*Sirf Gangaji hi pratyakṣa hai*).[2]

Coming out of the bazaar, the visitor finds herself in the presence of the Ganga with temples stepping into the river, the gurgling waters divided into multiple streams, crisscrossed by several bridges. On the ghats, pilgrims dip into the river, folding their hands in prayer and singing her praises amid a steady flow of devotional chants and the clanging of bells from the temples. Hawkers sell ritual objects such as flowers, candles, packets of prasāda, and conveniences such as plastic mats and drinking water. And many people who are elderly, forsaken, or physically handi-capped make a living from seeking alms, singing the praise of God, and soliciting divine beneficence for the addressee and her loved ones. Despite its tremendous asymmetry, this intimate communication evokes radical equality before God—where all are but desperate recipients and begging is no disgrace. *Snāna-dāna*, to bathe and donate, that is, to divest oneself of personal impurities and belongings alike, pithily describes the substance of the *tīrtha yātrā* (pilgrimage).[3] Willing recipient of the *dāna*, the ubiquitous alms seeker epitomizes the existential drama of giving, which organizes the entire sociality of the pilgrimage center and of the Kanwar as a pilgrimage.

The ebbs and flows of a transient clientele give Hardwar a seasonal pat-tern characteristic of many religious centers in India. It is a town pulsat-ing with religious and economic activity during certain times of the year, particularly on marked religious occasions. At other times, however, Hard-war can have the appearance of an elaborately equipped stage scene, where the main performers are yet to enter. Although the population density at Hardwar's ghats increases at the time of the Ganga *ārati* (prayers) every morning and evening, in general the "season" spans from April to October when the upper Himalayan shrines are accessible and heat in the plains spurs those who can afford to seek the respite of the Himalayas. Hardwar then becomes either a religiously significant stopover or, along with the adjacent town of Rishikesh, a primary destination. Yet it is the major pil-grimage occasions that truly provide Hardwar its exceptional quality: the preset annual pilgrimages of Baisākhi (April), Makar Sankrānti (January), MāhāŚivarātri (January–February), Ganga Dasaharā (May–June), and Kārtika Pūrñimā (October–November); the occasions of a solar or lunar eclipse, a Somavati Amāvasyā; and the great Kumbha festivals held every twelve years (a smaller version, the Ardha-Kumbha, takes place every six years).[4] During the frenzied activity on these occasions, the town partly takes on the character of each of these festivals—some of which are spe-cific to particular social groups and geographical areas—and their ritual and material requirements. It is also during these times that the paradoxes of an economy centered on religious activity come to the fore. The pilgrims' pious ideals and needs seem to become grist for the economic interests and the practical reason that dominates the orientation of the local providers of religious and market services who are highly reliant on these occasions of high traffic. This strange external duality repeats the duality internal to the pilgrims' performance.

HARDWAR AND ITS PARADOXES

In Hardwar's festive calendar, the entire lunar month of Śrāvaṇa, devoted to Lord Śiva, is considered particularly auspicious. The great Lord with his seat in Kailasa at the roof of the Himalayas, who is believed to have received the celestial Ganga on earth in his matted hair, is the predominant deity of Hardwar, or the gateway to Śiva. And it is precisely this unique association between Śiva and the Ganga that the Kanwar enacts, as pilgrims carry Ganga water for libations on Śivalingas across a large part of northern India. In the past, it is likely that the greater Kanwar celebrations took place at the time of MāhāŚivarātri in the month of Phālguna with a smaller version in Śrāvaṇa.[5] Speaking of the Pura Mahadeva temple, an important site for libations today, Atkinson noted in 1876, "Fairs are held here in Phalgun (February-March) and Sawan (July–August). The great fair is the one held in Phalgun called Shib Chandra or Shib Ratri, when the temple is sprinkled with water freshly brought from Hardwar and about 20,000 people assemble."[6]

Today, however, the scales have been tipped; although the Phālguni Kanwar continues to be practiced, the festival in Śrāvaṇa is by far the bigger phenomenon. While only a few thousand participate in the former festivity, the latter draws anywhere from five to twelve million Kanwarias. During the Śrāvaṇa festival, Hardwar and the adjacent shrines of Mansa Devi, Chandi Devi, and Nilkantha, as well as the town of Rishikesh, bustle with pilgrims; on certain days as Śivarātri draws near, one has to shove and jostle to find room at the ghats in Hardwar. While the pilgrims are occupied with bathing or saying prayers at the banks of the Ganga, visiting various shrines and temples, or gazing at the religious fare in the streets or collecting souvenirs, in numerous makeshift locations on terraces and in the backyards, in small open spaces and at street corners, one can see workers in hectic activity, busily constructing kānwaṛ structures. While some are engaged in making plain kānwaṛ structures, a significant portion of the kānwaṛs are more elaborate, with templelike structures appended to either side of the pole; some kānwaṛs can be enormous, for example, several people carrying a structure often shaped like a temple with a Śivalinga inside while others carry the water. Nevertheless, most pilgrims will further decorate their kānwaṛs, and some build the kānwaṛs personally with meticulous attention. Shopkeepers and hawkers are likewise busy selling water containers, canes, fabrics, flowers, ritual materials, and pictures and small statues of deities; and behind the counter in several shops, craftspeople weave nets of sturdy ropes for another important variety of kānwaṛ in which the pilgrim carries larger pots of water suspended on either side of a beam.

At this time, every inch of space in Hardwar jostles with religious or economic activity—religious to one, economic to another; an act of giving and sacrifice at one end or profiting at the other. Hardwar's eminence as a religious center and the bountiful religious merit it promises is rivaled only by its reputation for fraud and swindling. This reputation is as valid for facilities such as restaurants, lodges, tourist services, and shops that have few qualms about making a quick profit at the expense of a transient clientele as it is for the *pandās*—local Brahmin officiants of ritual service—who have been known to fleece their unwary and often desperate clients of their last penny. The pandās are often determined to make the most out of the indeterminate quality of religious goods and merit and the obligatory nature of ritual service. Likewise, in the caveat emptor ethic of the religious center, one may as easily be duped by the merchant as by the ascetic, whose affinity with criminals is legendary. Folk tales and rumors abound of criminals running from the law and hiding under the ascetic's garb; the ascetic's wandering lifestyle, shabby persona, and religious airs not only provide safe cover, but his iconoclastic behavior and repudiation of social norms may often be indistinguishable from the criminal's willful violation of social ethos. In the confounding impressions the religious center leaves on people, little separates the cynicism of the members of the nineteenth-century British ruling class from the contemporary Hindu pilgrim who, keenly aware of this social dynamic, unequivocally characterizes the place as an unrivaled conning hub.

These interactions are often defined by the paradoxical quality of faith, as in the following exchange at a flower shop, at the climactic moment when pilgrims were doing the mandatory prayers and decorating their kānwaṛs before beginning the journey. The shop had been set up in the central ghat (on which no shops are otherwise allowed) to meet the high, immediate demand on this occasion and was selling flowers at twice their price outside the ghat. It was early in the morning, and in the dark and drizzle, set to begin the pilgrimage, K and I were preparing our Kanwar—praying, decorating, and taking ritual baths. In need of some flowers, I went to the shop but lingered a bit, in two minds about paying the steep price. Just then, a customer turned back with the flowers he had purchased to complain that they were wilted. Shoving a replacement into his hands, the shopkeeper retorted harshly, "Calling the prayer flowers dry, are you! With that kind of faith, how do you expect your prayers to realize?" The person returned silently, almost contritely, I thought. Repulsed by this haughty quip, which transposed the flower seller's own unscrupulousness into the other's bad faith, I moved away from the shop only to return later to purchase a bowl of flowers, shying away from any observation on their quality or price.

Such flaws, however, can hardly tarnish the city's holiness. For all these aspersions, the place loses none of its power; indeed, in popular perception such concentration of vices may itself appear as an effect of the magnetic force of the place, much like hornets hover about sweets—the holy place attracts goodness and vice alike, and the two may become indistinguishable. The popular *māhātamya* (praise) genre of Paurānic literature extols places (as well as shrines and texts/mantras) for their powers and consequent efficacy in ensuring salvation, as well as for meeting the subjects' this-worldly desires. A number of such hyperbolic praise-texts—drawn particularly on the established Hardwar *Māhātamya* and *Māyāpuri Māhātamya*—extolling the miraculous powers of Hardwar in liberating devotees from their sins and meeting their desires are in constant circulation as books, pamphlets, and word of mouth.[7] In effect, the powers of the place are far too deeply embedded in the cultural imaginary to be disturbed by such observations. Overwhelmed by the encounter of the divine Ganga and the legendary holiness of the city of Hardwar, as

much focused on their deeper existential and social concerns and obligations that may have brought them to seek the blessings or the promise of
the great pantheon of Hardwar, for most pilgrims, these aspects are epi-
phenomenal. They are as inexorable as they are familiar and expected—
intensifying the factual order, such phenomenal surfeit may only enhance
the pilgrim's cathexis on her primary concerns. In the journey from Hardwar our thoughts were filled as much with this paradoxical co-presence
of conflict and piety, devotion and resentment, as by awe of the city itself.

TRESPASSING ON RELIGIOUS TERRAIN

As I was carrying the kānwar this morning, the third day of our journey,
K held the bag with our spartan belongings. We were entering the city of
Muzaffarnagar when suddenly the procession found itself blocked against
a rope held by policemen. The momentum had been stopped, so we were
stepping on one another's toes. It was a railway crossing, where the usual
barrier had failed to operate, and the police were filling in. As the crowd
built up, it was hard to keep balance. One had to ensure that the kānwars
did not get entangled, pass over or under anyone else's kānwar or body
part, or touch someone. Not trusting my ability to be able to pull off this
feat in the burgeoning crowd, K asked me to pass it over to him. But I
resisted; K I felt had been treating me with too much indulgence. A while
later, the Shatabdi Express, India's fastest train, thundered past us. We
had been walking on a narrow street, but now we seemed to have entered
a main lane of the city, a wide street with a median.

Soon, we were closing in on Śiva Chowk at the heart of the city. After
circumambulating this circle around a small Śiva temple, located at an
important intersection in the city, the pilgrims would spread into different directions. But Śiva Chowk was still about a mile or so away when
suddenly I felt a new burst of energy in the procession. There were a series
of loud exhortations and calls hailing Bhole Bābā: "Bam Bhole! Bhole
teri Bam!" (to the glory of Bhole); I suspected something.

The procession had been very lively and cheerful, very vocal, the first
day of our journey. Frequently, an enthusiastic pilgrim would raise a cry
hailing the pilgrimage or Bhole Bābā, exhorting the pilgrims to move
on, to which everyone would hail back in response. Along the way, as

described in Chapter 1, K and I had tagged along with a group of three pilgrims. We walked with this group for much of the first day before K and I had to back down since my body could not sustain the tempo. That burst on the first day, I thought retrospectively, had been unwise; it took a toll on my body. In the procession at large, the vivacity of the first leg of the journey was hardly there the next day. Although large mobile tableaux equipped with music systems and live performances formed part of the procession in stretches, most of the regular pilgrims on foot were not vociferous. After the initial enthusiasm, a practical attitude of making it to the destination was more conspicuous; the attitude was nevertheless supplemented by the cannabis many were rubbing with their hands as they rested along the sides of the street.

This morning, however, as we had crossed into the city from a side road specially earmarked for the pilgrimage, the mood had been very sober. One could hear the sounds of the pilgrims' flip-flops, the anklets some were wearing, the occasional swishes of the kānwaṛs, rustling leaves, some small talk among the pilgrims, and once in a while a call of "Bum Bhole" or "Bhole teri bum!" Not much seemed to have changed since about a century and half ago, when John Matheson, an Englishman traveling from Calcutta to Delhi, recorded:

> For each individual was not only attired but laden alike carrying over the shoulder a pole balanced by a covered *lota* or water jug hung at each end and ornamented with tiny flags and little tinkling bells whose sweet liquid tones appropriately announced the fact that holy water was being borne through the plains. The universal burden as we learned by enquiry . . . was indeed holy water from Hurdwar (that celebrated Gate of the Ganges where the sacred river is supposed to possess prime virtue ere it begins its course through the fields of Hindostan).[8]

Bayard Taylor and Reginald Heber traveled through central Uttar Pradesh and likewise observed groups of pilgrims carrying water from the Triveni at Allahabad and from Hardwar, respectively, in 1853 and 1825:

> The road was thronged with pilgrims returning from the Festival and the most of them women as well as men carried large earthen jars of Ganges

water suspended to the ends of a pole which rested on their shoulders. In spite of the toils of the journey and the privations they must have undergone they all had a composed, contented look as if the great object of their lives had been accomplished. . . . During the afternoon I passed many thousands who appeared to be of the lowest and poorest castes of the Hindoos. They all carried earthen jars filled with the sacred water of the Junction of the Ganges and Jumna which they were taking to pour upon the shrine of Benares or Byznath. . . . [After traveling 130 miles from Banaras] the road still swarmed with Hindoo pilgrims returning from Benares and Allahabad almost every one carrying his two jars of Ganges water.[9]

During the last week we have almost every day fallen in with large parties of pilgrims going to or returning from the Ganges as well as considerable numbers of men bringing water from Hurdwar. The greatest proportion of the pilgrims are women who sing in a very pleasing, cheerful manner in pass-ing near a village or any large assembly of people. Once as they passed my tents their slender figures, long white garments, water pots, and minstrelsy combined with the noble laurel like shade of the mango trees reminded me forcibly of the scene so well represented in Milman's *Martyr of Antioch*, where the damsels are going to the wood in the cool of the day singing their hymns to Apollo. The male pilgrims and those who carry water call out in a deep tone Mahadev Bol! Bol! Bol! in which I observed my Hindoo servants and bearers never failed to join them.[10]

In the middle of the sober walk when suddenly the slogans became frequent, louder, even somewhat strident, I raised my head out of my agony and looked around. My suspicions proved true; we were passing through a Muslim neighborhood. Yesterday evening also, I had noticed that when we entered a town with a predominant Muslim population, a few mosques conspicuous on the roadside, their minarets extending into the sky, the pilgrims' calls had become more shrill and loud. However, although the town was settled along the highway, the calls subsided soon and the pilgrims walked peacefully through most of the town until we reached Śiva Chowk, where a swirl of pilgrims boisterously circumam-bulated the temple, roaring slogans acclaiming Lord Śiva, many trying to get as close as possible to the temple. This time, K was decisive. He took the kānwaṛ from me while we went around the temple on the outer fringes of the crowd. "It would be crazy to try getting close," said K, with a veteran's sagacity; "it could breach [desecrate] our kānwaṛ." I nodded in affirmation and followed K, carrying the bag.

Despite such occasions where the simmering tensions between the two religious communities could surface, there were no immediate reports of any untoward incidents. The pilgrimage, it seemed, had passed more or less peacefully as it had in every other year, at least in this respect. Some usual conflicts between the police and the pilgrims were reported. Many times, the reason would be the pilgrims' resistance to the attempts of the police to divert them to alternative routes so that the disruption of everyday commerce could be minimized.[11] Reasonable as such diversions may be, for the pilgrim who is keenly aware of the long distance to cover, any detour is an extra charge on the body's finite abilities and increases the anxiety of making it to the destination in time without breaking down. I resented this forced detour when right at the beginning of our journey at Hardwar, we were sent snaking around the city, thus making us walk almost an additional one-third of the distance to the city limits. Thereafter, we were directed onto the canal road, which further increased the distance to Roorkee, the next major station, by about two miles. Although the actual difference was minor, many of my fellow pilgrims resented this and believed the canal route to be much longer; it meant more strain on the pilgrims.

Personally, however, I had always preferred this avenue stretching along the famous Upper Ganga Canal. Lined with trees for the most part, the passage was more serene and quiet than the congested main route that passed through dense habitations. As a frequent visitor to Hardwar I also realized that it was not significantly longer than the other route. And even as we walked rapidly, exclaiming continuously to the glory of Bhole Bābā and his followers, I often kept watching the impressive, swift waters of the canal.

TIME, DEATH, AND APATHY

I had been looking at two children swimming after a kānwaṛ floating in the canal. A pilgrim would have offered the kānwaṛ to the river at Hardwar, to ritually conclude a series of pilgrimages. It was rare for such an offering to make it this far, since usually it would be chased down within the town itself for the minor commercial value of the stick and possibly the baskets. The boys swam adroitly after the structure. No sooner had they made it to the bank after a successful chase than a corpse appeared, floating in the middle of the stream. The sight was shocking; it was the body of a middle-aged man of a relatively stocky build, the torso was bare, and he seemed to be wearing dark trousers and a belt. I looked around aghast as others gathered to watch; people speculated on the age, the dress, the circumstances of the death, and so on. The drift of the conversations was that he had probably been murdered and thrown into the canal. Another corpse floated by a while ago, some said.

The corpse was still in sight when I saw a policeman on the bank. He was looking the other way when I tried to draw his attention to the corpse. Without turning his head, he gestured with his hands to suggest, "Let it go on!" In the distance, the canal water whirled rapidly into an aqueduct, carrying the corpse along. Meanwhile, K and the others had outdistanced me by a margin. I walked quickly to catch up with them, when, yet immersed in that shock, I saw another policeman having chai at a roadside stall. I accosted him to explain that a corpse had just gone down the canal. Sipping on the chai, he said they would take it out downstream. As I left, I saw in the distance K looking askance at me. "Are you out of your mind, brother?" he asked in dismay; "are they fools to take note of this in their beat?" K felt embarrassed for my callowness in front of the other members of the group.

The *doab*, this vast, fertile plain between the two great North Indian rivers—the Ganga and the Yamuna—one may say, is numb to violence. In mythical time, it provided the setting of the legendary war described in the ancient epic the *Mahabharata*.[12] Historically, home to the capital city of Delhi, attacked by waves of marauding Central Asian armies, other subcontinental centers of power, and the British, the region has seen all the devastation, plunder, and bloodshed one has come to associate with the major seats of power and their often tyrannical regimes. Everything, however, pales in comparison with the indescribable carnage by the Central Asian plunderer Timur at the turn of the fourteenth century. After Timur ordered the slaughter of one hundred thousand people his forces had enslaved en route to Delhi, his men engaged in a complete massacre of Delhi that went on for several days, although Timur claims to have spared some of the Muslim communities. "After the departure of Timur," wrote the historian al-Badouni, "such a famine and pestilence fell upon the capital that the city was utterly ruined and those of the inhabitants who were left died, while for two whole months not a bird moved a wing in Delhi."[13] "Having put to death," as the plunderer notes in his autobiography, "some *lacs* of infidels, and idolaters,"[14] his army marched in separate wings along the Ganga and the Yamuna, taking "every fort and town and village," slaying every man they could, and making slaves of women and children. Timur goes on to give gory, self-congratulating accounts of this endless, religiously carried out carnage. And in this series, Timur would recall the massacre at Hardwar where "Hindu infidels . . . once every year come on pilgrimage" and where "a large number of infidels . . . had collected with their wives and children." Here, he added, "so many of them were killed that their blood ran down the mountains and the plain, and thus (nearly) all were sent to hell."[15]

Although sanitized and repressed in most narratives of national history, such traces of the past are by no means forgotten in collective memory. In the optimistic futurism of the state, there can be no time for mourning, for a memory that cannot be put immediately into positive use. Perhaps this is the divisive side of religion, where a state invested in a new future of unity and prosperity for its citizens is trying somehow to begin a clean slate. Yet, is this also not another side of the modern state's refusal or failure to register suffering, the denial of suffering, as it broadcasts its rosy visions amid radiant images of the present? Is this treatment of the past not a consequence of the same programmatic conception of time, where genocides and extreme social and economic destitution may all be condoned and denied in favor of grand visions of military might and economic prosperity? But there is no dearth of agencies—if any were required—to keep these memories alive, to enliven, stoke, and direct the flames of animosity they would effortlessly kindle centuries later. Thus, the excesses of Timur, along with those of other Muslim rulers or conquerors, serve as primary pedagogical material for right-wing groups. Almost all of the RSS's (Rashtriya Svamsevak Sangh) present politics, remarks Tanika Sarkar, "uses images of the past as both referent and justification: that is, most recommendations for present-day activity are projected as responses, reactions to the past. . . . There seems to be, thus, an unbroken, living dialogue with the past."[16] If the RSS has been able to sustain a divisive politics by dwelling excessively on a past it more or less constructs, part of the blame must be shared by secularist scholars who have tried to wish away or bury this past far too hurriedly.

But how different is Timur's use of a religious ideology in cultivating political legitimacy for his plunderous campaigns, the support of his subjects, and loyalty of his soldiers from contemporary power politics? Even today, so-called conflicts over religion, their momentum and expansion, the manner in which they are stoked, organized, and spread, inevitably implicate interests of power and politics. "*Religio,*" in its earliest meanings, according to Émile Benveniste, refers to scruples, hesitation, "a misgiving which holds back" in relation particularly to the divine, out of an apprehension of offending the holy, the whole, that which is wholly Other. *It is a subjective attitude that prevents as opposed to a sentiment that would impel to action.*[17] In the history of religions, rejection or renunciation of the order of social reality or power has been a key element. "An especially important fraction of all cases of prophetic and redemptory religions," says Weber, "have lived not only in an acute but in a permanent state of tension with the world and its orders."[18] Likewise, Robert Bellah in his impressive comparative study of the Western, Japanese, and Chinese societies, shows that a world-rejecting, contemplative attitude has been a fundamental, constitutive component in the history of all religions.[19] Nonetheless, power would leave no opportunity for harnessing, systematically engineering, or imposing every chance and means to further itself.

And insofar as it is the moral force called "religion" that humans find most inspirational, it is precisely religion that this power, whether of the politician or the plunderer, learns to most powerfully master—mastery, with terror and death always at hand. Thus, on Timur's command, to be executed on pain of death, even "Maulana Nasiruddin Umar a counselor and man of learning [a religious man, should we say?] who in all his life had never killed a sparrow . . . slew with his sword fifteen idolatrous Hindus who were his captives."[20] Although religion, in reference to such events, will be banished by whole political traditions and most academicians for its bigotry, statist power will continue to seduce scholars and politicians alike. In the "secular, independent state" of Uzbekistan, Timur would be recognized as a national hero; and quite befitting this farce, in central Tashkent his monument now stands in the place where Marx's statue once stood. On the other side, there would be the imperative of a responsibility to the past, to remember the sufferings of those who died, a long time ago, a felt duty to avenge the wronged against an oppressor and on behalf of an oppressed who would now be assigned, recognized, reached (politically, geographically) only in the sign of religion.

In any case, whether in a realpolitik that insists on capitalizing on this difference or a politico-academic imperative of secularization, it is religion that will be marked, targeted—a person's religion, or being religious *as such*. In the global politics of our time, this marking will often be as "radical evil," insofar as it always bears a reference to civilization, to a primordiality, a lack of morality to be defined by pure practical reason—that is, insofar as this religion is not the Christian religion.[21] And to the extent that in this sociopolitical context, any move at reconciliation, unification, or identification—say, in the name of a certain project, the future of the nation-state—is itself defined by the hurry and hubris of a restricted economy of this-worldly interests, there can be little possibility for an attitude, a space, or a time of forgiveness.[22]

Later, we came across news reports saying that six corpses had been floating in the canal, downstream in Sardhana. Four of these had been recovered by the police: first, a half-decayed body draped in white; followed by a child's and a woman's body; and immediately thereafter, a beheaded corpse. Residents reported having seen two others in the morning, but those could not be found. In the same area, a day later, residents also reported seeing two Kanwarias from Rajasthan who, involved in a nasty fight, had dragged themselves into the river and drowned. The police seized two kānwaṛs they found at the site, though they found no trace of the Kanwarias or their identities, only signs of a scuffle on the shrubs lining the canal.

Such incidents were not unexpected. With its deep and swift waters, the Ganga Canal, although the lifeline of this region—the doab, one of the country's most fertile agricultural belts—was also notorious as a place to dispose of bodies after a homicide. In my own village downstream, located close to the banks of the canal, although the street along the canal was the primary access to the village, it was hazardous in off-peak hours. Incidents of robbery and murder and sightings of groups of criminals were frequent. It had been like that as long as anyone could remember. Moreover, the waters were known to be turbulent, so only skilled swimmers would venture in. Not being advised of the dangers, the Kanwarias would swim in the canal or often use it for the meticulous ablutions required every time one had a meal or relieved oneself. Thus, there were several reports of pilgrims drowning, as well as of pilgrims saved by police rescue teams.

In any case, there were no reports of intercommunal conflicts by the time the pilgrimage was over (or so we thought). Despite record participation, with estimates varying from ten to twelve million pilgrims, the pilgrimage, so often chastised for its intolerance, had again been completed without any major incident of the notorious Hindu-Muslim conflicts that have been a defining feature of the nation's late colonial and postcolonial history. No such conflict during the pilgrimage had been reported until last year: a confrontation in Faridpur when a Kanwar procession passed through a predominantly Muslim village. Although dozens of people sustained injuries and several shops were gutted, there was no reported loss of life.[23] In view of the palpable tensions when passing through Muslim neighborhoods, where I thought a minor indiscretion could potentially set ablaze the thin veil of peace, the sustenance of intercommunal peace over the decades was a surprising feat of "tolerance."

The pilgrims I interviewed rarely brought up issues of Hindu-Muslim conflicts when narrating their pilgrimage, although cynicism over the politics of religion was common. One person remembered that the year after the infamous Babri masjid riots of 1992, "rumors had been going around that we had to be careful when crossing a particular Muslim village . . . warning us not to pass through it in the night . . . and, in fact, some corpses of Kanwarias were later found in the fields next to this village." The village was on a rural track about forty miles long that passed through several villages; this diversion off the main route was used by scores of pilgrims bound for the temple at Pura Mahadeva—including K and me. However, instances of communal harmony during the pilgrimage are also quite common. Many, if not the majority, of the kānwaṛs are made by Muslim craftspersons in Hardwar, Jwalapur, Meerut, and, in the case of the pilgrimage in Bihar, in Sultanganj. Although the considerations may be commercial, the craftspersons, mostly street vendors and laborers who shift into a somewhat more predictable and lucrative occupation for a few weeks, readily admit their own devotion during the activity—even as the Kanwar coincides with Ramadan, the holy month of fasting. As Tahir Hussain, a fifty-year-old artisan from the Gudri Bazaar area of Meerut says, "We don't make kanwars only for generating money. We do it more to help our Hindu friends, who undertake the arduous foot journey to express their devotion to the Almighty."[24] And another: "It is a labor of love. . . . We are proud of making kanwars and much more than the money we earn, it fetches us love and respect."[25] Likewise, a Kanwaria, in appreciation says, "It is most comfortable to use the kanwar made by Kalam [a Muslim]." And another notes, "Kanwars made by Muslim artisans are more attractive and of good quality. I simply go for their kanwar." Had peace prevailed during the pilgrimage, it would be just another of those times when a history of affiliation, toleration, and accommodation—mutual but by definition uneven, imbalanced—would have prevailed. After the Śivrātri libations on the day of the new moon, July 29, the massive festival concluded, or so we thought.

More than a week later on August 7, TV channels came alive with reports of intercommunal conflicts in Moradabad. A conflict had erupted between members of the two communities when a group of Kanwarias allegedly insisted on passing through a Muslim-dominated area that the police had barricaded. In the Moradabad region, the Kanwar libations were to be performed the next day, on the tenth day of the waxing moon. This was also the month of Ramadan, a period of pious fasting; in the evening, Muslims would be saying their prayers and breaking bread. In the conflict that evening, there was stone pelting from both sides, some people sustained injuries, and a motorcycle was torched. Despite reports of politically motivated provocations and the alleged complicity of key administrative officials, the police acted expeditiously to bring the situation under control.[26]

The pilgrimage finally concluded the next day with ritual libations in Śiva temples across the town. Yet again, the great festive celebrations had passed in relative peace. The pious rituals, at least of one group, were over. Now the normal political order could come to its own.

SECULARISM, POWER, AND
TRANSGRESSIONS OF THE SACRED

With assembly elections due in a few months, political interests seemed unwilling to relinquish such an opportunity; the very next day they would incite a much larger conflagration. Although laws controlling public assembly were in effect, a politicized administration permitted a large public assembly by the Sarvadaliya Hindu Mahasabha, a coalition of Hindu right-wing groups: the Siva Sena, Bharatiya Janata Party (BJP), Vishwa Hindu Parishad, and the RSS.[27] Several thousand people were assembled near a temple, and leaders from the different political parties made incendiary speeches. Once the riot began, people occupied a nearby railway track and began to smash things, and the leaders, noted a commentator, quickly took to their cars and left. And "as Muslims broke their Ramadan fast and began to gather for *namaaz* (prayer), a swirl of rumors hit the community, among them that a mosque had been set afire. Muslims led by community hotheads poured into the streets. The Hindu mobs followed."[28] Although a curfew had been imposed, the two sides are said to have fought pitched battles through the night, leaving behind a trail of destruction—houses and burned property, a police camp destroyed, and over a dozen seriously injured people. Moradabad remained at the edge of a major outbreak of violence for several days before the curfew on the city could finally be lifted more than ten days later.

On the Muslim side, a reporter thoughtfully observed after talking to various sections of the community, "Every riot has its genesis in the last riot. . . . The residue of the last clashes serves as a spark."[29] Only a month earlier, the Muslim community in a neighboring village on the outskirts of the town had had a violent conflict with the police, whom they blamed for desecrating the Koran when pursuing a criminal. Irrespective of its actuality (possibly a mere foil by an individual to escape criminal culpability),[30] the minimal evidence (the community went by the word of a twelve-year-old child, we are told), a wrong had been done the sacred, the holy Other—that which should have remained unscathed had been violated. It was a wrong that belonged to a pattern, a history, a demonic return of the same.

Twenty-two years ago, in the infamous Moradabad riots of 1980, the circumstances had been similar: a pig had strayed into the Idgah at the time of Id prayers. When a police officer on duty refused to chase it away, a war of words had ensued. The police and the assembled Muslims began to hurl stones at one another. Then the police opened fire on a congregation of about fifty thousand unarmed Muslims, including children, in the Idgah. People died from bullets and the ensuing stampede, and as they dispersed, they ravaged the adjacent habitation of the "Untouchables," from which the pig had apparently strayed in. The violence spread to the nearby villages and soon attained the complexion of a major Hindu-Muslim conflict. More than two hundred are said to have died in this conflict, which initiated a sinister series of riots that went on for a decade and continue to reverberate to this day.[31] Of course, the 1980 riot had its own precursors.

Whether in actuality or in rumor, by a mistake or inconsideration, malice or mischief, by an act lacking in faith, so to speak, at some point in the conflagration, the sacred had been violated. This warranted revenge on the guilty, even if at the cost of a sacrifice of the guardians themselves, the faithful who had allowed this to occur. But this responsibility cannot be simply reduced to a commonplace notion of time or immediate prov-ocation, for there is always an accretion of previous incidents, episodes, other times regardless of how distant they may seem: times when justice could not be done, scores remained to be settled, and a responsibility was owed to the holy Other and others who had suffered. Thus: Hindus and Muslims with their accusations and counter-accusations, since it is not a question of one event, one episode—the numbers are beyond count—one could go back a thousand years or just yesterday in memories that are as fresh as they are recollections made possible by the advances of technol-ogy, as much archaeological as sociopolitical.

In a recent study, Parvis Ghassem-Fachandi argues provocatively that political machinations explain only half the story behind the persecution of Muslims in contemporary India. In reference specifically to the 2002 anti-Muslim pogrom in Ahmedabad, Ghassem-Fachandi argues that the willingness of residents to be so persuaded to violence is inscribed in the culture, geography, and psychological material that has defined the texture of Hindu-Muslim relations in the city. In the refrain of political motives orchestrated by respondents on both sides, Ghassem-Fachandi sees an element of palliative rationalization that suppresses the more disturbing, intimate aspects of such violence for fear of "summoning a past that still lurks vividly in the present."[32] Today's anti-Muslim violence in India, according to this perspective, is driven by the desire for a homogeneous, pure nation through the excision of all that may appear foreign to this nation's body, its spirit. "The Muslim" has a particularly important place in the temporality of this national imaginary—it is the externality blamed for the primordial wound (figured mostly in terms of past "Muslim" excesses) in memory of, and in responsibility to which, the ("Hindu") majority unites in "its" nation. The annihilation of this intruder and persecutor, who lives alongside, would be the means as well as the end, the uniting force and the historical consummation, of the majority's nation. From the Muslim side, one story is of the resistance of a persecuted minority and the conflicts in relating to a nation identified with, and violently active on behalf of, an often despotic majority.[33]

Alternatively, as Sudhir Kakar insightfully argues, it is possible to explain mob rage psychoanalytically in terms of group narcissism, which involves the regression of the ego into a collectivity that may be traced to an earlier lack of distinction, during childhood, between the self and the world.[34] These conflicts evidence weakening of the reality effect during mass gatherings, whether pious or violent. Such instances can easily be the occasion for violence against another group, on which group members unconsciously project aspects of the self that are disavowed and which they seek to expel.[35]

Despite the importance of this explanation, which focuses on "primary" associations, communal conflict in India today has less to do with mob rage; rather, I would agree with Ashis Nandy that "the planners, instigators, and legitimizers of religious and ethnic violence" are secular users of religious forces and passions. Such violence may be located in the uncanny presence of what appears as another demonology, "the left-handed, magical technology" of modern statecraft. These conflicts are a consequence of the persistent "violence flowing from objectification, scientization, and bureaucratic rationality"; they are a product of a technology of "statecraft and political management," of modern elites' projects of nation building and state formation, of which the exploitation and effective disenfranchisement of a majority of the populace is but a counterpart.[36] These characteristics of an "internal colonialism" in India's contemporary social situation validates, as Nandy correctly argues, the sense in "philosophers, such as Hannah Arendt and Herbert Marcuse, that the most extreme forms of violence in our times come not from faulty passions or human irrationality but from faulty ideologies and unrestrained instrumental rationality."[37]

The neutrality of the government in the face of conflicts between religious groups, the necessity of maintaining an even hand in instances of religious differences, has been framed in Indian politics and in social theory in general via the notion of "secularism," a term added to the preamble to the Indian constitution by the Forty-Second Amendment in 1976. But this is a term, a social technique, with a very distinct European, and more broadly, Western provenance.[38] Thus, as Triloki Nath Madan shows, the notion of secularization may be traced right up to the Old Testament, to "a God who stands *outside* of the cosmos, which is his creation, but which he confronts and does not permeate."[39] This distinction between God and the sphere of human activity, where in Saint Paul's words, "all is permitted," was, however, "contained" in Catholicism, where earthly government was subordinated to the city of God.[40] The term "secularization" first appeared in political discourse during negotiations for the peace of Westphalia in 1648 after the wars of religion and referred to the transfer of land and property from the ecclesiastical authorities to the princes.[41] However, secularization during this time could not be understood as religious tolerance; indeed, this time "coincided with the reign of Louis XIV in France: a more cruel prosecutor of religious minorities would be hard to find in the annals of Europe."[42]

Aligned with the major theological reorientations brought about by the Protestant Reformation,[43] this political decision of transfer of worldly power and property into the hands of an autonomous secular authority would gradually evolve into a normative ideal during the French Revolution. Religion would then be explicitly characterized as a private matter in political discourse, as indeed it had already been tacitly in the paradoxical form of Protestant engagement in the world, lucidly described by Max Weber. Modern secularization theory, which basically involves the premise that this-worldly political and economic engagement would be—indeed should be—increasingly liberated from any trace of other-worldly responsibilities or recognition is a truism that translates modern Western history into universal fact and destiny.[44] This much should be common parlance today.

Beyond questions of historical prejudices, however, the epistemological criticism of secularization, as a notion and *eo ipso* as historical project, centers on the assumption of a scientific, technological order, of state power and market rationality as the final legitimate horizon of human existence and of social relations. This betrays a conceptualization and, consequently, a historical resolution and exorcism of religion drawn on a Cartesian rationality.[45] Not surprisingly, this sweeping *explanation* of religion shot through with a will-to-know, to analyze religion in the form of a discrete object, can predict only the final triumph of Cartesian rationality, of industry, the commerce between objects where religion itself, if it does not subside completely, will remain only another commodity in the marketplace. The facticity of the rational order will replace any other claim to order human experiences. The assurance of the marketplace, the form of the commodity, and the truth of its power can leave little doubt about the eventual universal ascendance of this proven social form. This totalizing economism as state policy and world ideal/future, a necessary corollary of the notion and project of secularization, which is but far removed from the reality of India's society and its diverse cultures, is the primary aspect of the strong resistance "secularization" has evoked in some of India's leading social thinkers. Ashis Nandy, perhaps the most vocal of these critics, declares decisively: "[I] am no secularist. In fact, I can be called an anti-secularist."[46] A critical assessment of the connotations of "religion" is vital to properly appreciate the reasons for this discontent.

OF TWO SIDES OF RELIGION

In discussing the etymology of "religion" in his excellent study *Indo-European Language and Society*, Émile Benveniste reports the curious history of the concept: "One fact can be established immediately: there is no term of common Indo-European for 'religion'" because "in the civilizations which we are studying,"—this, one must hasten to add, includes the vast expanse of habitation stretching from the Scandinavian Peninsula to the Gangetic valley—everything has been "imbued with religion, everything is a sign of, a factor in, or the reflection of, divine forces."[47] Thus, there was no need for a separate term to designate the group of rites, scruples, beliefs, or values that concerned the divine.

Only two ancient terms come anywhere close to the modern concept of religion—the Greek *thrēskeia* and the Latin *religio*. *Thrēskeia* may refer to observances or practices identified with foreign groups or cults; however, in other instances it designates all cults. Thus, Herodotus reporting on the rules of physical purity observed by Egyptian priests adds, "They observe a thousand other *thrēskeias*." This sense of observances, preparations, or hesitations that *thrēskeia* conveys is also, for Benveniste, the primary and "original" sense of the much more controversial—and, as far as we are concentrating on the politics of the present, consequential—etymological history of *religio*. For "originally *religio* did not mean 'religion'; that at least is sure."[48] The debate nevertheless is extensive and has been going on since the ancient period.

Since the ancient period, Benveniste tells us, two alternatives have been presented: one represented by Cicero (supported by Otto, Hoffman, and Benveniste himself) that associates *religio* with *legere*, "to gather, collect"; and the other represented by Lactantius (followed by Kobbert) who associates *religio* with *ligare*, "to bind."[49] In the first group of meanings, *relegere* is the sense of collecting once more, gathering again. Here, as Benveniste shows at length, *religio* is "a scruple which prevents and not a sentiment which impels to action."[50] The connection to *ligare* has a very different sense, one of being bound to God by a bond of piety. Unlike the pagan religions of old Rome, according to Benveniste, *religio* in this case is remodeled to fit the Christian idea of the bond of piety that links man to God, hence the modern term "religion."

In view of its historically specific nature, it is important not to lose sight of the Christian content of "religion" when using it as an interpretive heuristic for phenomena considered kindred. A minimal skepticism is required on observations concerning "religion" in different parts of the world across different cultures insofar as these observations are inevitably bound with the world dominance of Christianity, or Latin, particularly when one speaks of the secular, of the separation of religion from everyday practices. These are questions of hegemony, interpretive dominance, existential paradoxes, moral existence, an ideology that determines how the affairs of the world—from the most particular household activity in the most neglected part of the world to issues of global governance and state policy—are (an "are" that is obviously always an ethic, a "should be") managed or how obeisance should be paid and social relations valorized.[51]

Two things stand out when we speak of religion, the French philosopher Jacques Derrida suggests, in characteristically discerning fashion.[52] First, a holding back, hesitation, scruples, misgivings in reference to an Other, which is sacred, holy, unscathed, pure. A thousand rituals, observances, preparations, scruples, "the most meticulous care," rites of bodily purification, of the purification of thought, the sacred chantings when approaching this Other that must remain pure, *pavitra* (Sanskrit pure, sacred), holy, whole, which must not be violated. There is a wall of sanctions (*sanctus*) to protect the field and integrity of the *sacer*.[53] We have observed the importance of purifying rituals in Hindu religious practice; likewise, Jamsheed Choksy illustrates that notions of purity and holiness have been critical in the demarcation of ritual space among the Zoroastrians since the ancient period.[54]

Second, Derrida insists on distinguishing from the sacred—this holy (whole, in good health, intact) Other, indemnified by extensive injunctions, which seem to multiply by themselves through an automated repetitiveness—another element, a bond of faith between the faithful and the sacred. The bond of religion—whose separation, as *religare*, Benveniste traces to a Christian provenance—that links the faithful with that which is wholly Other is simultaneously the basis of the faith in one another, that is, the foundation of a social bond. Nothing without trust, without faith, a promise, a fiduciary bond—the ubiquity of an "I swear,"

"I promise," implicit or otherwise—on which rests a whole order of justice, from the constitution of a society or nation, a global community, to the smallest social exchange. There is no social possibility without a testimony, a declaration, a profession that refers back to a witnessing wholly Other where the difference between the interior and the exterior is radicalized, to an originary performativity.[55]

Of course, no sociality without faith; yet concerning modern global society, today one must first speak of the Christian faith. Kant says of Christianity that "of all the public religions which have ever existed, the Christian alone is moral."[56] In the schema of this great thinker, Christianity alone, in its universal message, the project of bringing God's kingdom on earth, and in the internal change it requires of its subjects so that each may become worthy of the love of God, can become a universal religion of reason. The Christian ecclesiastical faith alone does not seek favors from or an appeasement of the divine through gift, pilgrimage, penance, pious performances, or simply an external following of God's commandments. It seeks a moral "change of heart," a shift in intellectual disposition from all empirical or sensuous contingencies toward the continuous betterment of the individual whose previous guilt, or debt on account of the radical perversion of the human heart, would have been paid off by the unique sacrifice of the "Son of God." While for Kant, Christianity as a historical faith is not without its failings; it provides the only historical possibility for the evolution of a moral religion, that is, the religion of pure practical reason, according to which "*whatever, over and above good life-conduct, man fancies that he can do to become well-pleasing to God is mere religious illusion and pseudo-service of God.*" The principle is this: "It is not essential, and hence not necessary, for everyone to know what God does or has done for his salvation."[57]

This philosophical exposition of good faith is an insightful commentary on Christianity and the religious foundations of a certain "good life-conduct." At the same time, however, does not this moral religion defined by pure reason, by philosophy beyond all tenets of virtue, tradition, and contingent existence, also provide an exemplary illustration of the death of God? We see another illustration of this apotheosis of the manifest present in the Hegelian notion in which Christianity is but the last leap in the actualization of the Spirit as Absolute Knowledge. That is, out of the deepest kenosis, the diremption as much of God or the Absolute Spirit as of self-consciousness, rises the actualized identity of self-consciousness and the spirit where consciousness comes to realize, concretely and existentially, the spirit to be itself.[58] Whether or not one agrees with this macabre figure of the death of God, of all the Indo-European religions, Christianity with its morality most clearly exhibits the revulsion of Cartesian rationality to "superstition," miracles, and pious ceremonies in favor of a this-worldly ethic, which has supported capitalism with its all too this-worldly logic and for which perhaps the best apology remains Hegel's philosophical, ontotheological presentation of the historical unfolding of the World Spirit.

More than the dubious ideological horizons of secularism, however, the criticism of secularization in India and of a state policy directed by this abstraction is usually driven by its actual, historical failure in addressing or negotiating conflicts between religious communities in postcolonial India. Indeed, as Nandy argues, secular market rationality is a primary cause of these conflicts.

> Thanks to a few secretly taken photographs of some of the participants in the violence, one image that has persisted in my mind from the days of the anti-Sikh pogrom at Delhi in 1984 is that of a scion of a prominent family that owns one of Delhi's most exclusive boutiques directing with his golf club a gang of ill-clad arsonists. I suspect that the image has the potential to serve as the metaphor for the new forms of social violence in modern India.[59]

As Nandy argues, Hindu religious fundamentalism, fanaticism, or revivalism in India today is basically the doings of a psychologically uprooted urban middle class trying to beat the West at its own game: a "pathetically comic" mimicking through twin processes of (1) decontaminating Hinduism of all its folk attributes through semitization in the form of return to a putatively pure Vedantic Hinduism; and (2) a zealous nationalist pursuit of modern statecraft and technological power. In some astute psychological analyses of the Hindutva (Hinduness) movement, its discourses, and its primary ideologue V. D. Savarkar, Nandy has shown a zeal driven by the fetish of a masculinist nation so that "the Hindus can take on and ultimately defeat all their external and internal enemies, if necessary by liquidating all forms of ethnic plurality within Hinduism and India, to equal the Western man as a new *Übermenschen*." The inference is that religious violence in India has been increasing, most of it happens in urban localities or in surrounding industrial areas, and it has "something to do with the urban-industrial vision of life and with the political processes the vision lets loose."[60]

Nandy's understanding of religion in India, I believe, is original and far-reaching, from both a historical and theoretical perspective. In accordance with the autonomy of practical reason—where we know from as far back as Kant that it is an ethic that reigns supreme—this perspective steers clear of abstract modernization theories and the teleology of an instrumental rationality while registering subjective concerns that are as ontological and ethical as they are historical and sociopolitical. It should be noted that this perspective indeed recognizes the actual historical contributions of secularism in shaping possibilities of religious toleration, as well as of technological rationality, while refusing a social determinism driven by their logical extremes.[61]

One may refer here to the unconcealment, the disclosedness, *alēithia* of Being that Heidegger invokes in discussing the temporality of Dasein, "an entity which, in its very being, comports itself understandingly towards that Being."[62] As we know, Heidegger implies a radical questioning of the history of Western thought, its mode of unconcealing (in effect, obscuring) Being as the *Idea* and through calculations of entities as present-at-hand through a forgetting of the temporality of Dasein as being-in-the-world—that is, the one who primordially approaches Being—who finitely exists alongside and with others. It is not from a systemic perspective but from such recollection of the finitude of the human, a recollection of a human's existence in and of itself, that the religious attitude is being considered in this perspective.

Thereby, one finds that the conflict over religion—its momentum and expansion, the manner in which it is stoked, organized, and spread—almost inevitably implicates interests of power and politics; it is somehow also the consequence of an administration that refuses to defuse the situation, withdraws, takes sides, and at worst, is itself the assaulter.

"Initially the reaction," we often learn, "was not violent"; the situation was returning to normal when vested political interests "started mobilizing people, visiting door to door and distributing pamphlets."[63] And if, as a wide range of research shows, a fear of persecution by the other group has a role to play in inciting such violence, such anxiety is itself often the consequence of a lack of faith in worldly power, in a politicized, partisan administration that cannot be trusted, or alternatively, is always ready at hand and would not fail to capitalize from every opportunity.[64] "Every time there was some communal tension, the administration acted in a very partisan manner which led to a very strong sense of resentment against it."[65] In a state where a politics of religion and identity has been systematically engineered, cultivated through extensive organization by discursively mobilizing every incidence of difference, where power happens to produce itself democratically and ritually in election after election with every party trying to outwit the others in the diligent capitalization of differences, the communal riots are, at least in their frequency and the scale of violence, the product of a politics that is all too secular, lacking in faith, in "the fear of God," as a believer may say.[66]

CHAPTER 5

CASTE AND THE INFORMAL ECONOMY
Subversive Aesthetics of Popular Religion

> The fortunate is seldom satisfied with the fact of being
> fortunate. Beyond this, he needs to know that he has
> a right to his good fortune. He wants to be convinced
> that he "deserves" it . . . to be allowed the belief that
> the less fortunate also merely experiences his due.
> —Max Weber, *Essays in Sociology*

AFTER THE NIGHT'S delusional scare as a result of the thandai, the next morning we had covered some distance, and although still apprehensive about the reliability of my limbs, I was relieved not to have lapsed into a protracted fever. Both K and I felt that since I was unaccustomed to walking in flip-flops, I would need a pair of shoes. K had advised me to wear shoes from the beginning, but some other acquaintances had suggested that shoes would make my feet too hot. My zeal to approximate the rigor of the common pilgrim was also to be blamed. As we entered Purkaji, stretched along the highway like most towns here, under a scalding sun we wandered around looking for a place to eat lunch and a shop to buy a cheap pair of shoes. A community feast (*bhaṇḍārā*) seemed to be going on inside a temple, but it turned out to be only a resting place. However, we did find a shoe store and haggling over the price of a pair of shoes, I was struck by the salesman's remark: "We, anyway, quote *you people* the lowest price possible." As we bargained first over the shoes and then a pair of socks, he made the assertion several times, and I think quite sincerely, that the business never tried to profit from "us."

For the first time, I had been directly addressed as a Kanwaria. Although K and I, along with the other pilgrims, were Kanwarias—especially when walking there was almost no conversation but an exchange of the calls of "Bam Bhole!"—we never really lost our individual identities. Participants

132

interacted with ordinary familiarity when resting, although as soon as they lifted the kānwaṛ, a subjective attitude of pious sincerity and moral consideration would take over.

Thus, there was an internal complexity to the Kanwarias' interactions and performances; here, different temporalities stimulated, merged with, and substituted for one another. The Kanwar performances may by no means be removed from the participants' everyday struggles and responsibilities, although they may be engaged on a different, almost transcendental register. However, when the salesman identified me with a collective identity, I recognized "us" as outside the fold of everyday social interaction. It was the marked and distinct identity of a pilgrim, a bholā, a devotee of Śiva, participating in an ordeal in celebration of Śiva. The bholā belonged to the legions of Bhole Bābā. And it is indeed for the service of these bholās and to earn religious merit that Delhi businessmen—probably millionaires—may be seen on the route, lined up in their cars along with their families, distributing medicines and topical ointments and often themselves applying the ointments to the pilgrims' feet.

Although this does not quite amount to that vaunted cultural symbol and has functional evocations, it is important to note that "touching the feet" is a loaded symbol in northern Indian culture and, in addition to its religious connotations, is also emblematic of caste, gender, and age hierarchies. A devotee touches the feet of the deity and ideally, a child his parents', a younger brother his elder brother's, a married woman her elder in-laws'; a low-caste villager imitates touching the feet of higher-caste notables. In the extremely inegalitarian and hierarchy-conscious culture of northern India, more fortunate groups reproduce and maintain their status by keeping alive both precolonial and colonial practices; contempt for the poor, more broadly the multitude, characterizes the tenor of public interactions. In this context, such service and regard by the rich, perhaps upper caste, for ordinary folks, most of whom belong to lower socioeconomic groups, would be unthinkable outside a religious field. The pilgrims here are held in high esteem and can be served in humility precisely to the extent that they can be dissociated from their everyday persons and lifestyles and perceived as a godly group, their identities condensed into devotees of Śiva—like the *gaṇas*, Śiva's mythical legion.

For the rich devout, a class that revels in constructing ever more opulent temples, ordinary people would thus become respectable as devotees; everyday stigmas can be repressed once these people ascend into a religious aesthetic and ethos, into a sublime zone. Here, the aesthetics of two classes, of two cultures almost, can converge—at least at a formal level in the celebration of the same deities, the same myths or legends.[1] However, this transformation in social space, the territorialization of space by an undisciplined, lower-class habitus, under the authority of tradition and the sacred, also continues to be repugnant. Despite its massive following, the Kanwar is no less an object of contempt and disgust to both a middle-class sensibility and authoritative religion, which finds this unbecoming of Hinduism, betraying the refined global image it has assiduously cultivated.[2]

THE CULPABLE PILGRIM

Pilgrimages do not usually provoke adverse reactions. Instead, they often induce tender feelings—participants' motives are often deep and personal, their faith inspiring, their group behavior affable, their austerities and labors exacting. They evoke an ambience beyond social differences and discriminations, transcending historical tensions. Not surprisingly, the Turners, in their now classic *Image and Pilgrimage in Christian Culture*, perceptively described the phenomenon as liminal and an expression of communitas. Although anthropological research has also shown the many contests and conflicts over pilgrimage shrines and the role of institutional power, politics, and history, the aura of the pilgrims' piety and their good faith is rarely at issue.[3] From places widely dispersed geographically, historically, and culturally, scholarly narratives of pilgrimages abound with profound impressions of the sincere faith and inspiring performances the authors witnessed.[4] In many cases, these accounts seem only to transfer the equally evocative perceptions of the community. Such convergence of opinion looks all the more impressive in light of the geopolitical and scholarly controversies over the status and significance of religion itself. And even where scholarly accounts have been more critical, such as the cases of the Vaishno Devi and Amarnath pilgrimages in India, the popular perception is yet generally positive and one of adulation.[5]

In such a harmonious field, the Kanwar comes across as a rare and flagrant discrepancy. It is evident that the pilgrimage has a passionate following among broad sections of the populace. Accordingly, its performances and rituals are often inspiring and evoke compassion, and the participants' behavior frequently demonstrates their piety, labor, and suffering.[6] Nevertheless, antipathetic observations abound—it is common for the pilgrims to be characterized as "hooligans," "thieves," "unmannered," "disorderly," or "disruptive." Such characterizations are particularly common in English-language media and among the urban middle class in general, including on the Internet. Moreover, these appellations come from both the Left and the Right, from atheistic orientations as much as from religious authorities. A secularist observer from the Left dismissive of this "puerile" practice writes,

> In most cases he [the Kanwar pilgrim] is not a person devoted to religion. Usually from the urban fringes, or poor, low middle class habitats, he prays infrequently, and *he reads and understands the religion even less*. . . . In most cases he is a person who has no respect or say in his community. . . . [While, in the pilgrimage] he is urged to eat more. . . . At times his feet are washed and bandaged by ladies who would not care to employ him as domestic help in normal settings. . . . The present socio-religious subaltern assertion may become a political assertion in the days to come. To paraphrase Sartre's analysis: the character of that political assertion will be Fascism.[7]

Likewise, the Sankaracharya of Sardapeeth, one of the highest authorities of institutional Hinduism, is quoted as saying,

> "They are presenting a distorted picture of Hinduism where recreation has taken over devotion and bhakti," he [the Sankaracharya] said, lashing out at the Kanwar. "What kind of faith and worship is this?" he asked . . . elaborating that Hindu scriptures do not mention any Kanwar Yatra. It is a tradition, which has grown on the basis of hearsay.[8]

In both these authoritative voices, the Kanwaria's religion is a poor, botched, illegitimate version —it is "puerile," lacks the composure of adult rationality. This is a religion commingled with local customs and personal desires, an example of ritual miscegenation. Proper religion, on the other hand, would be unadulterated, a detached, serene exercise concerned either, like Vedantic religion, with metaphysical truths and eschatological questions or with pure devotion in the manner of *bhakti*. It would be a distinct sphere of activity to be practiced under the guidance of virtuoso religious leaders in accordance with canonical texts. The Kanwaria's religion, its poor taste, thus disgusts both the authoritative representative of religion and the teleological vision of the intellectual of the Left.

Such aversion to mass religiosity falls along expected lines. It reflects pervasive sensibilities, an embedded aesthetics, widely shared across the ideological spectrum—from the Left to the Right, from political and religious elites to social scientists, from classical religious texts to the contemporary sociology of religion. Hence, the remarkable indifference in sociology to the significance of mass religiosity, except for its putatively retrogressive, reactionary, or resentful push as seen in the extensive discourse on religious fundamentalism.[9] Likewise, in Weber's classic studies, although Asiatic religions are categorized simply as other-world oriented and exponents of a "flight from the world"—opposed to the this-worldly asceticism of Protestant rationality—mass religiosity everywhere is interpreted as primarily oriented toward magic, in expectation of immediate, "solid goods in the world." As magically oriented, mass religiosity is irrational; only the religion of the virtuoso offers possibilities of a "rational ethic" for social life: "The religion of the virtuoso has been the genuinely exemplary and practical religion."[10]

Furthermore, in this conception, religion is a distinct realm of social life that "receives its stamp primarily from religious sources. . . . Other spheres of interest could only have a secondary influence."[11] The Weberian perspective centered on Western exceptionalism, which would give rise to capitalism—a cultural phenomenon of "*universal* significance and validity"—employs an almost tautological definition of rationality, specific to capitalism and the Protestant ethic.[12] This perspective is untenable in the context of the Kanwar pilgrimage; as opposed to such a typology, the pilgrimage must be understood in terms of a performative rationality.

This chapter relates the performativity of the pilgrimage to the controversial nature of the event, the revulsion it frequently provokes in the English-language media and to a hegemonic sensibility. It analyzes the af-

fective divergence between the millions that the pilgrimage mobilizes—
as well as among the pilgrims themselves—and those dismissive of the
phenomenon, many of whom seem to indeed find it revolting. I argue
that such revulsion to the pilgrimage has, at its base, an often aesthetic
distaste—a rejection at once sensory and ideological ("moral and physical
disgust" in Breuer and Freud's words).[13] The Kanwar allows the habitus of
a huge but invisible majority to occupy center stage. Here, the otherwise
suppressed, inferior habitus of the majority pits itself as absolute, occupies
the highways, and performs its ethic under the full splendor of the public
gaze. The dialectical constitution of the pilgrimage is thus a site of political conflict. This conflict is not so much between progressive forces and
a retrogressive religious or cultural belonging, as a teleological reasoning
may conclude; rather, it demonstrates a conflict between a dominant habitus and its ideal values and a lower-class existential aesthetics performing
a very different ensemble of life concerns and obligations.

THE CARNIVAL: ENJOYMENT AND DISGUST

Kanwar processions are quite a carnival. The kānwars are often ornately
decorated. Many are quite elaborate, and some are enormous. In addition to the walking pilgrims, the pilgrimage includes heavily decorated
Jhānkīs (tableaux) on wheels, illustrating mythic episodes in various art

FIGURE 5.1. *Kānwars with templelike models*

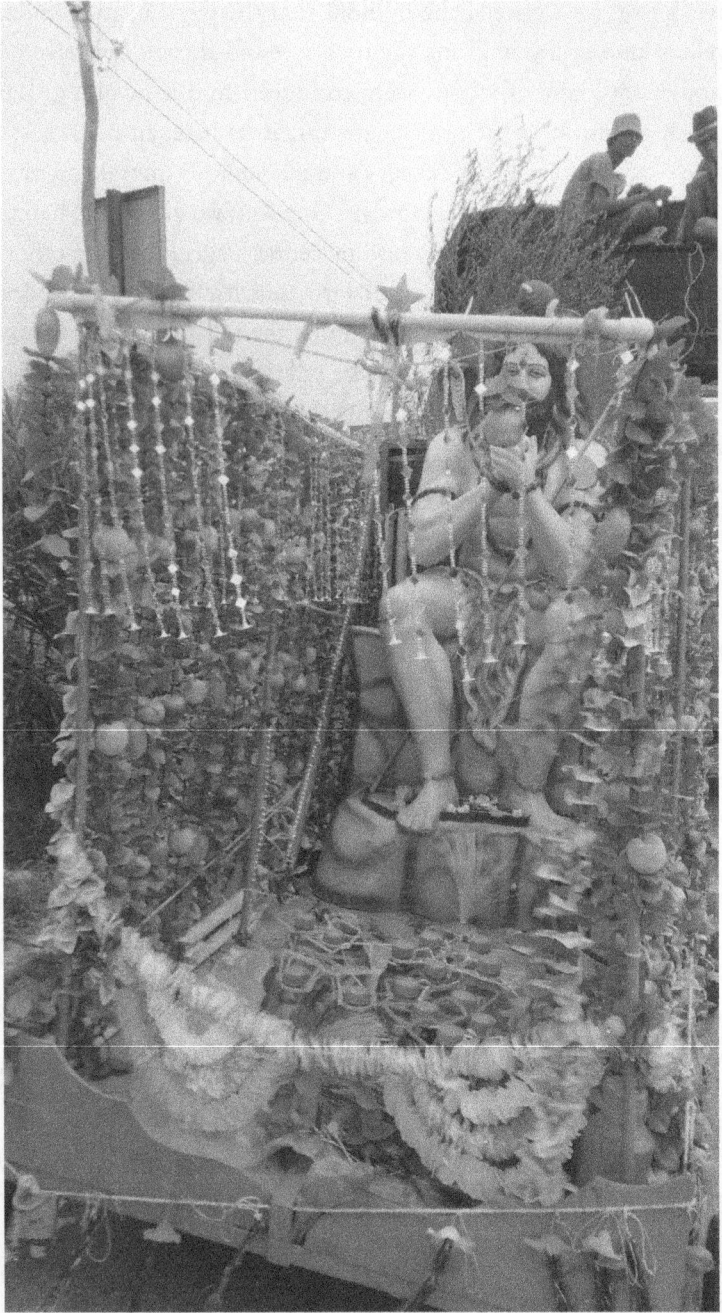

FIGURE 5.2. *A kānwaṛ tableau showing Śiva smoking cannabis*

forms such as sculpture, paintings, and live performances. The Jhānkīs, accompanied by performing artists and a continuous stream of often lively, high-decibel music, create quite a spectacle and attract much fanfare. The large kānwaṛs and tableaux are financed collectively by groups. While liquor consumption is a strict taboo, a good number of pilgrims, as we have seen, make the journey under the effect of cannabis products, which are regarded as things Śiva himself relishes. En route, transit camps provide resting space and occasionally food and medical assistance. This is more fuel for the critics' rhetoric, who see only vulgar, intoxicated gluttons delighting in free food and service.

Even as a large number of the pilgrims had been diverted by the police to the canal-side street from Hardwar, the main carnival with larger, elaborately decorated kānwaṛs and Jhānkīs, accompanied by small trucks and tractors, had continued on the national highway. Despite the restrictions, pilgrims diverted to the canal side would often find a way to the main pageant. The street by the canal, called the Kanwar *patri* (lane), had been specifically developed over the last few years to free the highway, but it was too narrow to accommodate the procession. More important, the carnival required the audience from the numerous towns and villages, the almost uninterrupted rows of habitations and markets along the highway. Many of the troupes would thus make strategic halts to pass through the towns during the evenings when whole towns would descend into the streets to cheer their ornately lit tableaux, the live performances, the spectacle of their labor, the frequent sport with the onlookers, and boisterous music themed on Śiva, the Ganga, and the Kanwar itself. At the many camps alongside, volunteers served free food and drinks, thus creating a seductive environment of celebration and gaiety. Channeling the carnival via the low-profile back street would thus strike at one of its core elements. The administration's efforts at diverting the carnival were to no avail; it underestimated the phenomenon's intersubjective dimension, the interaction necessary between the carnival and its audiences.[14]

Walking by the canal side, we had remained rather oblivious of the main carnival until the second morning when, at Manglaur, about twenty-five miles from Hardwar, the two routes intersected. Now that we had crossed into the state of Uttar Pradesh, no police manned the intersection, leaving us free to choose our route. Here we took the high-way—the road was much wider, the number of pilgrims had multiplied, numerous large kānwaṛs and tableaux dotted the stretch, some rested along the sides of the street sides, and others matched pace with the walking pilgrims with intermittent stops. For large kānwaṛs, usually four or eight pilgrims—and if the structure is prone to imbalance, another two to four to keep it vertical with the aid of ropes—carry the kānwaṛ, while a truck loaded with supplies, music equipment, and a generator follows behind. On a scaffold on the vehicle, or on another platform ahead or be-hind it, there could be actors depicting Śiva or Pārvatī, sometimes posed, performing only a few characteristic motions, and at other times, dancing and acting or singing from scripts. Other members of the troupe may dance in front, usually not in rhythm with the music, much in the manner of an ordinary Indian wedding party. These impromptu dances and songs make little devotional pretense except for an exaggerated gesture here or there following the mention of a divine name or act in the song or script.

There is little to differentiate the religious occasion on this score, the dances being only another means for the exhilarated participants to prac-tice or show off their favorite steps. And frequently, with little regard for the music, the dance steps would imitate the flirtatious or sexual banter between a heterosexual couple characteristic of Bollywood—here usu-ally by male participants, some acting male roles and others, female. The gendered suggestive banter is often imposed on the characters of Śiva or Pārvatī, their conjugal life, or the mundane exchanges between a fictional bholā and *bholi* (his wife), for example, on the subject of their desire for the pilgrimage or common aspirations. Such performances are iter-ated in a prolific number of video albums on religious themes. Whereas some songs are based on pop albums with a countrywide appeal, most are composed by numerous local artists in dialects such as Khaṛi Bolī and Haryānvi. The scripts, usually drawn on a mythological repertoire or familiar and customary tropes of everyday life, are hardly inventive; the music likewise is either rudimentary or copies of Bollywood tunes. Because there is little copyright enforcement, there is a vast amount of overlap among the albums. Many are released by T-Series or any of a number of smaller companies that have imitated its business model.[15] In catering to market demands, these video albums simultaneously work out the desires of young women and men aspiring to Bollywood ego ideals, their rags-to-riches stories, and the fantasized glitter of their lives. The wish for an unexpected windfall, an unlikely yet tantalizing turn of fortunes, is of course always an additional lure; the desire for recognition of one's talents can be equally conspicuous.

While devotional music following sacred chants and the poetry of renowned historical figures such as Surdas, Tukaram, and Kabir may be played at hours of prayer, most albums draw on folk renditions of Paurāṇic myths, imagery from the Kanwar pilgrimage itself, and common themes and episodes of domestic life set to a blend of Bollywood musical scores. The songs may thus include eulogies of the Kanwarias, including their piety and suffering during the pilgrimage, the kānwaṛ decorations, their love and appreciation for Bhola, their appeals to Śiva and his kindness, the conjugal games between Pārvatī and Śiva, and episodes from the *Śiva Purāṇa*. Despite the thematic diversity, however, there is little artistic virtuosity; the lyrics may seem repetitive and predictable, the voices are often unrefined, and the derivative music may be dissonant. The impressive variety of themes that seem to convey real feelings and social concerns are as if transformed into a singular, boisterous effect with little discrimination.

However, some songs with a clearly pop quality and often drawing on Bhole's inebriated aspect are widely popular, and a few even have a rustic charm. The refrain of one popular song is as follows: "Nilkantha pai chadh kai pī gayā ek bāltī bhāng; O Bholā nu matkai; O Bholā kyun matkai" (He went up Nilkantha and had a bucketful of bhāng; therefore Bholā struts; O why does Bholā strut?). Another popular song in the last few years has been the lively "Babam Bam" by the pop singer Kailash Kher, a prominent Bollywood artist hailing from the adjacent town of Meerut. The song is structured as Pārvatī's address to Śiva, expressing her desire to live with him, and Śiva's riposte in which he discourages her because of his life in the wilderness and his disagreeable form covered with ash and snakes. Interspersed in the song are praises of Śiva and, importantly, the alliterated refrain "Babam bam, Babam bam Babam bam bamlehri" in a very fast tempo.

Such racy numbers exhorting the pilgrims themselves to swing to the tune and sashay after an intoxicated Bhole Bābā obviously strike a chord with pilgrims, many of whom—especially the younger—are likewise intoxicated. Videos of such songs may show actors representing Śiva and Pārvatī. Śiva's character is often dressed in a tiger-skin-printed wraparound, a wig of matted hair tied on top, numerous rudrākṣa (Rudra or Śiva's teardrops) necklaces, and with snake replicas around the neck. Pārvatī is usually dressed in a sari and blouse in the manner of North Indian housewives; at times, the blouse is skimpy and the sari short, imitating the depiction of goddesses and mythological characters in epical TV serials such as the *Ramayana* and the *Mahabharata*. This conjugal play may thus often have a titillating effect. Other variations of the theme may involve child actors, with a male child acting as Śiva, the female as Gaurā/Pārvatī—the former craving for bhāng and asking her assistance in preparing it, the latter refusing. The songs clearly enact the playful, often fractious, exchanges of domestic life in stereotypical gendered forms.

At a basic, visceral level, this indiscriminate folk religiosity of the Kanwarias offends middle-class sensibilities or taste. Such offensiveness becomes particularly disturbing in the context of identifications stemming from a national belonging or with the putatively sublime spirituality of an ideal Hinduism, with its Vedic rituals and Vedanta metaphysics, the image it has assiduously crafted internationally. These performances claim to represent *one's* religion, the most sublime of cultural identifications, in the most crass and distasteful manner, giving a lie, as it were, to ideal imaginaries of the future of the (postcolonial) nation libidinally driven by a past constructed as at once golden and traumatized.[16] Offensive and uncanny, this representation expresses precisely what is sought to be repressed.[17]

In addition, the Kanwarias' occupation of public spaces, particularly roadways, disrupts routines and inconveniences the urban middle class, provoking their resentment. There is thus a collective notoriety to the festival, an aura of scandal. A livid middle-class commentator from Delhi notes,

> Kanwarias, the name could send jitters down the spine of any civilized person. These hooligans have no ethics and have no rules to follow.... People who pay

tax in numerous forms, who pay toll tax to use a petite road made out of their own money are left with JAMS, snail speeds and MESS when these people with no work at home hit roads in the name of God! Does the Linga God not accept my prayers? He does! I am a Shivite and I know how dear is my God to me.... But does that need a show off on the road? ... A dirty number show ... a dirty political motive is what I sense behind the hooligan carnibal [*sic*]! [18]

Equally angry with this ritual miscegenation and occupation of roads, another argues:

They are a strange mix of tradition and modernity—men wearing Nike shoes and gaudy saffron vests walk or trek and occasionally stop to take rest. The resting places are audible before they are visible, with loud, garish devotional music being played over cheap amplifiers. Number of *Siva Bhakts* can be seen there squatting or resting on makeshift tables or cots and engorging themselves at the *Bhandaras* sponsored by the local traders. Recently Kanwarias blocked the Delhi-Mathura highway.... Seven *Kanwarias* were recently run over by speeding vehicles in three mishaps, which sparked the protests.... All this points to one disturbing phenomena [*sic*]—the lumpenization of piety. And that is frightening.[19]

Although the pilgrimage indeed creates business for trading and religious communities, since a large part of the financial operation is in the informal economy with limited revenue accruals to the state, the state sees little advantage: "The State Government has planned to consider Kanwarias as non-tourist arrivals as they create more law and order problem than the revenue they generate. The law and order problem caused by Kanwarias can be gauged from the fact that most of the foreign tourists prefer to stay away from Hardwar and Rishikesh during the Kanwad Mela."[20]

The traffic disruptions and detours for four or five days at the height of the festival are important—perhaps not as much in the dimension of the Real as for their symbolic dissonance. The pilgrims' intrusion disrupts routine perceptions of rights over public spaces, of an assumed function of roads; otherwise unshaking beliefs in one's prerogatives are challenged, and identifications with statist, instrumental rationality, and one's status as a rightful subject are suddenly breached. The inconvenience, however, does not explain the disgust—it is at most a discursive referent, a prop, for an upsetting affect caused by an affront to one's sensibilities.

The disgust instead, I would argue, is in the necessity of rejecting and dissociating from the lowbrow culture: its often gaudy aspect; the remixes of loud, raunchy Hindi film songs to which the Kanwarias dance; the frequent references to Śiva's conjugal life in the songs and slogans; the lascivious themes of many of the plays and dances either performed live or on videos; the ambiguous sexualities of the actors; the suggestive bodily gyrations of males performing as females or females as males; and the garish makeup. Such promiscuity is an affront to cherished identifications and aesthetic ideals; it upsets one's imaginaries—national, local, and historical. This distaste or disavowal is personal since there is a merger of identities—a historical, national, religious belonging-together. It comes across as the uncanny, recurrent, inexorable return of what one seeks to dissociate from, perhaps a past, an ascribed stigma, a lower part, a behind, sexual or excretive, to identify elsewhere in a national imaginary, a future, an image in the world. Yet this abyssal, obscene thing presents itself as religion, as sublime, thereby shamelessly mixing things. *It is the abject.* Then we have the genius of Kristeva:

> I endure it, for I imagine that such is the desire of the other. A massive and sudden emergence of uncanniness, which, familiar as it might have been in an opaque and forgotten life, now harries me as radically separate, loathsome. Not me. Not that. But not nothing, either. A "something" that I do not recognize as a thing.[21]

> What disturbs identity, system, order and does not respect borders, positions, rules. The in-between, the ambiguous, the composite. The traitor, the liar, the criminal with a good conscience, the shameless rapist, the killer who claims he is a savior. . . . Immoral, sinister, scheming and shady.[22]

THE POLITICS OF INDISCRIMINATION

If the performances here are disgusting to some, for others they express the anxieties, desires, and obligations that define the tenor of everyday life. Weaving in the radical antinomianism of Śiva, these performances, as I have argued in previous chapters, express and sublimate the complex social affects that mark the subjective existence of a large number of people.[23] Striving for uncertain success in highly informal conditions where there is much left to chance, and usually at a critical life turn, these performances often demonstrate an anxious plea to supernatural benevolence. At the same time, they compete with the dizzying novelty and disparity of commodity-mediated social relations, which they are to outshine and to resignify—to "master," to use a Freudian term.[24]

In the Kanwar, one finds (not unlike the modern market perhaps) a near lack of reserve and minimal normative regulation in performing to or supplying desires. Thus, the proliferating video albums, while catering to market demands, simultaneously work out the desires of young women and men. The Bollywood star, her absolute success, is among the supreme fetishes of many a young person, grappling with the suspect rationalities of a highly unorganized social order. Unlike the huge odds of attaining a celebrity career, such albums provide bountiful opportunities with minimal restrictions; set in the name of God, these performances seem to as much provide an avenue for these desires as perhaps to transcend them. The relaxed sensory regulation here corresponds with the lack of social divisions in the pilgrimage itself, where people, irrespective of caste, class, age, and, to a large extent, gender, merge in the singular identity of the bholā. The suspension of otherwise rigid caste identities is notable in this context, since caste ideology in India today often operates practically as an aesthetic differentiation.

Contrary to these normative discriminations, one finds in the pilgrimage a radical intermixing, a lack of differentiation. Outside and away from one's fixed identities and historical trappings, in a context of anonymity, an undifferentiated monism where Bhole Bābā is the only reality, caste identities are no longer recognized. Likewise, in the pilgrims' actions, and not unlike Saivite or Tantric antinomianism, judgments over distinctions between the "low" and the "high" and the sacred and profane, between the devoted ritual and the frivolous action, the saintly and the petty, are to a large extent suspended: "One cannot judge another person's *śraddhā* [faith] from their external actions." One after another, my respondents refrained from judgment on the quality of the other's faith.[25] "This is Bhole Nāth's great fair; you may expect people of every kind," one said. However, if among many pilgrims sharing the intensity of a common phenomenal experience there is a deference to this intermixing of the sensible, the lack of discrimination in the pilgrimage—"oh, they say anything that comes to their mouth," blithely said Shamli, a young female pilgrim, without a hint of disapproval—this very intermixing and indiscrimination to which caste and class significations are never missing makes the pilgrimage an anathema to others.

And at times things may appear very mixed. Thus, a member of a group of young, economically destitute pilgrims from the Dalit community (outcasts or "untouchables," traditionally identified with scavenging) boasted, "We brought a very large and excellently decorated kānwaṛ. After winning a game of gambling, we decided to put all the money into it." The Kanwar offerings were done at a temple the community had constructed a few years ago. What may seem, from one perspective, as a banal "show off" is also on another dimension an intervention in a historical struggle, a group assertion in the context of a history of oppression, of exclusion—above all, from temples—which goes back to the very beginning of (historical) time as much as it repeats itself every day in the smallest interaction and is, perhaps as frequently resisted.[26]

And if in some cases, such indiscrimination shows a collapsing of time, others more clearly manifest negotiations in the present: "Yes, kids like this, such people go for the Kanwar. They don't get food at home and are therefore attracted to the free food at the camps. . . . You see, my own kids, I have two. They will never go for this, because they get everything they need at home," a woman interjected as I was discussing with Sundar, a boy thirteen or fourteen years old, his experiences in the pilgrimage. Now in ninth grade, he had been going on the pilgrimage for three years. The eldest of three children whose father is informally employed as a salesman in a motorcycle shop, Sundar said he dreamed of bholes going for the pilgrimage, and when he asked his mother, she agreed to let him go with the elders. "No, we only ate at restaurants; only rarely would the leader let us make a halt," Sundar told me later. "[But] we danced and had a lot of fun," he said, referring to the children in the group. . . . I was wearing *ghungrus* [musical bells worn around the ankles]. . . . I liked their sound." Another pilgrim, a young adult attending college, added, "I had the same dream. . . . I saw bholes going on the pilgrimage." This was an observation several others had made. The festival reflected a collective mood: a time, a season—marked by the pleasant showers after months of scalding weather—when a multitude, and many in one's circle, set out for the glorious, legendary city of gods, Hardwar, to tread the long way back home in memory of that adorable deity Śiva. The desire was irresistible. As Basant had said, "It gives me goose bumps; tears well up in the eyes."

In an economy where the formal sector is but inexistent and lack of institutional regulation the norm—where more than 90 percent of people are informally employed—Sundar's desire and the relaxed control of the family are no aberration.[27] Instead, by addressing and negotiating these relaxed norms, also represented in the relative lack of norms of the pilgrimage, one will learn, face, and play with the prospects of a future that is very likely to be as undefined and uncertain. Whether they work as real estate agents or petty swindlers, small entrepreneurs or self-employed, or unemployed skilled or unskilled workers—except for a few government jobs and fewer formal private-sector jobs that too are often informally distributed—adroitness in dealing with informality will very likely determine one's life chances.[28] However, precisely this extent of informality and uncertainty leads to anxious overcontrolling, obsessive attachment to an ideology identifying extensive behavioral regulation, studiousness, and discipline as conditions for success. And in the tenuous gains this success would make and anxiously safeguard—perhaps not without guilt, but inflexibly and accusingly—amid a sea of destitution, as though ready to devour, the other with its threat of contamination will have to be kept at a distance, as abject. Thus, the frequent parental admonition: "Do not mix with *those, other* kids!"

This negative perception shows the moral ambiguities associated with the gaiety and carnival atmosphere of the pilgrimage, which seems out of character with accepted religious conventions. This is evident in the ambivalent perspectives of many of the pilgrims themselves: "Three or four decades earlier, it would be only a few people—one or two from our whole village—who would make the pilgrimage to fulfill a vow. . . . Now it will be hard to find a family without a participant. . . . It is hard to explain. Call it a herd mentality if you wish; it is hard to say." These words of one respondent, who has himself made the journey several times, echo the views of many others likewise amused by the explosion of the phenomenon and admit the ambiguity of their own motivations. For many, the increasing numbers correspond with a dilution in the intensity of the event; there is a levity to the occasion, a carnivalesque atmosphere. One common complaint is that "there are too many young people on the pilgrimage—they have turned it into a carnival. They take bhāng and make merry. The festival is therefore earning a bad name, despite a large number of seriously pious devotees." Some consider that there is only a small percentage of devoted pilgrims, the rest being miscreants; for others a handful of bad apples are responsible for spoiling the occasion and its reputation.

Yet I rarely found a person who would name someone either in his group of pilgrims or acquaintances who could be blamed of levity of faith or ritual insincerity. It was more a vague feeling that seemed to vanish in the context of the dense situatedness and historicity of any specific individual. In addition to the seeming abandon and gaiety of the celebrations, the pilgrimage, along with its toil and penance, also amply demonstrates the ritual intensity and good faith of the participants. Thus, in most cases, the vow of the pilgrimage comes to be pronounced in the immediacy of overwhelming agonies and apprehensions. For example, Bimala's elder son ran away from his family after a domestic conflict. In a family immersed in the throes of poverty, when the father who had promised to bring the arduous Khaṛi Kanwar died of sepsis, compounded by alcoholism, before he could fulfill the promise, the mother was haunted in her dreams and had to set out on the journey herself. Another example is the unfathomable agony of the parents I met at the Bilvakesvara temple in Hardwar, whose only child had been returned home with no chance of survival—the doctors having given up—but who miraculously revived as the parents prayed to Bhole Bābā in a frenzy, avowing the labor of a Kanwar. In their unceasing gratitude, the parents have been coming yearly for the Kanwar ever since. Other examples are the anxiety of the father who vowed a Kanwar because he was concerned about the future of his son who had an infirm leg, and Samli, the destitute mother anxious over her daughter's polio-affected limbs. A brother implored Bhole Bābā to be generous to his sister, childless after many years of marriage. Another respondent who wished likewise for his friend's childless daughter—whom he had adored and entertained since she was herself a child—has been bringing Khaṛi Kanwars for five years.

CONTESTED TRADITIONS

We have seen previously that the pilgrimage provides an occasion for expressing, sublimating, and mastering desires, aspirations, and obligations that command little consideration in the everyday social context. At the same time, however, the Kanwar has strong contentious tendencies, which are perhaps most evident in the conflicts over territorial rights— particularly the occupation of the roads. "They refuse to yield even an inch of the road," a news report claims in amazement.[29] Another commentator, likewise, avers: "The Kanwarias have also become very aggressive. They just walk wherever they feel like, cross roads where it suits their fancy. . . . And god forbid if a Kanwaria is hurt in an accident. All hell breaks loose."[30] And yet another finds it "unusual" that when "seven Kanwarias were recently run over by speeding vehicles in three mishaps," they sparked protests leading into "burnt buses, blocked roads," and clashes with the police.[31] This resentment clothes itself in the rhetoric of national loss, public good, and "proper religion" violated by irrational actors. Thus, a state bureaucrat deplores the disruption of commercial life as irreligious: "Religion never allows anyone to cripple life."[32] Another person comments, "What intrigues one is the sudden increase in the number of Kanwarias of late and their aggressive behavior, the last thing that one would associate with a religious congregation."[33] While this imperative of "common interest" and "public good" seems reasonable, it is oblivious of any specific genre of concerns and suffering, notwithstanding a widely disreputed polity and administration, its criminal disregard and injustices.

It is important to consider the other perspective. First, the violent reaction to pilgrims being "run over by speeding vehicles" itself requires little specific explanation. Not limited to the Kanwar, such incidents reflect the common animus over the usage of limited, poorly managed roads—between speeding cars and other vehicles, their negligent drivers, and an often destitute pedestrian traffic—that tips over a threshold of tolerance during such unfortunate yet common episodes. For example, two weeks after our Kanwar libations, in one of the research towns a child on his way to school was crushed by a speeding bus, provoking wide public reaction. Cars and buses were burned, shops and police stations gutted, and the demonstrators chased the police. The situation was controlled only after a curfew and a parading of especial forces. In a place where police action is almost thoroughly governed by its rent-seeking character and the legal system is more or less ineffectual, witnesses often assume the role of the agent of retributive justice.[34] In the Kanwar, since the huge numbers of pedestrians share a common, religious identity and normal traffic conventions—in which pedestrians have neither rights nor respect—are suspended, traffic accidents become marked. Group psychology and the possibility of a few incendiary characters among such vast numbers may lead to further aggravation.

At a more specific level, however, the speeding traffic, its effortless hubris, and unquestioned right over space or roads is quite the opposite of the Kanwaria's difficult, painful treading over endless space, anxiously protecting the sacred water in the containers, and upholding its ritual status. The spilling of the water, even its minimal violation—say, by a traffic indiscretion—would destroy all the merit of the act, the immeasurable labor and cathectic investment that goes into it. And insofar as one's most intimate worries and concerns seem to hang on this precarious and difficult ritual act of getting the water safely to the shrine, such an incident could be ominous, disastrous. "When a Kanwaria's water gets spilled, he is unable to move . . . gets stuck to the ground, as if he had lost everything . . . prepared to die," I was frequently told by witnesses.

These contentions, however, should not be perceived as discrete; they are on a continuum with, and transfer the affects of, everyday life. The refusal to "yield an inch," as the previous report claims, has to be seen in the context of embedded power relations, where cars move effortlessly—in an expression of what looks like the mocking comforts of life for a small minority—even as a vast number of people drag themselves through the struggles of life in dire and humiliating conditions, often silently bearing the ailing, emaciated bodies of their children and their disillusioning futures (or continually witness such suffering). In the public space of the road, its rights, in the daily conflicts it hosts, two different worlds ceaselessly cross paths every day. In the Kanwar this balance is upended.

Effectively then, in the Kanwar a huge but otherwise invisible majority territorializes public space. This shift, lacking the form of a great endless wave of protest movements, massive demonstrations, or open revolts,
becomes feasible through the means of an antinomian religious tradition.
The religious performance invokes an ethic, a past, a culture, a higher
order; it invokes the Absolute without betraying the subjects' jouissance.
And it is precisely this pitching as absolute, ethical, and religious by what
is abject and unsightly—culturally inferior, tasteless, overindulgent, in-
discriminating, characteristic of those *other* castes or groups—that the
ideologies that construct dominant perceptions find most consternating.

The disgruntlement caused by traffic inconvenience, the detours one
may be forced to make for a few days in a year, cannot be extricated from
an aesthetic intolerability of this abject other that presents itself in the
name of one's own culture and religion. Here, the Left and the Right
agree to a surprising degree. The repulsion is an effect of this unusual,
unseemly mixing of the sensible—kānwaṛs decorated "with multi-hued
cheap plastic festoons and toys, Pokemon *dumroos*," "pilgrims engorging
themselves at the *bhandaras*"—that presents itself as absolute, transcendental, and a representation of *one's own* identity and religion.[35]

The Kanwar thus becomes the place, voice, acts, and opportunity of a
majority, which although obviously numerous remains invisible, nonin-
trusive, unheard if not silent, and somewhat suppressed much of the time.
The difference is striking. Instead of the apparently smooth operations
of daily commerce with all their silences and inequities, another order
of concerns, desires, responsibilities, aptitudes, habits, and worldviews
authoritatively takes over the space. This intrusion becomes particularly
annoying in its occupation of the highways, as a complacent worldview
that usually keeps its thin veneer of order intact, despite gross inequities,
excesses, and the silent, inordinate suffering of the multitude, is forced to
give way to the existential concerns and the habitus of the majority.

The revulsion caused by the Kanwar is provoked by such unusual,
unseemly mixing of the sensible; it has as its base an aesthetic distaste,
a rejection, at once sensuous and ideological. The aesthetic chasm here,
however, builds on India's caste heritage—a differentiation between the
subtle and the gross, the pure and the abject, which is simultaneously

aesthetic and metaphysical. Vulgar taste, poor manners, and tendency to excess after all are simultaneously the defining characteristics of the "low" castes and the ideological moral ground defining their "inferior" status. In the Sudra, the quality of *tamas* (darkness) predominates, teaches the Lord in the *Bhagavad Gita*, which makes them "unsteady, vulgar, obstinate, deceitful, malicious, lazy, down-hearted, procrastinating."[36]

NEOLIBERALISM AND THE STIGMAS OF NEO-CASTEISM

As we have seen, religious performances such as the Kanwar function as occasions for participants, here mostly lower-class young males, who are facing and anticipating the social expectations and excesses of a highly hierarchical society to cultivate social and self-recognition. They are also cathartic events that at once subvert normative protocols and the imperatives of daily commerce and give expression to repressed anguish. In these practices, one sees a lower-class habitus, clearly reminiscent of indiscriminate taste and practices identified with the caste abject, presenting itself as legitimate *representations* of Hindu religion.

Said one of my respondents, "There is no 'high-low' here; *jati* [caste] does not matter. . . . Of course, everyone is a Hindu." Caste difference turns secondary to the category of the "Hindu," construed in an alternative structure of difference both within the nation—say, Hindu, Muslim, or Christian—and internationally in terms of "Indian" identity. If caste identity and anxiety are embedded in the structure of India's traditional, sedentary society, the "Hindu" identity is an effect of a nationality and personhood navigating the culture and time consciousness of a dynamic, global society. The "Hindu" is the new one—condensing both national and personal identity—and calling for solidarity in the face of difference, where the marked "high-low" must be transcended for the cause of Hindu national solidarity. Yet, much as a transcendental cause and moral duty bound the ancient caste divisions, the new unity is conditional on another abject in the form of a treasonous other. While the respondent took pride in this performance of Hindu faith and identity, it is precisely as betrayal and denigration of Hindu culture and its noble identity that the phenomenon also arouses moral revulsion and disgust in others.

The disgust they provoke may be well described using Kant's formulation. "Disgust," says Kant, is aroused by a unique "kind of ugliness,"
with an artistic object "insisting, as it were, upon our enjoying it, while
we still set our face against it."[37] In the Kanwar, what arouses disgust is
precisely the certitude of the practices, the actors, their shameless claim
to sublime, religious merit, showing such contemptible lack of discrimination and respect that only the caste unworthy may be capable of. It is
the profanation of Hinduism, a treasonous defilement of Hinduism, of its
ideal image in the world and a pure ancient past that it has painstakingly
salvaged from the debris left by the historical traumas of Islamic occupation and English colonization.[38] The act is as morally unforgivable as it is
aesthetically abhorrent. From being identified through closed caste mark-
ings of a premodern society, the abject here is the constitutive externality
of a new national and Hindu consciousness.

National self-consciousness, however, itself transfers the anxiety of
social and self-recognition in the liberal capitalist context of a highly un-
equal, poor, and hierarchical society. It is an identity anchor in hopelessly
challenging social conditions, where one must frantically kick to barely
stay afloat in a sea of poverty while struggling with moral and existential dilemmas. The abject here is a stigmatized other—overdetermined at
once as social and economic failure, moral degeneracy, aesthetic offensiveness, bad habits—whose company and mere thought must be shunned to
accomplish a meaningful life.

Thus, it is increasingly in the context of an aesthetics of morality
shaped by the imperatives of national identity and neoliberal certitudes
(of work, discipline, and spectacular commodities) that caste is evoked.
The rationale of just deserts underlying the caste system is reinvoked in
a different paradigm.[39] The collective memory of caste works as a metaphysical and historical reserve that can be mobilized toward a consciousness (conscience) of distinction in the context of new exclusions. If it
were a moral aesthetics and its correlated economic distinctions that caste
substantiated in the traditional society, it is precisely as the implicit but
substantive reason for moral and aesthetic distinctions and economic exclusion that it is now invoked. Thus, the dynamics of Sanskritization of
particular social groups, which the anthropologists have shown so much

interest in, are not nearly as important as the binary distinction between the cultured, or the *sanskrit*, and the uncultured, one not fit for *samskars* (sacred rites), which has served as the condition for social exclusion and the concomitant accomplishment of social and ego integrity since antiquity. In classical Hindu society, this exclusionary reference is usually the Sudra. Hence, Śaṃkara in the *Vedanta Sutra Bhasya* states:

> The Sudras have no such claim [to knowledge].... The Smriti prohibits their
> hearing the Veda, their studying the Veda, and their understanding and per-
> forming Vedic matters, (as), conveyed by the following passages: "The ears of
> him who hears the Veda are to be filled with (molten) lead and lac."... "His
> tongue is to be split if he pronounces it; his body is to be cut through if he
> preserves it."[40]

And the Manusmriti states: "One occupation only the lord prescribed to the Sudra, to serve meekly even these (other) three castes."[41] India's sedentary, closed, but heterogeneous society established a thorough, unbreachable system that is as gratifying to the "included" as it threatens to annul any being that ponders challenge. The excluded, of course, do not exist; they are marked only by absence, as darkness is but the absence of light.[42] Sudra or Candala, the abject of the caste structure, is an overdetermined negativity—deformed and unpleasing to the senses, sinister and shady, dirty in manners and by life station, indolent, ignorant and obtuse, condemned by the gods. She is a deformity of both matter and consciousness accountable to her own moral depravities, karma, in a timelessness spread over an indefinite number of lives.[43] Although specifics must vary, the exclusive function of caste powerfully elucidates contemporary racial exclusions.

Today, as racism has evolved into a new social form identified as "neoracism," cultural difference has become the primary focus of racial difference while, at least in public discourses, biological arguments have diminished. Likewise, sweeping political and economic changes of the last several decades have transformed caste relations and sentiments substantively enough to warrant a term such as "neo-casteism." It is appropriate that these neologisms indicate newness; yet these social changes also bring into light new dimensions of caste and racial relations per se. The prefix "neo" simultaneously marks a social phenomenon and an analytical step. Thus, neoracism, while indicating a new phenomenon, also directs attention to issues of culture, economic status, and disposition in explicit forms of racism, previously occluded by discourses of biological difference. This revealing feature is particularly true for caste; the changing profile of contemporary caste practices helps address many of the persisting puzzles of India's timeless caste structure.

Mediated by hegemonic nationalist and neoliberal ideas, neo-casteism operates as pervasive and insistent exclusion of the habitus and popular culture of the poor and downtrodden as contaminants and risks, simultaneously to the nation and its cherished projects and to personal ideals and desired life courses, whether for the individuals or their loved ones. These anxiously guarded exclusions are the condition for certitudes that can weave together nationalist ideals with comforting narratives of self (ideal ego) and desired life courses and objectives, whether or not they are realistic. For the most part, the harder it is to realize these objectives, the more anxiously one upholds them to foreclose the threat and greater likelihood of being rendered abject; in conditions of widespread and growing poverty and unemployment, such an outcome is highly probable. The social patterns previously designated "caste" now cannot but express themselves in the new legitimacies of nationalism and neoliberal references that equate morality and propriety with economic success and a culture of high consumption, and poverty and deprivation with corruption of character and a lack of work ethic. Notwithstanding inflections from the specifics of India's postcolonial nationality, obviously neither nationalist nor neoliberal imperatives are confined to India. Rather, they constitute a dominant ideology that increasingly orders moral and social considerations in societies across the globe. As it happens, exclusion is increasingly a defining feature of these societies. Caste as much as racial exclusions increasingly must be constructed, practiced, and thus conceptually constituted not through a social logic that focuses on division but in a sweeping discourse that putatively incorporates everyone.

That discourse today is neoliberalism, especially of the Chicago School variety, simultaneously an economic doctrine, a political strategy, and a moral and aesthetic horizon.[44] In this hegemonic global discourse, economic logic provides a universal grid of intelligibility for any kind of social practices, from family and marriage to work, crime, and state justice.[45] This discourse would conceive the human in totality as herself a form of capital—*human capital*, a product of investments in education and upbringing, or the natural merits of genetic ability, and wages as the income earned by this capital.[46]

Racial and caste ideology and practice inevitably combine interests of politico-economic domination in a normative morality and aesthetics. If earlier race and caste practices were produced by the dominant discourses of their age, colonial liberalism and Brahminism, respectively, today both neoracism and neo-casteism are aligned with the common global hegemony of neoliberal ideology. The sweeping, exhaustive nature of globally hegemonic American neoliberalism, its singular emphasis on wealth accumulation, also means that its exclusions will be that much more compulsive, the race of its abject that much virulently patrolled.

Several scholars have drawn attention to the emergent dystopian characters of contemporary societies, where beyond a core of people with full-time work and secure, embedded life-courses—a sphere of meritocracy and equality between the sexes, kind and gentle in its relationships, with life exigencies covered by comprehensive insurance—lies a growing outgroup. As Jock Young elucidates,

> The outgroup becomes a scapegoat for the troubles of the wider society; they are the underclass who live in idleness and crime. Their areas are the abode of single mothers and feckless fathers, their economics that of drugs, prostitution and trafficking in stolen goods. They are the social impurities of the late modern world. . . . This section of the population has a large ethnic minority constitution, creating the possibility of easy scapegoating and of confusing the vicissitudes of class with those of race.[47]

This is surprisingly evocative of Dalit poetry in India, for example, Vijay Tendulkar's following description of the world that shapes the ruminations of the famous Dalit poet Namdeo Dhasal:

> This is the world of days of nights; of empty or half-filled stomachs; of the pain of death . . . of overflowing gutters . . . of the jobless; of beggars; of pickpockets; of Bairaga swamis; of a hashish cot and a beautiful child asleep on the

edge of that cot and a tubercular father ... of hermaphrodites; of home-brew liquor ... of smuggling; of naked lives; of opium ... where children cry near-by, where prostitutes waiting for business sing full-throated love songs.... Dhasal says, here all seasons are pitiless, here all seasons have a contrary heart.[48]

From this perspective, the abject is not just a particular, stigmatized demographic minority but indeed a majority obliged to negate itself by the imperatives of a collective morality.[49] No wonder that cultural iconoclasm and profanation of cultural artifacts with their pervasive meaning-loaded presence are inevitably the first targets of subaltern resistance groups. Not surprisingly, the Dravida movement of the late nineteenth century consciously rejected Sanskritizing values. Likewise, the Dalit Panthers asserted new cultural imperatives that "exploded their subaltern world into a complacent middle class, upper-caste consciousness."[50]

What David Goldberg has to say about racialized exclusions in conditions of contemporary neoliberal hegemony may be said for the overdetermination of exclusion over multiple axes in more or less any epoch:

Those thus seen as threatening to disrupt these authorized economic, informational, and cultural flows, movements, placements, and positionings—the media of value and significance, of capital, after all—become more or less racially marked, racial rogues, mutant states. The racial marking of the targets serves to rationalize—both to economize and legitimize—the invocation of *violence*. ... [Race] sustains systematic social conditions of exclusion, and the varieties of a more or less visceral violence underscoring and extending them. ... A state of exception licenses the state ... to treat such subjects in any way deemed necessary to restrict, restrain, or disappear them.[51]

Characterized as much by the working as the consuming disposition, moral irreproachability expresses itself aesthetically. The lesser race is marked by dubious behavior, poor consumption, and poor presentation of the self. Where work was a necessity, and surely also a theological value in nascent capitalism, it was not at any great scale a disposition or trait that defined one's *mode of being* itself so much as it does in the advanced neoliberal economy. Where morality came to center on the appropriateness of such disposition, racial separation became imbricated within its attendant economic and aesthetic evaluations. This social order motivates the body of the nation through imperatives of material and cultural progress, simultaneously advocating a "pragmatic" social stratification in which the previously natural and hereditary differences in social ranking give way to a logic of differences apparently earned in a social space defined by "freedom." The individual body remains a significant site for studying and validating race in addition to cultural practices; yet what the body now more than ever marks and represents is a purported lack of cultural achievement, whereby power can continue to assure itself of being "Good" in the medium of an aesthetic that putatively manifests the spirit of the age. The correspondence with the word of the Lord in the *Bhagavad Gita* and the *Manusmriti* is striking: the Sudra is disposed to "covetousness, sleepiness, pusillanimity, cruelty, atheism, leading an evil life, a habit of soliciting favors, and inattentiveness." *Tamas*, the quality predominant in the Sudra, "has the character of an indiscernible mass" and cannot be fathomed by reasoning or fully known.[52]

Aesthetic repulsiveness is merged with moral and intellectual degeneration; collapsed into a group essence, this combination operates as an enduring ideology of caste discrimination. The Kanwar then effectively subverts the hegemony of this moral order to carve a space and time for *other* concerns to perform and exist in an alternative mythical and practical medium in—as Chapter 6 demonstrates—all their radical vitality. Yet few would see such phenomena as an example of "resistance." Notwithstanding the complex social conflicts apparent here, religious practices are rarely treated in sociological scholarship as forms of resistance because the notion of resistance in the social sciences is normatively framed by embedded ideas of individual freedom and historical liberation; religious actions are more likely to be characterized as "fundamentalist" than as instances of social resistance. But it is to resistance that we must refer to understand these subjectivities in their anticipation, mastering, and opposition of oppressive and humiliating conditions. Questioning the teleological, modernist paradigm that commonly frames instances of resistance, in the next chapter I make a case for an alternative hermeneutic that would embed these practices in moral philosophy, existentialist literature, and psychoanalysis.

CHAPTER 6

WISHFUL NIGHTMARES
Triumphant Neoliberalism and the Resistances of Religion

> We do not want to know anything about the anxiety, the distress,
> the paradox.... We carry on an esthetic flirtation with the result.
> —Kierkegaard, *Fear and Trembling*

"MY LIFE HAS BEEN a series of struggles, moving from one crisis to another, but Bhole Bābā has helped us stay aboard ... very often from the verge of a breakdown," Shailesh had reflectively observed. Shailesh was about thirteen or fourteen years old when his father's disfigured corpse was found on the nearby railway track. Using a forged birth certificate, he was able to find a job replacing his father. This provided succor to a family that included four younger siblings and the widowed mother. Twenty years later, Shailesh recounts several tales of the harrowing times he and his mother had gone through. The series of adversities that encumbered his memory include the recent deaths in traffic accidents of his youngest brother-in-law and a cousin who had mentored him on his first Kanwar pilgrimage, as well as the endless ongoing expenses for his spouse's fertility concerns. But it was his father's death that Shailesh mostly dwelled on during his conversation with me:

> They said, *babaji* [father] might have been drunk and may have walked onto the railway track, probably suicidally, but that can't be true. All his things, a box of cigarettes, eyeglasses, et cetera, were found neatly placed in his shoes [on] one side of the track. Which man bent on suicide has the care to empty his pockets and neatly place things aside? ... Several years later, in a dream ... that repeated several times ... God [Bhagvan] showed me very clearly

what transpired that evening. . . . My mind would be tense . . . as usual, I went to sleep humming the name of God . . . "Aum Namah Sivay!" . . . He showed me the events of that tragedy, saying this was how it happened. I saw everything very *clearly* in full *detail*, as if in a movie. . . . Father walks out after closing the government ration shop (which he used to run as a part-time job), with shop collections from the week. (It used to be about twenty to twenty-five thousand rupees, which in those days was a large amount.) As he comes out, he is invited over by a group of people sitting outside a liquor shop in that market. This includes a leader, the person in charge of the whole market. There, they make shots of liquor and give my father a poisoned one. When he fell unconscious, they took all his money and laid him on the railway track close by. I saw everything very clearly . . . saw them serving him liquor and carrying him to the track.

Shailesh continued, "In numerous crises, on so many occasions, I have had to run till the last minute from one place, one person to another and yet another for a small amount of money for my sisters' weddings and on other occasions, but, God be thanked, our heart's desire has finally, always been met . . . *automatically*." As for so many of my respondents, for Shailesh the eventual emergence of a path, "God wishing," has attained an axiomatic status. Such resolution has the tenor of a wish.

The wish, as we know, denotes the temporality of a sign that gathers the subject in an irreducible tension; the fulfillment of the wish, as Freud tells us through the pleasure principle, is the resolution of a tension.[1] This is a resolution already half inscribed in the mode of time, in the finitude of matters: for example, a marriage may already be fixed, a body revives, and there is death. But it is momentary, for waiting on it is another wish, another responsibility, as much in the form of a "coming due" as a futurity already weighing in on the present. If this repetitive wishfulness has something of the pleasure principle, it also responds to a beyond of the pleasure principle—the death drive, the temptation to give up.[2] As Freud shows in the dream "Irma's Injection," which is the fulcrum of his theory of wish fulfillment in dreams, at issue—"the artisan of the dream"—is a subject so mired in his obligations or responsibility that the necessity of exculpating himself pushes him to the verge of the "Real." The "Real"—

that is, a formlessness, the raw flesh of the mouth, nose, sexual orifices, death, to the dissolution of the symbolic order such that the symbol, paradoxically, comes forth in its vertiginous arbitrariness. It pushes the subject to a point of breakdown, where one interpreter after the other—Erikson, then Lacan—is left wondering, how, possibly, did Freud not wake up in the middle of the dream.[3]

Freud's dream, "Irma's Injection," narrated at the beginning of his thesis in the *Interpretation of Dreams*, is the launching pad of this text, which is of seminal significance to the history of psychoanalysis. The dream had to do with the events of the day when Freud inquires of Otto, "a younger colleague," and one of his "best friends," who had visited Freud's patient Irma in the countryside, how she was doing. "She is better but not altogether well," replied Otto. The words, especially Otto's tone and expression, somehow disturbed Freud very much; he sensed in these words a reproach to the effect that he had perhaps promised too much. "The very same evening," says Freud, "I wrote down the history of Irma's case, in order to hand it, as though for my justification, to Dr. M., a mutual friend, who was at that time a leading figure in our circle."[4] Among other several intricacies of the dream, which require the reader to closely read the dream text itself, it is important to note that in the dream, the episode evoked the case of Matilde, a patient who had died of diphtheria, for which Freud blamed himself and his overeagerness. Freud's eldest daughter had the same name as the patient who had died. The daughter herself had had a weak development and as a child almost died from the same disease. Freud would continue to worry over her health for a long time.[5]

Thus, one must be careful not to be deluded by the simplicity, the familiarity of this word "wish" to expect transparency and thereby the possibility of a neat classification of its "object"—such as whether the objective is "mundane" or "soteriological," centered on "needs" or "wants."[6] Phenomenologically, however, the association of wish with simplicity is not without significance; it indicates the relieving quality of the wish, which is precisely relief from a tension—relief proper and therefore possible only through a performance that will deliver on it.

The wish is to be exculpated (of guilt and bad faith), says Freud.[7] In Freud's Irma dream, it meant "exculpated," in a context where a defense against an aspersion on professional integrity and an innuendo of over-ambition rapidly involutes into a drama wherein the accountability for the particular patient was merged with the case of the patient who had died from a professional oversight; in turn it associates Matilde with the daughter who almost died of diphtheria. The associations of this disease, Lacan tells us, run amok in this dream.[8] Matilde for Matilde, a tooth for a tooth: here one finds inscribed an order of responsibility that will only find its proper voice in psychoanalysis several chapters later in the *Interpretation of Dreams*—in the dream of the unfortunate father shaken out of his slumber by the address of his dead child, "clasping his arms and calling out reproachfully, 'Father, don't you see that I am burning?'" The child's corpse was in fact burning in the next room.[9] Freud recounts in chapter 7:

> For days and nights a father had watched at the sick bed of his child. After the child died he retired to rest in an adjoining room leaving the door ajar, however, so as to enable him to look from his room into the other where the corpse lay surrounded by burning candles. An old man who was left as a watch sat near the corpse murmuring prayers. After sleeping a few hours the father dreamed that *the child stood near his bed clasping his arms and calling out reproachfully, "Father don't you see that I am burning?"* The father woke and noticed a bright light coming from the adjoining room. Rushing in, he found the old man asleep and the covers and one arm of the beloved body burned by the fallen candle.[10]

One must decipher a similar order of responsibilities in Shailesh's life. Far removed from the "hierarchy of needs" of a Cartesian individuality, on the level of subjective historicity one finds here a being that becomes, recognizes itself, only in the obligations that it enacts—whether in reference to a younger sister, an infant brother, a worried mother, a father killed, unrequited, haunting[11]—and insofar as one's responsibility to each, all, of them remains infinite and impossible to deliver on. Such running from one person to another, one place to another, is as much a running amok forced by circumstances, the *hic et nunc* of a personal history, as it is a drama of the subject who thus enacts itself, finds its gatherings in the recognition of a body of witnesses. It is an appeal to a crowd as much for assistance as to understand and bear witness to his exemplary state, his efforts, that he was not guilty on account of not having tried. In the dream of Irma, with Lacan's guidance we find Freud likewise appealing to one person after another, frenetically gathering a crowd to assist him and equally to witness and testify to his good faith.[12]

For Shailesh, the pilgrimages, as I have noted previously, perhaps had the significance of a rite of passage. The labor and pain of the pilgrimages doubled as an embodied demonstration of resolve and fortitude, repetitions of everyday adversity in an intensely physical form, on faith's celebrated ground. The pilgrimage, not unlike the dream, allows the subject to persist within a performative relational ethos and address responsibilities and desires against the force of a hegemonic discourse of exchange and self-interest. The figure of Śraddhā, as we have seen, is thus ubiquitous in the narratives of Kanwar participants, such that it appears as much a quality of the act as of the person herself. And the act of faith, Kierkegaard has told us, involves an order of responsibility beyond any determinate morality:

> Abraham did not speak. He spoke neither to Sara nor to Eliezar nor Isaac. . . . He *cannot* speak, therein lies the distress and anxiety. The relief provided by speaking is that it translates me into the universal. . . . Abraham can describe his love for Isaac in the most beautiful words. . . . But this is not what is on his mind; it is something deeper, that he is going to sacrifice him because it is an ordeal. No one can understand the latter, and thus everyone can only misunderstand the former.[13]

If Kierkegaard's reference lies in the exceptional events surrounding the sacrifice of Isaac, it also illustrates the "most common and everyday experience of responsibility."[14] The paradoxes of responsibilities that support the symptomatic investments of faith and are performed here cannot be framed in the Universal and are therefore beyond speech. And *here*, it is also a responsibility to he who is dead, unrequited, the father whose place one has come to occupy, in a twist of fate that inculpates one in the very discharge of one's obligations.

Lacan asks, again in the context of Freud's Irma dream, how is Freud content "at this first step in his demonstration, to present a dream which is entirely explained by the satisfaction of a desire which one cannot but call preconscious, and even entirely conscious?"[15] Lacan then goes on to ingeniously amalgamate into Freud's explanation another order of significance, suggesting in this dream—that is, the analyst's, Freud's, dream—the desire to know. Yet Lacan himself has said, in just the previous seminar, "In fact, we don't always know if it [desire of the dream] should be located on the side of the unconscious or on the side of the conscious. And whose desire anyway? And above all, from what lack?"[16] Unconscious, conscious, preconscious—these remain qualities of the subject's temporality. The dream here seems to perform, repeat the concerns and obligations that occupy the subject—a temporal entity—in all the freedom and vitality of the imaginary register, insofar as this latter bears in a primary medium (images) the exigencies, the charges, the responsibilities transcribed in the subject's waking mode.

Unhinged from a hegemonic discourse, in this pause from the time of reality, the dream is the splendor, if tragic, of the unfolding of the subject in its immediacy. The subject is tied to the dream; what takes place here has a veridical significance. "Freud addresses the subject in order to say to him the following, which is new: *Here, in the field of the dream, you are at home.*"[17] And "here" in the dream as much as in these religious performances, one finds an implicated subject, performing to one's relations, responsibilities, and desires and living a fate that is one's alone.

Social scientists avoid using the term "resistance" for such religious phenomena or thinking of them as moral protests. Instead, this scholarship prefers to read here a reactionary politics frequently summarized under the pejorative label of "religious fundamentalism."[18] In these formulations, such phenomena are effectively retrogressive expressions of an inability to surmount past affects and prejudices and embrace futuristic horizons. Even in the subaltern studies literature, where such phenomena are ubiquitous, they are usually seen as substitutions for other, explicit social and political causes and interests. For example, although James Scott in his now classic *Domination and the Arts of Resistance* frequently refers to religious expressions, practices, and movements, in his examples the adversary and the social cause are usually clearly identifiable and the social oppression explicit.[19] The religious expressions are at most of secondary interest. Subaltern scholars such as Ranajit Guha also find religious movements as perhaps the most frequent expressions of resistance, but they likewise underplay their semantics and maintain the focus on specific oppressive groups such as the colonists and feudal authorities.[20]

Thus, extant literature provides little precedent to employ the analytic of "resistance" to understand a contemporary phenomenon such as the Kanwar in sufficient theoretical detail. Yet it is precisely in reference to such particularity of the subject, to this crowded solitariness that "discourse shuns" but that is manifested in the symptom, that the "moment of resistance" appears in psychoanalysis.[21] Psychoanalysis: perhaps the only discipline that has given systematic, protracted attention to the profound paradoxes of subjective temporality, the finitude of human life, in defiance of the systematic prioritization of abstract collectives and the teleological projects of modern thought whose time knows no death.

An analysis of the social form would be a hollow exercise in syllogisms and platitudes unless the analyst can relate to the actors, the subjects that are its players.[22] It would be unwise for the ethnographer to disregard the subject and deny her significance for a vague, poorly conceived impulse of generalization. Following the psychoanalytic understanding of resistance and its coincidence with transference, this chapter aims at another relation of the subject, and of ethics, in the pilgrimage. Departing from metaphysical understanding of consciousness and recognition, it asks us to witness the subject in her relational disposition—invested as much in her worldly responsibilities as in mythical or transcendental imaginaries—to arrive at another (say, half-anthropological) model of recognition. We thus find resistance in the radical experience of responsibility for the death, suffering, and desires of others and also that a fundamental abandon, a complete gesture of death and renunciation—that is, absolute resistance—may shadow the subject's demand for, and pleasure in, goods. To approach "resistances" in the finite temporality of individual existence rather than the teleological paradigm of historical duration, we must rethink resistance.

RETHINKING RESISTANCE

The notion of resistance has had a pivotal—if sometimes confounding—role in most lines of social thought in the twentieth century, from theoretical explorations in cultural studies, political philosophy, and feminist studies to the more empirically centered observations of disciplines such as anthropology and political science. Once the fault lines of a political imaginary and praxis dominated by teleological arguments became apparent over the course of the century, new developments in Left thinking gradually shifted attention to the cultural domain. A rediscovered Antonio Gramsci and Louis Althusser both showed the grip of dominant ideologies in the cultural constitution of individual subjects and thereby the difficulties and importance of engendering a critical class consciousness. Although acknowledging the role of ideological forces and apparatuses in popular consciousness and individual subjectivity, New Left scholars such as Stuart Hall, Tony Jefferson, and Dick Hebdige sought to demonstrate that youth popular cultural practices were also sites of resistance.[23] Nevertheless, the constitutive role of power and ideology in the very interiority of the subject has been hard to challenge, since the subject could not presumably preexist the social and discursive conditions of her production. A similar tussle on the credentials of resistance has ensued in ethnographic narratives.

Noting in resistance studies the tendentiousness of a scholarship as against a coherent pattern of the empirical situation, the anthropologist Lila Abu-Lughod warned against the "romance of resistance."[24] Local resistance to a particular order of power exercises by a group of subaltern subjects, the ethnographer observed, was often motivated by another often far more insidious system of power relations, such as the pervasive ideologies and machinations of global capitalism. With a similarly critical stance, Douglas Kellner describes readings of resistance in anthropological narratives as "fetishizing," while Susan Gal argues that these studies betray an ahistorical notion of self and personhood without regard for cultural differences.[25] Equally assertively, others would valorize resistance to instead criticize these disavowals as symptomatic of a scholarly fad—the putative "crisis of representation" characteristic of the postmodern turn—which they manifestly disapprove of. Thus, Susan Seymour advocates a stoic moral stand, where resistance should refer only to conscious, intentional acts of opposition by subordinate individuals or groups "against a superior [sic] individual or set of individuals."[26] Sherry Ortner, on the other hand, argues that the problem is not conceptual but of ethnographic thinness. Resistance studies, the author avers provocatively, are thin "because they are ethnographically thin: thin on the internal politics of dominated groups, thin on the cultural richness of those groups, thin on the subjectivity—the intentions, desire, fears, projects—of the actors engaged in these dramas."[27] Yet this long tally of concerns itself would suggest that the apparent lack of research "quality" perhaps reflects a more fundamental epistemological impasse.

Grappling with this paradox, contemporary theory often asks for a departure from binary categories of "domination" and "opposition" to invoke instead Foucault's studies of power and agency.[28] Such an epistemology of power and agency, as illustrated, for example, by Judith Butler, itself, however, inevitably slips into the dilemma of the kind that Abu-Lughod observed. Butler argues that the power assumed by the subject "cannot be thought of as a) a resistance that is really a recuperation of power or b) a recuperation that is really a resistance. It is both at once, and this ambivalence forms the bind of agency."[29] In Butler's Hegelian project, much like in Abu-Lughod's empiricism, the analytical endeavor comes to an impasse, an intransigent state where power and resistance, master and subject, become inextricable. The dialectic is blocked; it does not offer an immanent resolution.

Is this, then, the nature of the subject, of the signified, its originary involvement in potentially repressive power, so to speak, or is it a consequence latent in the discourse, an inevitability produced by a mode of signification that, despite all the disavowals on the part of these scholars, remains binary: power/resistance?[30] In other words, in what manner is the resistance of the discourse of the human sciences complicit in the resistance attributed or denied the research situation?[31] In an apparent inversion, Abu-Lughod suggests that incidences of resistance may be more useful as a diagnostic since they invariably signal the presence of "power."[32] However, does not such a proposition turn resistance—and could we not thereby say, the subject herself—into a function of power, making her temporally subsequent? What assumptions of *time* operate here; what notions of psyche, subject, and freedom are at issue?

I would argue that this epistemological confusion is a consequence of a flawed notion of resistance. Liberal ideals of progress, universal emancipation, and individualism embedded in commonplace discourses are more active in these arguments than scholars of resistance would admit. Despite the authors' equivocation and the inevitable multiplicity of voices, the notion of resistance at play here belongs largely to a positive hermeneutics, defined by universalist ideals of "progress" and "Good." This abiding romance, rush of the Universal, can have little patience for the particular, for the finitude of human existence; at an important level, it involves a forgetting of death. This discourse, as I have argued consistently here, often functions under the cover of a grand ethic and project of emancipation defined by a universalism of which the dialectic of the Hegelian World Spirit remains perhaps the most eloquent representative.[33] Philosophical specificities aside, a number of key determining prejudices of Western thought—including its teleological biases and the abstract orientation toward the object (or other) as present-at-hand—that inevitably implicate knowledge in the instrumental perspective of power continue to have a determining influence in Marxist and New Left thinking as well as in social scientific discourses.[34]

Restricted to a binary treatment of "power" and "resistance" framed in a normative analytics, this scholarship somehow fails to witness the subject in her particularity, in her embeddedness in the world as someone implicated, caught in the game—in the mode of a being at stake.[35] Furthermore, this emphasis on a universalist project is hardly accidental, consequent as it is to a mode of recognition characteristic of Western metaphysics, a historical failure to recognize the other, her desire, of which the discourse of the human sciences more or less unsuspectingly partakes. Thereby, this discourse also errs in recognizing the resistance of the subject.

It is possible to see in such a universalist project—whether one understands it through the stoicism of a Kantian moral imperative or the perfection of a Hegelian telos—the goodwill of a constructive futuristic involvement, the mission of a conscious, positive construction of history. Notwithstanding the formidable risks of such a project, this is an orientation that deserves credit at the level of social structures. More disturbing, however, is the transposition of this sociohistorical imperative into a commentary, frequently consecrated by empirical data, on individual psyche and behavior, with minimal psychoanalytic and philosophical inputs. Consequently, the human subject comes to be imagined, constructed at the seam of the two primary tendencies of social scientific scholarship: a search for stable, underlying structures in the "spirit of science" and a critical orientation involved in the investigation with an expectation of, an eye for, change and progress. A complementarity of forms is assumed—equivalence between the subjective and the objective, between the metaphysical good and good tidings from the research object.[36] More than a trace of the romance of realism persists in this rendering of the Hegelian speculative project in empirical particulars.[37] Hegel, the philosopher, one must say, continues to be at work, historic or not.

These embedded biases toward "externality" and historical time to the exclusion of the lived, suffered time of the subject have been profoundly brought to attention by thinkers such as Schopenhauer, Nietzsche, and Kierkegaard and developed systematically by Heidegger in *Being and Time*. The temporality of Dasein—being-with-one-another in relations of care, concern, and solicitude—Heidegger showed, comes prior to history or world-time.[38] Heidegger's radical reformulation of the philosophical project, together with the new fronts opened by Freud, laid the ground for far-ranging epistemological developments, particularly in the form of work often glossed under the title of "poststructuralism."[39] Although the New Left built on some of this thinking, particularly through Lacan, Althusser, and, more recently, Slavoj Žižek, the mainstream of the social sciences—encouraged at least in part by academic cultures of high expertise and narrowing disciplines—has usually scoffed at such philosophical "jargon." In the process, social scientists have unwittingly tied themselves to irresolvable binaries of "structure" and "agency."[40]

To address the resistance in the religious practices and subjectivities under consideration here, one must conceive of resistance in reference to the moral and existential anxiety of being-in-the-world instead of the aloof Being of historical time. In addition to the obvious platform of Heideggerian thought, this analytical movement incorporates a return to Kant's emphasis on the moral imperative of being human. If Kant, however, bracing against the charges of an "empiricism in its naked superficiality," found himself advocating a categorical moral imperative beyond the pathos of human existence and radically removed from any sensate considerations, it is the moral quality of being-in-the-world that has been the focus of the current work.[41]

If the order of obligations and motivations that guides Shailesh, for example, and the religious performances and expressions here are hard to qualify as resistance in progressive scholarly discourses and the universalist politics of liberation it vouches, it is precisely in terms of resistance that psychoanalysis asks us to understand them. The "resistance" of psychoanalysis and the context of "transference" it warrants provide a medium both to analytically depart from the pervasive powers of discourses, practices, and institutions so well characterized by Foucault and other scholars and to understand the subjective significance of religious practice.[42]

RESISTANCE AND THE MYTHIC DISCOURSE

In a seminar on Freud's paper "The Dynamics of Transference," Lacan notes the coincidence of "resistance" and "transference" in psychoanalytic practice.[43] Here, resistance is the name for the turn in the subject's discourse as it approaches what Lacan calls the "pathogenic nucleus." "Resistance is the inflexion the discourse adopts on approaching the nucleus."[44] While deferring interpretation of the signifier, "nucleus,"—for "the value of the object may be a purely tactical one and may perhaps emerge only in this one battle"—one should note that precisely at this point, in a process Freud described as transference phenomenon, the subject begins to take a special interest in the analyst.[45] At other places, Lacan argues that the only resistance is the resistance of the analyst; it is the insistence—even the "ill will," the "biased belief"—of the analyst that produces resistance.[46] Resistance, let us say then, is the resistance to discourse whether it takes the form of the analyst's insistence or is the discourse that speaks under the name of the subject as a representation of the subject. "It is worth recalling that the first resistance analysis faces is that of discourse itself, insofar as it is first of all a discourse of opinion, and that all psychological objectification proves to be intimately tied to this discourse."[47]

Hence, the common refrain of the Kanwar pilgrims: "Bhole Bābā knows your heart's desire much better than you do yourself." The trust in

God's understanding is a verdict on the failures, the apathy of ordinary discourse, of profane community, its routine lack of time and care, its inability to empathize and come anywhere close to the paradoxes that bind the subject. As discussed previously, the ubiquity of expressions such as "Bābā has invited," or "an invitation has been received from the Mother," in North Indian pilgrimages indicates the particularity of the address. However, as in all instances of the symptom, the tables are turned; it is a question of being the object of the other's, the deity's, desire—a desire that harbors the subject's symptom. Likewise, Sered observed that in the discourses of women visiting the cults of the three Rachels in Israel, the word "understand" was "reiterated with particular fervor and frequency": "only Rachel really understands my suffering."[48] And Willy Jansen and Meike Kuhl, speaking of cross-religious female interest in Marian shrines, note that pilgrims see Mary as someone who can "understand" and address their suffering in its felt intensity by virtue of their identification with Mary's womanhood and her subservient status.[49] Such singularity of address, the symptomatic community it heralds, is equally evident in the attachment of the intensely marginalized labor force in the Sertão (northeastern Brazil) to Saint Francis of Wounds, as it is in Obeyesekere's account, in Sri Lanka, of the Muslim ecstatic Abdin's "abject surrender" to "Skanda, the great Hindu-Buddhist god, the son of Siva himself."[50]

Gayatri Spivak has illustrated the impossibility of representation (in language) of the subaltern subject in the discourses of first- and third-world intellectuals.[51] However, while Spivak's primary reference is to the subaltern as a collective identity, a class, or a gendered class, where it is the matter of the single subject, psychoanalysis tells us unequivocally that the subject is to be encountered in the moment of resistance. Resistance here is the resistance to representation—of a memory, a moment, a subject (subaltern, if one will) inscribed as a loss in representation. Precisely at the instance of this loss—the repressed, in the Freudian vocabulary—in proximity to it, the subject invests itself libidinally in the person of the analyst, seducing, inveigling, and calling on the other to bear witness. What is important in transference, the key moment of the psychoanalytic experience, is the particularity of the relation, the call for a symptomatic community that nevertheless has a special halo of recognition since it is a community with the psychoanalyst, as the "one supposed to know." It occurs at the cusp of the subject's recognition of her own condition—although insofar as this condition is cognitively unavailable. "Analysis is an experience of the particular."[52] Unlike recognition in dominant discourses of knowledge complicit in power formations, their metaphysical or sociological grounds, we can locate the emergence of the transference phenomenon in the ability of the analytical situation to interrupt in a tongue "that can be understood in all other tongues" and yet be "absolutely particular to the subject," the self-alienation imposed by the master's discourse.[53]

A partial introduction to Lacan's quartet of discourses—which can only be half true because of the mythlike contradictory emphases of Lacan's illustrations—may be useful. Using a quartet of signifiers and discursive positions, in the *Other Side of Psychoanalysis*, Lacan has provided an excellent figurative demonstration of the manner in which the analyst's discourse subverts the discourse of the master.[54] In this seminar in 1969–70, in the aftermath of the political events of the previous year, Lacan addressed the frequent question about the political significance or stance of psychoanalysis. He posited four divisions in the discursive field, discourse being "certain fundamental relations," "a necessary structure that goes well beyond speech" but "which literally would not be able to be maintained without language."[55] Among these, the discourse of the master is the dominant ideological frame that reduces the subject to her institutional or functional identity—say, woman, thirty-seven years old, married, retail clerk, and so on. The subject is reduced to a functional slot in the dominant version of social reality as a battery of signifiers—in Lacan's terms, the symbolic order or the field of the big Other. Lacan calls this the master's discourse insofar as it is bound up with the interests of the ruling class but also as an allusion to and subversion of the maneuvers of philosophy, in particular the teleological logic of Hegel's master-slave parable that explains knowledge as the dialectical historical product of the working consciousness. Instead, Lacan quips: what work produces "can certainly be truth, it is never knowledge—no work has ever produced knowledge." Knowledge in the sense of the master's knowledge relates to the worker's know-how only in the form of a cunning appropriation, its "theft, abduction, stealing."[56] This form of knowledge "rejects and excludes the dimension of truth" and is "fundamentally tautological," more or less a tool of exploitation. In the master's discourse the subject happens to be configuring itself by the semblable of its place or status in the historical designs of the master's interests (surplus value, or surplus jouissance, as Lacan calls it).[57]

The analyst's discourse responds to, indeed subverts, the realization of the Hegelian dialectic of self-consciousness (as the strict commensurateness of the universal and the particular) as fundamentally disjunctive of the subject.[58] Thus, the dialectic—which is, of course, not related to Hegel and the World Spirit alone, as it implicates an entire tradition of Western metaphysics—betrays itself as the master's discourse.[59] Analysis inverts the discourse of the master, to reveal its cache, make it legible. In saying to the subject, "Away you go, say whatever, it will be marvelous," analysis "introduces him [the subject] to the language of his desire."[60] Analysis thus elevates to the surface the fantasies that the master's discourse (which would but like him "to be like everyone else"), by definition, excludes; it works with the "debris of this knowledge" rediscovered as the unconscious. And much of this work involves return to the mythic, insofar as its bundle of contradictions, in the foreignness to the discourse of science, leads us to something of the order of truth. These are inevitably vague truths, half truths, flashes of truth—as in a dream—that are doomed to fade away since they are at odds with a formidable adversary in the form of the domination of "reality" by the master's discourse. The moment of transference when the subject *resists* a commonplace interpretation of his symptom, terms that would deliver him back to the master's system, and instead transfers his desire to the person of the analyst as someone who may know better is key to the analyst's ability to intervene in a state of affairs where recognition is so often tied to appropriation.

One of the first things one can say about the relation with the deity, like that with the analyst, is that it is an address in the particular. Addressed here is a figure who *knows*, as much in the particular as she is master of the universe itself. Evident in this reiteration of the difficulty of *understanding* is a resistance to discourse, insofar as discourse and the manner in which it inscribes relates the world, affects the subject. Instead, we find signifiers that symptomatically engage the subject by their relation to *her* "pathogenic" condition. Above all, these signifiers bring about a different relation of death, the finitude of human existence precisely in the context of, in difference with, the infinite power of mastery that drives Western metaphysics, from Plato to Hegel, and a fortiori the History that materializes it—which is today more or less the History of the world. They are the call of a different order of temporality. Unlike the latent cognitivism of metaphysics, the symptom is in the manner of a being-in-the-world. It is an embodied difference, a performance that fundamentally implicates the subject in her particularity, whether to be hailed or denounced, praised or stigmatized—simultaneously embedded and transcending, remarked one commentator.

The mythic idiom of the pilgrimage allows such particularity while subverting discursive hegemony. In its ability to artistically play discursive opposites, the mythic allows alternative forms of subjectivity and opens additional possibilities of experiencing time and space.[61] Anterior to the binary split that often defines discourse, it funds the play between good and bad, between power and opposition, between pleasure and death;[62] to use the Lacanian vocabulary, it provides a locale for the rapture of jouissance. "Everything that can be said about myth is this, that the truth reveals itself in an alternation of strictly opposite things, which have to be made to revolve around one another."[63] Contrary to a detached universalist project, the mythic addresses a subject implicated in the game. Here one may subsist with the imperatives of being in the game, of keeping the performances—that is, life—going, without holding back from an utter disregard for life; seek goods at the same time as renouncing, ask for favor and protection while yet being outrageously sovereign. For Śiva or Bholenath (the Guileless Lord), the great renouncer is also the epitome of generosity, the all giving—much like the pilgrim, the bholā, who identifies with the Lord in this duration:

> Great you are my Lord
> you have not a dime in your treasure
> Settler of the three realms

Śiva, you live in the wilderness . . .

You have many names, honorable Shankar

"Naked" is the best of them . . .

Lord of the three realms

Yourself a seeker of alms . . .

So generous you are the great Giver

You kept not a dime for yourself.[64]

Far from normative expectations of giving and taking in familiar processes of measured exchanges, this "giving" operates amid highly precarious material conditions. These narratives reflect a pervasive sense of anxiety, which is not difficult to understand amid the massive deprivations of contemporary India. The dreadful uncertainty of life is reflected in the dread that seeks the grace and protection of God almost continuously, from every direction: "May the destroying Rudra protect me from destruction . . . from all kinds of afflictions . . . from the north . . . the east . . . the west . . . the south . . . at the beginning of the night . . . at all times."[65] Shailesh says, "For as long as I can remember, I have never gotten out of bed without chanting the *Hanumāna Calisa*. . . . I know it by rote."[66] Sankaṭ Mocan, the one who wrestles with troubles, Hanumāna (a manifestation of Śiva) is a guardian deity frequently invoked for his prowess.

Thus, suffering is widespread. Yet it behooves the ethnographer to note that what one sees here, in the radical relation to the deity, is an arrogant, sovereign affirmation of one's suffering, as illustrated, for example, by Lacan in "the resistance of the *amour-propre*. . . . I can't bear the thought of being freed by anyone [in this case, by any ordinary terms or relations] but myself [or here, by the Supreme]."[67] In the ordeal of the Kanwar, in its banter and wagers, in the anxious expressions of self-affirmation, I have argued, one finds a repetition of messages exchanged with a dominating neoliberal ethos. To practice and prepare—"walk through"—however, as we know is only one part of Freud's articulation of "repetition."

Eventually, in perhaps the culminating expression of this theme, in *Beyond the Pleasure Principle* Freud will ponder over repetition in the context of a dialectic of renunciation and desire, of rejection and anticipation, which will have nothing less than quiescence or death for its transcendental reference. And in yet another profound turn, Lacan will reinterpret the death drive, echoing Sade, as the desire for the ex nihilo, the desire to destroy and "begin again."[68] Repetition thus is also to strive to *master*—master, with nothing less than death, sovereignty, and absolute renunciation at hand. Not a moment passes when the slave who sets out to prepare and work does not have her masterly mantle by her.[69]

The anxious repetitions of the economy, the following through of its directives, the apparent willing subjection to its refusals, exclusions, and excesses is no less attended by an imperative of rejection, destruction, and affirmation of sovereignty. After all, it is the destructive signifier of Śiva, where the *imagos* of destruction and death converge in abandon, that attracts the pilgrim.[70] As if nothing less than this figure—which gains as much from the destructive instincts that, as Lacan shows, are anchored in fundamental images of the mutilation and evisceration of the human body commonly found in the human psyche as it does from history, a rich and varied scriptural tradition celebrating such images—would meet the pilgrims' demand.[71] Only Śiva, presenting the ashes of all presence, the detritus of forms, can go past the subject's defenses.[72]

The Freudian notion of the death drive, articulated as the beyond of the pleasure principle, helps elucidate the attachment to Śiva, the compulsion behind these repeated pilgrimages. It is the same desire for the ex nihilo as articulated by Sade, which funds all production but is also the beyond, the destruction of all production. Sade exclaims, "For nature wants annihilation; it is beyond our capacity to achieve the scale of destruction it desires."[73] Yet, as Lacan has demonstrated, the drive is historical; its reference is strictly "outside of the natural world" and, coupled here in the desire to destroy, "is also a will to create from zero, a will to begin again."[74]

As we saw in the previous chapters, the resistances seen in the pilgrimage are evident in so many resistances to the pilgrimage. The apparent absurdity of the phenomenon, whether in relation to religion, institutional morality, or economic sense, makes it suspect to a liberal ethos. Thus, the aggressiveness, hubris, the offensive penance of these Śaivite pilgrims makes them an anathema, as much to the "middle-class" sensibility of English-language news media as to the figureheads of orga-nized religion and the state. These normative liberal impressions lead into strong repressive feelings and action against the pilgrims.

Sitting next to me, two policemen speak in unison: "During the pil-grimage, we allow them to create all the disorder they wish. Challenging them during the festival is unwanted trouble. . . . We just ask them the name of their village, town, anything. But swiftly after the Kanwar is over, the police swoop in on their location irrespective of how far they may live. No Kanwar then to their aid! . . . Just pick them up." Whether interpreted as acts of the "lumpen proletariat" or "hooligans" or reactionary religious fanatics, in a society flush with images of mass-mediated consumption amid widespread deprivation, these are performances of the underprivi-leged. In contemporary India, steeped in power relations whether in a capitalist, statist, or feudal mode, where a large majority of people live under very precarious circumstances and high levels of insecurity yet are burdened with many responsibilities, such expressions of the death drive function to affirm the subjects' sovereignty. If this journey in the name of Śiva occasions an aggressive vindictiveness in one instance, in the other it connotes (to follow another of my respondents) "spiritualism"—a turn away from the cacophony of common desires; if it occasions an other-worldly gift to the gods in one instance, in another it evinces binding, this-worldly obligations to one's dear ones.

THE "HIDDEN TRANSCRIPTS" OF
THE ETHICAL SUBJECT
In his excellent treatise *Domination and the Arts of Resistance,* James Scott, focusing on the social performances of the hidden transcripts of subor-dinate social groups, frankly admits that his analysis is predominantly focused on relations of personal domination. The hidden transcripts sub-vert relations of personal domination to voice, perform, and assert the dialectical experiences and consciousness of oppressed groups in forms and spaces that avoid the dangers of overt encounter with power. This interesting formulation is, however, "less relevant to forms of impersonal domination . . . by say, scientific technique, bureaucratic rule, or by market forces of supply and demand. Much of Michel Foucault's work bears on

those. . . . There is something qualitatively different about claims to authority based on impersonal, technical, scientific rules."[75]

This divide that Scott admits is, I would argue, more a conceptual problem than a question of actual social differences. It is as much a consequence of Foucault's rather pervasive formulation of power as of Scott's anecdotal, if evocative, approach. Foucault's overwhelming interest, as we know, is in the genealogies and structures of modern social control; questions of agency or resistance are secondary to his interests. Scott, however, is more interested in subtle anecdotal illustration than in theoretical formulations; to his credit, such delimitation helps him ward off the teleological reifications discussed earlier. To proceed further, without submitting to overdetermining teleological frames, as we have seen in the case of the Kanwar participants, we must draw the problematic of resistance to the complexities of subjectivity in the phenomenological and psychoanalytic corpus.

As the previous conversations should show, it is not possible to recover the subject and her resistance without an unqualified prioritization of her time, the horizons of her own finite existence bound in relations of care and obligations. From an analytical perspective, this time comes before any expectations of sacrifice for an abstract collective history, which itself can only be a motif in her own temporality. As Scott notes eloquently,

> We know relatively little about a Malay villager if we know only that he is poor and landless [that is, in abstract terms]. We know far more about the cultural meaning of his poverty once we know that he is particularly in despair because he cannot afford to feed guests on the feast of Ramadan, that wealthy people pass him on the village path without uttering a greeting, that he cannot bury his parents properly, that his daughter will marry late if at all because he lacks dowry, that his sons will leave the household early since he has no property to hold them, and that he must humble himself—often to no avail—to beg work and rice from wealthier neighbors.[76]

On a theoretical plane, the Heideggerian moment in Western philosophical thought is a sine qua non for the epistemological departure necessary in this case, from the abstract notions of poverty and class to the profundity of lived time. Note that, every time, it is in the necessities of existence, whether in meeting one's obligations to loved ones or in the struggles of going about life in a dignified manner—concerns often shared with a social group—that Scott finds expressions of resistance. This is also precisely why he finds that there is very little of hegemony in actual social existence.[77]

In view of the observations on Kanwar participants, it is no surprise that it is on the subject of ethics that Mahmood in her study of the "piety movement" in Egypt finds herself forced to question the liberal or progressive notions of agency and resistance.[78] It is the ethical subject behind Muslim women's religious practices, Mahmood would argue, that liberal and progressive conceptions of subjectivity based on notions of "choice" and "free will" are unable to address. These perspectives gloss such religious practices as oppressive insofar as the women are seen as subjects of "custom, tradition, transcendental will, or social coercion" instead of exercising their own choices out of "free will." Mahmood instead argues that "socially prescribed forms of behavior constitute the conditions for the emergence of the self as such and are integral to its realization."[79]

Situating herself in a tradition of "positive ethics," with its roots in Aristotle, Mahmood argues that morality should be conceived not just in terms of "rational content" but in the dispositions, "procedures, techniques, and exercises" through which the specific self affectively realizes itself in varying social conditions. For Mahmood then, it is only in the context of a particular habitus that ethical being can be understood.[80] According to Aristotle, "Moral virtue comes about as a result of habit.... For the things we have to learn before we can do them, we learn by doing them.... We become just by doing just acts, temperate by doing temperate acts, brave by doing brave acts."[81]

Although I believe Mahmood dismisses Kant rather too easily when laying the blame on him for displacing an Aristotelian tradition emphasizing the embodied ethics of virtues and practices with an ethic elaborated through critical reason, the anthropologist makes an important theoretical intervention in critical scholarship. In emphasizing the ethical motivations of a subjectivity that consciously and with protracted effort cultivates a moral disposition grounded in customs and practices, the author throws into question a pervasive liberal discourse of "choice" and "self-interest" uncannily complicit in a hegemonic capitalist economy driven by exorbitant mythologies of desire and consumption. Echoing William Connolly, she reasons that political judgments "do not simply entail the evaluation of abstract moral principles, but issue forth from 'visceral modes of appraisal' that draw their force from an inter-subjective level of being and acting."[82] This is a conclusion we can clearly expect from the temporality of Dasein discussed earlier. However, we must proceed further.

The issue is not limited to the ethic and labor of a mode of embodied customary existence, as Mahmood avers. The resistances to a hegemonic capitalism, which has (neo)liberalism as its choice voice of discursive articulation, are no less elaborate and subtle than the multifarious forms—political, economic, moral, and cultural—in which this discourse expresses itself. The question then would be not only of cultivating customary practices but also of "inventing," excavating new discourses, customs, performances, and rituals of not only a disciplined disposition but also a destructive disposition now specific and targeted, now generic and radical. Then we must go back to "resistance," as Scott illustrated, but with the insights we have from Kant, Heidegger, and the psychoanalytic corpus. We must then conceive of resistance not in a hermeneutic predicated on an abstract teleological universal Good but in the temporality of being-in-the-world. Such a conception is necessary not only to theoretically situate Scott's "hidden transcripts" but also to address the anthropological and feminist disaffections with the notion of resistance.

Insofar as it is an instance of the subject, resistance cannot be reduced to a power effect, whether as reiteration or opposition; it will have to be read in the difference—say, in a complex of form, force, and repetition—that enacts the subject, as much in her attention as in her forgetting, in her refusals as in her silences, in her symptoms as in her appropriation of symbols. It must be witnessed in a temporality incommensurate with the historical progression of a universalist dialectic and the specific metaphysical pursuit or renunciation of the good(s) it entails. While it might be possible to question the value of such performances on the measure of a visionary universal Good, at the same time, one also finds that such sovereign renunciation including invocation of the figure of death also radically interrogates the universalist dialectic, which governs a certain concept of resistance, and of power.

Thus, if going by the discourse of the social sciences and its metaphysical presuppositions true resistance is impossible to find, it remains, from another perspective, ubiquitous and radical. The subject may be imbricated in power ab initio, but she no less participates in a fundamental rejection of its metaphysical foundations and the economy of its history. Bringing the lessons of psychoanalytic practice to my critical ethnography, I have tried to show here that such rearticulation of resistance is indispensable for a radical epistemology that can encounter the new, global infrastructures and certitudes of repressive power and violence.

CHAPTER 7

WAR, NATION, AND
THE HUMAN AS A THING

But what does this "reifying" signify? Where does it arise? ... Why
does this reifying always keep coming back to exercise its dominion?
—Heidegger, *Being and Time*

IN HIS LATER WORK, beginning with the 1975–76 lectures, Michel
Foucault spoke of society as being in a state of perpetual war; flipping
over Carl von Clausewitz's formulation, he described modern politics as
war by other means. Since the end of the middle ages, "history" transi-
tioned from stories of the life and feats of the sovereign to an account of
racial struggle or war between the races. We are, Foucault says, "at war
with one another; a battlefront runs through the whole of society, continuously and permanently. ... Peace itself is a coded war."[1] Marked first as
distinct and of foreign origin, the other race eventually came to indicate a
subrace, a deviant, inferior entity infiltrating into the social body and pos-
ing the one true race a biological and moral threat. The state of war thus
seamlessly alternates between targeting the enemy outside and the enemy
within.[2] The United States is certainly a historical example of this state of
perpetual war—from the many international wars to wars "against crime,"
"against drugs," "against terror," along with a litany of racial persecutions.
In view of this ubiquity of war terminology in the political consciousness,
it is to be expected that the idiom of war should be the first recourse of
American social scientists trying to explain contemporary religiosity. The
generously corporate-funded Fundamentalism Project (1987–95), which
symptomized and defined religion as fundamentalism for the academy as
much for the neocolonial empire, is a paradigmatic example of such mo-

bilization of war ideas. Editing the work of more than a hundred scholars apparently representing the diversity of religious movements worldwide, Marty and Appleby stamp much contemporary religiosity across the world as (in the last instance), "fundamentalist." The following then is more or less true for all of these religious movements:

> "Modern" is a code word for the set of forces which fundamentalists perceive as the threat which inspires their reaction. . . . *Fighting back.* It is no insult to see them as militant, whether in the use of words and ideas or ballots or, in extreme cases, bullets. . . . Next, they *fight for.* . . . Fundamentalists *fight with* . . . resources which one might think of as weapons. . . . Fundamentalists also *fight against* others. . . . Fundamentalists also *fight under* God.[3]

This war cry obviously warrants a response, a call to arms, especially when the aggressor is supposed to be a fanatic, they who despise (our) freedom (and freedoms), people out of joint with Time. The counter-aggression answering this war cry is a moral duty—as much to protect the self as a responsibility to Time, to History, to all the moral and political imperatives contained in the notion and the metaphor of the World Spirit, in and beyond Hegel and philosophy. It is a duty to the bigots themselves and those counted among them, a duty to protect them from themselves—for they know not what they do.[4] Indeed, they *cannot know*, since knowledge, which appears in the light of reason, is precisely what is lacking, shut off. Wars then are called for to give light an opening, another chance, the Spirit some hope.

These representations of the other are obviously corollaries of the representations of the self, of the ego and its ideals in the form of the West: secular, academic, enlightened, and knowledgeable. In some sense, this is a battle of lifestyles—"style" as simultaneously model, desire, and fact, built within the aesthetic an ethic, a notion and imperative of the good. "The Good, of course, is always beautiful," says Plato; as for the Kanwarias—"they are so dirty," sneered an acquaintance.[5] The issue with the authors of "Fundamentalisms" is that they show little consideration (beyond occasional slips) of the implication of the self, its own desires, fears, and "fundamental" misrecognitions—say, in the vicissitudes of market fundamentalism, state terrorism, or Cartesian individualism —in the construction of the other as uncompromising, a stickler for "fundamentals," "which often turn into icons, fetishes, or totems."[6]

In this work, I have labored to throw a little light, illustrate the "reason," in some of contemporary religious practice. I cannot say that the Kanwar practices are representative of religious subjects in general; my conclusions on the epistemological prejudices of the social sciences, however, are much more generalizable.[7] The religious other here is but a curious object of analysis—rather ignorant and superstitious, lacking refined sense. In this perspective, insofar as this contemporary religion is fundamentalist and not traditionalist, it is not so much radical evil but resentment—they who cannot themselves bear the "burden of individual freedom" resent our freedoms.[8]

I have argued that this interpretation is inseparably implicated in the practices and discourses of power. The problem is pervasive, an insidious habit of thought, where "every relation between the same and the other, when it is no longer an affirmation of the supremacy of the same, reduces itself to an impersonal relation with a universal order."[9] Continental thought has shown a systematic critical awareness of this problem, at least since Kierkegaard. Thus, Kierkegaard's deep suspicion of Hegelian systemicity, the denial of interiority for the sake of a rather comic exteriority in the Hegelian edifice,[10] his concern for the ordeals of the "particular" in opposition to the "esthetic flirtations with the result" encouraged by a shallow emphasis on universality.[11] But it was Heidegger who shook the foundations of Western thinking in systematically questioning the thinglike treatment of the other, the individual—the question of the human's Being "has remained forgotten, and that this Being is rather conceived as something obvious or 'self-evident' in the sense of the *Being-present-at-hand* of other created Things."[12]

This apathetic treatment of the individual as just another entity, a thing, a commodity, immediately, completely present, at hand, as an object of the cognition, is obviously convenient to statist rationality of regulation and government, to those that govern. It is tailor-made for, and a consequence of, the extreme dissymmetries of power that have as a rule been characteristic of world history. This is as clearly seen in Foucault's unrelenting illustrations of the collusions between power and knowledge as it is in Lacan's insistence on the role of the master's discourse in the production of knowledge and in our understanding of the subject. Social scientific certainty and reassurance, as represented in the fundamentalist discourse, for example, likewise rests on a fundamental immobilizing of the subject, making out of her life practices a "social fact," thereby annulling the anxiety; "for anxiety is invariably the result of a certain mode of being implicated in the game, of being caught by the game, of being as it were at stake in the game from the outset."[13] The consequence is a privileging of the telos, the generality, as opposed to lived, suffered time, a system of thought based on the cognitive at the cost of material conditions. It speaks from the side of sovereign power, its paternal dictum, "cashing in on that capital, taking account of it, giving accounts and reasons, upholding" its reasoning."[14]

This epistemology for the most part encourages a treatment of the human being as a thing, all transparently present right here and without any proper temporality, an insignificant entity in the great scheme of history. Her time or being here "is a commodity, no more, no less so than is the sugar. The first is measured by the clock, the other by the scales."[15] The construction of religious subjects as fundamentalists, notwithstanding specific empirical facts, is built essentially on such habitual conceptions of being. The necessity of alternative constructions of being is not a question merely of academic importance (if there is such a thing). Our assumptions about subjectivity legitimize or challenge political and ethical operations of enormous social and historical importance.[16] From events in recent history, we know that these operations tend to become all the more polarized, stark, and real on the issue of "religion," to unfold dramatically in the form of major tragedies, wars, and bloodbaths.

I also suggest that my observations here not be interpreted through a prism of cultural relativism. Whereas this work surely draws from ethnographic observations and participants' narratives in an Indian pilgrimage, it only formulates itself in dialogue with strands of "Western" thinking by differentiating in certain instances, aligning in others. It intends to therefore not culturally distinguish Indian society or consciousness but highlight the factuality of the subject that is ignored in dominant liberal discourses and, consequently, in contemporary sociological studies of religion. At the same time, these critiques of Western thought or "metaphysics"—a system of thought centered on the cognitive, meta, beyond of the materiality of being in the world—would be no less true for Indian thought. Here too, for example, Upanisadic thought constructs a whole moral and theological edifice of caste, karma, reincarnation, and a Supreme Being (Brahman) rather oblivious of, if not justifying, the suffering of ordinary beings.[17]

In this work, I have attempted to read the participants' religiosity and performances by breaking through or merely resisting—in some sense always a vain effort—certain habits of interpretation promoted by a dominant epistemology, whether we call it Cartesian, empire-driven, or a nexus between the master's discourse and the discourse of the university.[18] An alternative approach, informed by psychoanalytic theory and existential phenomenology, reveals these subjects not as fundamentalists and bigots but ordinary young men and women seeking ways to countenance their obligations and master their anxieties in the middle of precarious material conditions and an unforgiving social system. Religion, its ethic and order, is being called on here to provide some existential meaning and predictability, the possibility of trust, community, and hope, however illusive, in circumstances otherwise conditioned to bolster a state of paranoia.

I may be asked, where does the discourse of "Hindu nationalism" or "communalism" employed in South Asian studies fit in this representation of contemporary Hindu religiosity? In one sense, I believe, this field is surely part and parcel of global cultures of social scientific knowledge production.[19] The broader motifs of religious fundamentalism, modernization, and secularization have been as important to many of the important works on South Asian religion and society, such as by Thomas Hansen, Arvind Rajagopal, Christophe Jaffrelot, and Peter van der Veer, as to scholarship in the United States.[20] But the field has its specific historicity, formulations, and moral obligations situated in colonial and postcolonial history and politics. Following on the constructions of communalism, against civic social relations, this literature focuses on Hindu nationalist assertion driven by anxieties based on a colonial history and opposition to Muslims.[21] This perspective created valid and interesting insights: majoritarianism in postcolonial India, the suppression of

Muslims, and the demonic force of the nation, a mystical community that comes across as much as a futuristic project as it congeals around an imagined past. These illustrations emphasize the analytical strengths of Anderson's *Imagined Communities* but also its limitations, because the paradigm ignores colonial turmoil and traumas, postcolonial struggles, and the novelty of the imaginary force, the compulsions, of the new southern nations.[22]

"Hindu nationalism" may mean one of two things. First, a moderate version referring to an embedded partiality whereby putatively secular, Indian nationhood has habitually defined itself in the symbolism and desires of a Hindu imaginary. More disturbingly, however, it is a proto-fascist ideology that aggressively claims the identity, space, and consciousness of the nation exclusively for the Hindus through enunciations, rituals, and a politics of exemplary disavowal of the other. The nation here is the desire of a majority zealously pursuing an ideal image and place in the committee of nations (and races) based on projections of a golden, if traumatized and violated, past and a glorious but threatened future. The Muslim (like the Jew in Europe) has a particularly important place in the structure of this ideology; he is the marked (chosen) agent and constant reminder of the deep gash in the past, the barbaric violator whose very presence mocks the sacred body and future of the nation. The construction as much as the presence of the Muslim is the lack, the real that allows the necessary misrecognitions facilitating this ideological fantasy to persist. The elision of the Muslim is primary; but insofar as it cannot be done, it reveals the lie of the fantasy as such and brings the subject to face his castrated condition.

Such Hindu-Muslim antagonism is perhaps borne from layers of historical sediments that morphed into the culture, geography, and psychological material of communitarian relations.[23] It is no less the consequence of nation formation during the tumultuous days of the national socialist disaster, and a global discursive environment charged with the cultural nationalism of Johann Gottfried von Herder and Johann Gottlieb Fichte, as well as the specifics of the hubris and governmental practices of colonial *divide et impera*.[24] The notion of the nation, this particular consciousness, emerges in the context of a nation already in ruins, a wreckage of colonial humiliation with a deeply uncertain future. It is thus quite evident why a rhetoric of national spirit and will that called for loyalty, determination, sacrifice, and "patriotic enlightenment" of the masses through education to be rewarded with national greatness should have been so persuasive to a generation of national activists, including Vinayak Savarkar and Keshav Hedgewar. It will give rise to a discourse of national purity and essence, a matrix of belonging, rather farcical disciplinary regimens, and Hindu nationalist organizations such as the RSS and Jan Sangh (later the BJP), bound as much by the threat and guilt of degeneration as by fantasies of future glory mirroring projections in the past.

The path to the (future) nation, as fantasy object, will be forked. On one side will be a social democratic project of pragmatic and planned development, led mostly by liberal, educated elite and premised on themes of religious tolerance and ethnic inclusion. Religious belonging and nostalgia of the elite will be an influence here as well but balanced by universalism and a discourse of inclusion. On the other hand grows a more or less unabashed and xenophobic sectarianism, performing and stoking the religious sentiments, fears, and guilt of the Hindus as the true national community, the Muslim but a scapegoat. Both these projects are led by elites, but Hansen rightly observes, citing Tocqueville, that democracy inevitably entails "a process of questioning and subversion of social hierarchies and certitudes that over time produces an altogether different society."[25] Thus, the centrist Congress Party, unable to routinize the charisma of the early elite leadership and lacking much internal democracy, has gradually lost its eminence and its constituency of voters to regional, populist parties. Thanks to greater internal democracy, however, the BJP has been able to actively construct its constituency, the political feeding into the ethnic, the cultural, reengineering it and appropriating it into its design.[26]

Insofar as the stakes involve political fortunes and fantasies of the nation's future and existence, every conceivable device is used in these programs of indoctrination and polarization. And pilgrimage has surely been a primary tool of mobilization of religious nationalism, especially during the last two decades as these sectarian forces have gained momentum. In a country where the sacred is widely dispersed, often identified not so much by explicit uniqueness but "in a context of polycentricity, plurality and duplication," the landscape imaginarily charged and historically contentious, the trope of the pilgrimage—an affirmative, religious treading of this landscape—is of immense symbolic import to the construct of the national imaginary.[27] Since the late 1980s, Hindu nationalist organizations, such as the BJP and the Vishwa Hindu Parishad (VHP), have eagerly mobilized the pilgrimage motif, the *yatra*, in presenting this political project as a sacred journey to India's pristine future, traversing her timeless geography. Perhaps the most significant of these events was the Rath Yatra (Chariot Journey) in 1990 led by the BJP leader Lal Krishna Advani. It traveled some seven thousand miles from Somnath (site of a famous temple destroyed by Mohammad Gouri) to Ayodhya, identified as Rama's birthplace and site of the controversial Babri Masjid. Advani rode "atop a DCM-Toyota flatbed truck decorated to look like an ancient chariot, with cutouts and designs of lotuses [the BJP's symbol], lions, and the ancient mantra, Om."[28] Throughout the journey, Advani and other BJP leaders addressed the crowds that gathered eagerly, often possibly to simply witness the spectacle, on loudspeakers with their politico-religious messages. The Rath Yatra is believed to have done much to create a mass base for Hindu religious nationalism.[29]

There are a legion of such examples, from across the country and the world, where social and political organizations have directed popular interest in pilgrimage and sacred sites to their own perspective and interests.[30] The symbolic and practical political significance of the control and transformation of religious shrines for ruling political groups is well established in scholarship.[31] All evidence suggests a complex, dynamic relation between political forces and popular religious idioms and practices. Frequently, the latter are part of the cultural repertoire that political power, ruling or aspirant, mobilizes to gain support and legitimacy among the people. The BJP mobilized the cultural memory of pilgrimage into a political project, its leaders the champions of the sacred cause. Social movement literature describes this phenomenon as "framing."[32] In this theory, we may say, the BJP frames itself as a representation of Hindu interests, even as it frames the "Hindu" and her or his interests in accord with the expediency of its political project. The "Hindu" is constructed as an ideal subject of the party, much as the party is an ideal representation of the interests of this subject—a correspondence of images.[33]

Such politics of polarization mobilizing religious sentiments, which can give a visceral force powered by deep psychic feelings of resentment, guilt, and sadomasochistic temptation, is a serious challenge to Indian democracy, with possibly grievous consequences.[34] The scholarship on Hindu nationalism has powerfully demonstrated these legitimate fears, founded on a real history and equally real possibilities of religion-based violence, frequently in collusion with the state. Hindu nationalism with its powerful cathexis around colonial and historical injuries, real or imagined, has frequently attempted to assert itself through an exclusionary, retrogressive figure of cultural essence with obvious affinities with European fascism.[35] The 2014 ascension of the BJP to power, along with the once unthinkable rise of an extreme divisive figure like Narendra Modi, who is blamed for the 2002 pogrom in Gujarat, to the office of prime minister and the ambience of animosity and cultural narcissism that has followed give this problem unprecedented urgency today.

And these powers have surely mobilized the motif of pilgrimage, whether in the form of the sectarian mobilization of Advani's Rath Yatra or tactical interventions in contested national boundaries as seen in the politics of the Amarnath and Vaishno Devi pilgrimages.[36] The party-led assertion of national identity becomes one with the individual's search for, and affirmation of, cultural identity ostensibly under duress of globalizing social conditions. This is also true of the BJP and VHP's calculated postures in support of the Kanwar pilgrimage and the assertion of the Hindus' right to public space and time for performing their religious practices, particularly in instances of conflict with the administration. These organizations clearly also contribute materially in the form of rest camps and medical supplies for the pilgrimage.[37]

Yet such focus on "religious nationalism," that is, primarily on religion as represented in political parties—their ideologues, institutions, agendas, and activities—also runs the risk of determining interpretations of popular religiosity based on the machinations of power politics. In the very magnitude and inevitable complexity of their social contexts, popular culture and religion surely must exceed the statist, power-oriented referents of nationalist ideologies. To absorb the density of the phenomena, the manifold concerns of religious practitioners into a single, statist idiom would imply a failure to distinguish different dimensions and scales of the social event; it would also imply an analytic itself focused on power, incognizant of the many other forms of subjective investments popular religiosity may perform or represent. It is important to analytically separate the ideological representations of religion as only one dimension, albeit important, of the phenomenon.

For all its possibly good intentions, I believe the discourse on Hindu nationalism has attained something of a hegemonic status in the study of religion in India. Where its message is important, it surely shares the familiar traits of social scientific studies I have described in this book. Here too, a certain passion of the universal, the Good, is impatient with the pains, the cry, the ordeals of the subject, the existent being who becomes as if a thing of the political elite's power and intentions. There is an emphasis on effects and ends, which, as Kierkegaard said, does "not want to know anything about the anxiety, the distress, the paradox."[38] This, in turn, I think is involved in the many alienations of, and thereby the many resistances to, the social sciences. It thereby shows its "fundamental" affinity with the broader motifs and politics of notions such as religious fundamentalism, modernization, and secularization, which surely are part of this literature too. Scholarly choices in our era must be constantly on guard, since it is hard to judge when the zeal for justice, in its many involutions in the discourse and economy of the university, imperceptibly inverts into injustice. (And I dare make any such claim for my own work in this book.) For Creon too was on the side of the Good!

As a festival of the dominant Hindu community identifying with the nation, the Kanwar pilgrimage may therefore—especially under right-wing political influence—easily turn out to be an expression in exclusion and symbolic repression of other communities. Yet in recent times the state is increasingly the agent of a transnational capitalist class and the ideals and images fetishized by neoliberal discourse. Though in a sense only a more vigorous continuation of the social processes witnessed in the older project of postcolonial state building by denying communities, the confluence of the national and the neoliberal—in India most clearly evident in its right-wing political parties—ensures that the community or the nation may now be affirmed only through economic success.[39] Citizenship literally has to be earned. The Kanwar may thus be seen both as an assertion of one's claim to an increasingly alienating nation—its time, space, and culture—by mobilizing the (religious) symbols in which this claim most forcefully resonates and a demonstration negating the new criteria of citizenship and status, that is, wealth and possessions and the comfort and luxury in which their value evidently lies.

The research presented here has shown other multiple dimensions of these ostensibly Hindu religious practices as they perform the precarious informality of the participants' life; the demanding performances here repeat, perform, and sublimate the excesses and aspirations of being in India's contemporary conditions. For the participants here, often living under conditions that are simultaneously precarious and challenging, under constant exposure to and risk of death, disease, and debilitating poverty, the pilgrimage devoted to Śiva—in whom dread, death, and gaiety are inextricably bound together—we have seen is at once an expression of anxieties, responsibilities, and desires. The Kanwar is then effectively the institution of a phenomenon, which is no less the invention of a genre to performatively respond to current social and economic paradoxes and intimate personal concerns. The importance of the religious development is not so much in that it provides the subject with a distinguished signifier (or "identity") but in the various operations through which it intervenes to renegotiate or reconfigure an existing system of signifiers, and consequently the subject's social existence. I have asked in this work only for a little patience for the particular from the social scientist, lest we too in our passion for the Good, like Creon, pronounce a second death on those who have already been sacrificed.

NOTES

ACKNOWLEDGMENTS

1. Findings and parts of this project have been previously published as "Work, Performance, and the Social Ethic of Global Capitalism: Understanding Religious Practice in Contemporary India," *Sociological Forum* 28, no. 2 (2013); "Precarious Life and the Ethics of Care: Subjectivity in an Indian Religious Phenomenon," *Culture and Religion* 12, no. 4 (2011); "Beyond Religious Fundamentalisms: An Analysis of Resistance in the Kanwar Pilgrimage in India," *Subjectivity* 7, no. 3 (2014); and "Religious Practice and the Phenomenology of Everyday Violence in Contemporary India," *Ethnography* 15, no. 4 (2014).

INTRODUCTION

1. Sāvan or Śrāvaṇa usually falls about July–August in the Hindu lunar calendar. Hardwar is a renowned Hindu pilgrimage center. It is the first major town on the banks of the Ganga after it enters the plains in Rishikesh. Hardwar is also one of the four sites where the great Kumbha festival takes place every twelve years. For more on Hardwar, see Lochtefeld, *God's Gateway*.

2. When capitalized and without diacritics, "Kanwar" refers to the pilgrimage, while the "kānwaṛ" is the device that the pilgrims carry. The pronunciation is the same. "To bring the Kanwar" is an idiom meaning to undertake the pilgrimage.

3. See "Kanwar Mela Passes Off Peacefully," *Pioneer*, August 9, 2010. Lochtefeld suggests that the Hardwar Kanwar may have been "transported" in the 1980s by Hindu nationalist groups from a similar phenomenon in Baidyanath (in Jharkhand state). See Lochtefeld, *God's Gateway*. Although there are many similarities between the pilgrimages at Hardwar and Baidyanath, which suggest communication between the two phenomena that may well have reinforced the Hardwar pilgrimage, Lochtefeld's claim about conscious transportation of the pilgrimage is rather speculative. On the contrary, my informants provided several examples of people, often in their own family, who had undertaken the pilgrimage much before the 1980s. There are also sufficient historical data from colonial records to establish the existence of the Hardwar Kanwar at least from the early nineteenth century. See, for example, Heber, *Narrative of a Journey*; and Atkinson, *Statistical, Descriptive and Historical Account*.

4. The pilgrimage is differentiated into types, loosely by levels of difficulty. Thus, the Jhūlā (Hanging) and Baithī (Sitting) Kanwars are the most common. The Jhūlā Kanwar requires that the kānwaṛ should never be placed on the ground and must be kept suspended, ideally on a fruit-laden tree, but since these are supposed to have become rare, on wooden or metal railings set up at camps. In the Baithī Kanwar, the device can be set on

the ground as long as the place is clean. In these cases, the water vessels are usually too heavy to be suspended. The Kharī (Standing) Kanwar requires that the device be borne on the shoulder throughout the journey and therefore requires assistance from another person, either a companion or a random stranger. In the Daṇḍavat (Prostrate) Kanwar, a companion carries the kānwaṛ while the pilgrim advances, moving along the ground one body length at a time. In one variation called Dāk (Mail/Relay) Kanwar, groups of young, athletic men, accompanied by supplies in motorized vehicles, run relays with the sacred water and often have prior commitments to cover the distance within a brief, defined period of time.

5. The Kanwar is governed by many, though often variable, injunctions: for example, when shifting between shoulders, the kānwaṛ may be moved only around the back; the water pots should never hang below the waist; one should not pass under the cluster fig tree; it is imperative to take a bath after using the toilet; neither the pilgrim nor his family is to abuse or hit any living beings during the pilgrimage; family members at home are not to eat fried or spicy food during the pilgrimage; the pilgrim should not enter home (domestic life) before the ritual is completed, that is, until the libations at the Śivalinga have been performed. Pilgrims generally go in groups, usually with a leader to ensure that pilgrimage rules are adhered to, since a breach would violate the kānwaṛ's integrity, destroying the merit of the act.

6. Berger, *The Desecularization of the World*, 7 (emphasis added).

7. See Giddens and Hutton, *On the Edge*; Kinnvall, *Globalization and Religious Nationalism*; and Robertson and Chirico, "Humanity, Globalization, and Worldwide Religious Resurgence."

8. Giddens, *Runaway World*, 4.

9. Ibid.

10. See Mahmood, *Politics of Piety*; Martin, "From Pre-to Postmodernity in Latin America"; and Casanova, *Public Religions in the Modern World*.

11. See, for example, Asad, "The Construction of Religion."

12. See Turner, "Reshaping the Sociology of Religion."

13. See Heidegger, *Being and Time*, 487.

14. See, for example, Young, *The Exclusive Society*. See also Bourdieu, "The Essence of Neoliberalism"; and Goldberg, *The Threat of Race*.

15. Benveniste, *Indo-European Language*, 516.

16. Kant, *Religion within the Limits of Reason Alone*.

17. See Benveniste, *Indo-European Language*, 516–28.

18. See Benjamin, "Critique of Violence." See also Agamben, *Homo Sacer*.

19. See Kant, "An Answer to the Question," 17.

20. Gay, *The Enlightenment*.

21. Rousseau, *The Social Contract*, 120.

22. For arguments on differentiation and secularization, see Durkheim, *Elementary Forms of Religious Life*; Berger, *The Sacred Canopy*; Casanova, *Public Religions*; and Beyer, *Religions in Global Society*. See also Wilson, *Religion in Secular Society*; and Luckmann, *The Invisible Religion*.

23. See Bellah, "Civil Religion in America"; and Bellah, *The Broken Covenant*.

24. Casanova, *Public Religions*, 31.

25. Weber, *From Max Weber*, 293–94.

26. See Durkheim, *Elementary Forms of Religious Life*.

27. See Foucault, *The Birth of Biopolitics*. See also Becker, "Nobel Lecture." For a rational choice theory of religion, see Stark and Bainbridge, *A Theory of Religion*; and Stark, "Micro Foundations of Religion."

28. See Casanova, *Public Religions*; Marty and Appleby, *Fundamentalisms Observed*; and Berger, *Desecularization*.

29. Berger, *Desecularization*, 11. See also Bruce, *God Is Dead*; Yamane, "Secularization on Trial"; and Demerath, *Crossing the Gods*.

30. Berger, *Desecularization*, 11.

31. See Chapter 2 for an analysis of the severe cognitive biases of the idea of "uncertainty" in sociological theory, especially the theories of modernity and globalization influenced by Anthony Giddens.

32. Berger, *Desecularization*, 2; and Bauman, "Postmodern Religion?," 74.

33. Bauman, "Postmodern Religion?," 73.

34. Ibid., 72.

35. See Kant, *Essays and Treatises*, 2:76; Hume, "National Characters," 235; and Eze, "Introduction"; and James Mill, cited in Goldberg, *Racist Culture*, 34.

36. Pritchett, "Who Is Not Poor?"

37. Berger, *Desecularization*, 2.

38. Bauman, "Postmodern Religion?," 70.

39. According to Jacques Lacan, the "symbolic," "imaginary," and the "Real" are three interwoven dimensions of subjective experience. The "symbolic" is largely the meanings and identities attributed by the dominant social order, while the "imaginary" includes fantasies and the dreamlike attributes of psychic life. The "Real" is the traumatic core to the particular existence, which escapes both the ability to symbolize and to properly imagine. See Lacan, *The Ego in Freud's Theory*. For a critique of the notion that religion is primarily motivated by human frailty and fear, see Durkheim, *Elementary Forms of Religious Life*, 225.

40. The elevation of religious "compensation" to the level of principle, as we see in Stark and Bainbridge's widely cited "new paradigm," may to an extent be seen as the explicit formulation of the metaphysical assumptions of most sociological theories of religion. See Stark and Bainbridge, *A Theory of Religion*.

41. See Durkheim, *The Rules of Sociological Method*, 52 (emphasis added).

42. See Craib, *Experiencing Identity*; and Bourdieu, "Vive la Crise!"

43. See Asad, "The Construction of Religion." For examples of nuanced anthropological and philosophical treatments of "religion" as a category, see Mahmood, *Politics of Piety*; and Derrida, "Faith and Knowledge."

44. For the "postmodern" characterization, see Bauman, "Postmodern Religion?" For work that characterizes religion as premodern, see Springett, "Religious Fundamentalism." See also Beyer, *Religions in Global Society*; Lechner, "Global Fundamentalism"; and Marty and Appleby, *Fundamentalisms Observed*.

45. See, for example, Gary Becker, the most reactionary of the Chicago School neo-

liberals, boasting in his Nobel lecture on the widespread adoption of his theories in sociology, among other disciplines. See Becker, "Nobel Lecture," 403. See also Stark, "Micro Foundations of Religion." For a compelling analysis of Chicago School neoliberalism, see Foucault, *Birth of Biopolitics*.

46. Stark and Bainbridge, *A Theory of Religion*, and Stark, "Micro Foundations of Religion," exemplify the former; Iannaccone, "Introduction to the Economics of Religion," illustrates the latter.

47. See Giddens, *Modernity and Self-Identity*; Lechner, "Global Fundamentalism"; and Kinnvall, *Globalization and Religious Nationalism*.

48. See Fabian, *Time and the Other*; and Clifford and Marcus, *Writing Culture*.

49. Max Weber's *The Religion of India* is a consummate example of his exceptional ability to connect the psychic, moral, and material dimensions of human subjectivity and situate them socially and historically.

50. See Weber, *The Protestant Ethic*.

51. See Craib, *Experiencing Identity*, for an insightful critique of sociological method.

52. Heidegger, *Being and Time*.

53. See Hegel, *The Phenomenology of Spirit*.

54. See Derrida, *Dissemination*; and Heidegger, *Being and Time*.

55. Heidegger, *Being and Time*, 480, 499.

56. Kant, *Critique of Practical Reason*, 99.

57. Ibid., 102.

58. Scott, *Domination and the Arts of Resistance*, 24.

59. Durkheim, *The Rules of Sociological Method*, 52 (emphasis added).

CHAPTER 1

1. See "Dak Kanwar in Progress, Pilgrim Count in Hardwar Tops One Crore," *Hindustan Times*, Delhi, July 27, 2011; and "High Security at Kanwar Mela for Shivratri," *Hindustan Times*, Delhi, July 28, 2011.

2. Śivalinga is the iconic representation of Śiva in the phallic form.

3. Across India, many rivers are identified as variants of the great North Indian Ganga, often with subterranean connections (see Feldhaus, *Connected Places*).

4. See Heber, *Narrative of a Journey*; Atkinson, *Statistical, Descriptive and Historical Account*. See also Taylor, *A Visit to India, China, and Japan*; Parlby, *Wanderings of a Pilgrim*, 260; and Lockman and Jesuits, *Travels of the Jesuits*, 274.

5. "Kanwar" in this monograph henceforth refers only to this particular pilgrimage.

6. See Atkinson, *Statistical, Descriptive and Historical Account*, 310.

7. Lochtefeld, *God's Gateway*, 193.

8. See "Kanwar Mela Begins," Hindustan Times, Delhi, July 14, 2006; "Dak Kanwar in Progress"; and "High Security at Kanwar Mela for Shivratri"; and Purnima S. Tripathi, "The Long Walk for Worship," *Frontline* 21, no. 17, August 14–17, 2004.

9. Hobsbawm and Ranger, *The Invention of Tradition*.

10. "'No *tīrtha* like the Ganga,' said Brahma," the *ṛṣi* (sage) Pulastya recounted to Bhīṣma, narrating the merits of different pilgrimage centers at the request of this great hero of the *Mahabharata*. See Vyasa, "Book 3: Vana Parva."

11. See, for example, Marty and Appleby, *Fundamentalisms Observed*; and Beyer, *Religions in Global Society*. See also Kinnvall, *Globalization and Religious Nationalism*; and Robertson and Chirico, "Humanity, Globalization."

12. The ecological fallacy is perhaps as germane to the sociological method as it is seen as a lurching threat, a recurring caveat in sociological training. For more on the pervasiveness of the ecological fallacy, see Van Poppel and Day, "A Test of Durkheim's Theory of Suicide"; Alker, "A Typology of Eco-logical Fallacies"; and Robinson, "Ecological Correlations."

13. See Foucault, "Truth and Power," 300, 304. Among the many profound illustrations of the role of power in knowledge production in the social sciences, see Derrida, "Structure, Sign, and Play," 278–94; Lyotard, *The Postmodern Condition*; Derrida, *Dissemination*; Heidegger, *Being and Time*; and Lacan, *The Other Side of Psychoanalysis*.

14. See Mahmood, "Secularism, Hermeneutics, and Empire," for the insidious connections between imperialism and the discourse of religious fundamentalism. Also see Hunter, "Ted Cruz Vows to 'Carpet Bomb' ISIS Until He Finds Out 'If Sand Can Glow in the Dark,'" Dailykos.com, December 8, 2015, http://www.dailykos.com/story/2015/12/8/1457863/-Ted-Cruz-vows-to-carpet-bomb-ISIS-until-he-finds-out-if-sand-can-glow-in-the-dark.

15. See B. Turner, "Reshaping the Sociology of Religion," for the many limitations of contemporary literature in the sociology of religion.

16. These ethnographies express social concerns as diverse as the trauma of colonization among the Maoris in New Zealand (Sinclair, "Mission to Waitangi"), historical identifications with the suffering of slave ancestors in Ghana (Schramm, "Coming Home to the Motherland"), economic suffering and social humiliation in Brazil (King, "Pilgrimages, Promises, and Ex-votos"), and gendered oppressions in Europe and the Middle East (Jansen and Kuhl, "Shared Symbols"; Sered, *Women as Ritual Experts*).

17. See Kant, *Religion within the Limits* and *Critique of Practical Reason*.

18. See Bharati, "Pilgrimage in the Indian Tradition"; Gold, *Fruitful Journeys*; Eck, *India*; and Bhardwaj, *Hindu Places of Pilgrimage in India*.

19. Other scholars critical of the "religious fundamentalism" thesis have suggested a similar recourse. For example, Bernice Martin, in "From Pre- to Postmodernity in Latin America," argues insightfully that Pentecostalism in Latin America allows a structural negotiation of social change, which is analogous to the role of Protestantism in facilitating capitalism in Europe and the United States.

20. See Weber, *The Religion of India* and *From Max Weber*.

21. Weber, *From Max Weber*, 289. See also Asad, "The Construction of Religion."

22. Durkheimian structuralism has had an influential status in interpretations of Hindu religion and society through the works of scholars such as Louis Dumont and McKim Marriott. Dumont's thesis presenting the Hindu society as essentially hierarchical and other-world oriented has been extensively debated over four decades of research and continues to be a contentious topic. See Dumont, *Homo Hierarchicus*; and Marriott, *Hindu Transactions*. The structuralist tradition itself has been criticized for focusing on untenable grand theses to unravel the "mysteries" of Hindu society and religion. See, for example, Lutgendorf, *Hanuman's Tale*; and Hausner, *Wandering with Sadhus*.

23. See, for example, Marty and Appleby, *Fundamentalisms Observed*; Beyer, *Religions*

in Global Society; Kinnvall, *Globalization and Religious Nationalism*; Lochtefeld, *God's Gateway*; and Robertson and Chirico, "Humanity, Globalization."

24. See Turner and Turner, *Image and Pilgrimage in Christian Culture*; Coleman and Eade, *Reframing Pilgrimage*; and Morinis, *Pilgrimage in Latin America*.

25. Eade and Sallnow, *Contesting the Sacred*.

26. My problem with the idea of "anomie" is somewhat similar to the questions Donna Gaines raised in her excellent study of the suicide of the Bergenfield County teenagers in *Teenage Wasteland*. The issue was not that they were not integrated into the moral order; rather, they were perhaps too integrated into the mores and expectations of a totalizing social order, which held little promise. The suicides were more fatalist than they were anomic.

27. See Blumer, *Symbolic Interactionism*; Cerulo, "Identity Construction"; Cooley, *Social Organization*; Goffman, *The Presentation of Self*; Geertz, *The Interpretation of Cultures*; V. Turner, *Dramas, Fields, and Metaphors*.

28. Butler, *Gender Trouble*.

29. See Geertz, *The Interpretation of Cultures*; and V. Turner, *Dramas, Fields, and Metaphors*.

30. O'Flaherty, *Dreams, Illusion*, 117–19; Schechner, *Performance Studies*, 114.

31. Schechner, *Performance Studies*, 113–14.

32. Śaṃkara, *The Mandukyopanishad*, 76.

33. Hegel, *The Phenomenology of Spirit*, 86–92.

34. See Heidegger, *Being and Time*.

35. Ibid., 289.

36. See Heidegger, *On the Way to Language*, for a brief look at his "Eastern" connections.

37. See also Young, *The Exclusive Society*.

38. See Karl Polanyi, "*The Economy as Instituted Process*," 29–51.

39. "Those working in unorganized enterprises or households, excluding regular workers with social security benefits, and the workers in the formal sector without any employment/social security benefits provided by employers." National Commission for the Enterprises in the Unorganized Sector, *Report on Conditions of Work*, 3. According to the data based on the 2004–5 National Sample Survey (NSS), of a total working population of 457.5 million, 422.6 million (92.4 percent) are informally employed (4).

40. See Freud, "Remembering, Repeating and Working-Through."

41. Performance in the religious field then was "a piece of real experience, but one which has been made possible by especially favorable conditions." Ibid., 154.

42. On the different but morally equivalent fields of action and toil potentially available for life practice in Indian metaphysics, see Patrick Olivelle's excellent thesis on the origins of the *Āśrama* system, *The Āśrama System*.

43. On "sovereignty," see Bataille, *The Accursed Share*.

44. See Bayly, *Recovering Liberties*.

45. I remember vividly from about two decades ago how my maternal grandfather—an Arya Samaji from a village close to Kamarpal's—had sharply, and very unexpectedly, reprimanded a young relative who had ventured to enthusiastically describe his maiden Kanwar journey (uncommon in those days) to the old man, hoping for a pat on the back.

46. Lacan, *On Feminine Sexuality*, 123.

47. Lacan, *The Other Side of Psychoanalysis*.

48. Ibid., 31–38.

49. Bataille, *The Accursed Share*.

50. See Bourdieu, "The Essence of Neoliberalism; *See also* Goffman, *Asylums*.

51. Yaspal used the English word "spirituality."

52. See Singh, "Religion and Neoliberalism."

53. Heidegger, *Being and Time*, 378.

54. This was also evident in K's interest in pets—dogs, horses, calves—which had to be lean and pretty, as well as his fantasies of love interests.

55. See Benveniste, *Problems in General Linguistics*.

56. Weber, *The Protestant Ethic*, 17.

57. We may think of "work," either under the gaze of an apparent master or the very conditions of existence prescribed by the greater Master—be it God, Nature, or Death. In the Hegelian dialectic one clearly witnesses how it is in an experience of trembling and fear under the threat of annulment, and in the presence of an other who one must eventually come to recognize, that the human consciousness is shaped simultaneously as work and as knowledge. Whether knowledge abstracting as "science" can ever represent in good faith, in the form of absolute knowledge instituted in the state, as Hegel would have it, the know-how, and the suffering, of the working is questionable. Nevertheless, this combination of work, or *techne*, and the knowledge assumed to be fully representing it and the essence of the working being (morally assured as a common condition shared by both the master and slave) more or less saturates the dominant idioms of the social field in which the actor must exist. See also Lacan, *The Other Side of Psychoanalysis*.

58. See Foucault, "Society Must Be Defended."

59. Young, *The Exclusive Society*.

60. On "informality," see Böröcz, "Informality Rules"; and Polanyi, "The *Economy as Instituted Process*."

61. Śaṃkara, *The Mandukyopanishad*, 3.18.

CHAPTER 2

1. See McGee, "Desired Fruits," 71; and Pearson, "*Because It Gives Me Peace of Mind*."

2. For use of market reason in the sociology of religion, see Stark and Bainbridge, *A Theory of Religion*. For a critique, see Martin, "Pentecostal Conversion."

3. See Mauss, *The Gift*.

4. Derrida, *Given Time*.

5. Moreno Arcas, "Murugan," 33.

6. Mauss, *The Gift*, 45 (emphasis added).

7. In *Dissemination*, Derrida provides an incisive exegetical meditation on time, gift, and Being and on Mauss's text.

8. J. L. Austin calls such speech acts "commissives." See Austin, *How to Do Things with Words*, 157–58.

9. On "sublimation," see Freud, "On Narcissism"; and Lacan, *The Ethics of Psychoanalysis*. On votive rites, see McGee, "Desired Fruits," 71.

10. Benveniste, *Problems in General Linguistics*, 230–31.

11. Monier-Williams, *Sanskrit-English Dictionary*, 1095.

12. Benveniste, *Indo-European Language*, 138.

13. Ibid., 141, citation from *Rig Veda*, 1.104.6.

14. Ibid., 143.

15. Having made the remark, Nancy acknowledges the problems of such an overdetermined interpretation. "When someone says to his gods: 'Here is the butter. Where are the gifts?' it may be that we do not know what he is saying, since we know nothing of the community in which he lives with his gods." Nancy, "The Unsacrificeable," 26.

16. See Harman, "Negotiating Relationships with the Goddess," 32.

17. See, for example, Stark and Bainbridge, *A Theory of Religion*; and Iannaccone, "Introduction to the Economics of Religion."

18. Eck, "The Goddess Ganga," 148.

19. Eck, *Banaras*, 139.

20. See also Durkheim, *Elementary Forms of Religious Life*, 217–41.

21. See Kristeva, *The Portable Kristeva*, 429. Also see Kristeva for a description of performance as a play of the disjuncture between the time of ordinary social life and the atemporality of the unconscious, performance analogous to the fantasy, "torn between the atemporality of the unconscious and the forward-moving flight of the story" (449).

22. See Benveniste, *Indo-European Language*, 470–71, 470–75.

23. Ibid., 471.

24. Ibid., 475.

25. See Benveniste, *Problems in General Linguistics*, 229.

26. Likewise, Harman observes in the context of vows to a South Indian goddess "to take a vow to the goddess and to fail in its performance is to place yourself in great jeopardy." Harman, "Negotiating Relationships," 31.

27. Yet, at the same time, if there are contingencies that make the pilgrimage in a particular year particularly inconvenient, it is not uncommon for a votary to beseech the deity for forgiveness with a promise of doing the pilgrimage on another occasion.

28. Kakar, *Shamans, Mystics, and Doctors*, 44.

29. I owe the "arc" analogy to an observation by Elin Diamond of Rutgers University during a discussion on this project.

30. In feminist literature on votive rites, such centrality of the other, generally a loved one, is an important figure. See Pearson, *"Because It Gives Me Peace of Mind"*; Pintchman, *Women's Lives*; and Sered, *Women as Ritual Experts*. Speaking in a context of Jewish women, for example, Sered notes, "In numerous rituals—spontaneous, formal, private, and communal—they guard over the living, dead, and unborn people . . . the health, happiness, and security of particular people with whom they are linked in relationships of caring and interdependence" (10). See also Mahmood, *Politics of Piety*.

31. McGee, "Desired Fruits," 83.

32. Lacan, *The Ethics of Psychoanalysis*, 261.

33. Kinnvall, *Globalization*, 4–5.

34. On the centrality of the notion of "identity" in contemporary scholarly understanding of religion, see, for example, Robertson and Chirico, "Humanity, Globalization";

Giddens, *Consequences of Modernity* and *Runaway World*; Berger, *Desecularization*; Kinnvall, *Globalization and Religious Nationalism*; and Beyer, *Religions in Global Society*.

35. See Bendle, "The Crisis of 'Identity.'"

36. See Giddens, *Consequences of Modernity* and *Modernity and Self-Identity*.

37. Giddens, *Modernity and Self-Identity*, 61.

38. This particular account of the ego as an agency capable of disengaging from the turmoil of the id and rationally adapting to the social environment is a legacy of the ego-psychology tradition mostly developed in the United States under the influence of Anna Freud, Heinz Hartman, and Erik Erikson. The perception of the therapeutic goal of attaining a healthy, well-developed, well-adapted ego so pervasive in contemporary cultural practices is itself largely a correlate of this model. See Bendle, "Crisis of 'Identity.'"

39. See Groarke, "Psychoanalysis and Structuration Theory," for the primacy of cognition in Giddens's theories despite Giddens's own occasional statements to the contrary. Also see Craib, *Experiencing Identity*.

40. Giddens, *Modernity and Self-Identity*, 58–61. These presuppositions disregard such long and established traditions contesting "reality" as feminism, Marxism, and postmodernism, along with other traditions in psychoanalysis itself.

41. Bendle, "Crisis of 'Identity,'" 13.

42. Lacan, *The Ego in Freud's Theory*, 148.

43. Heidegger, *Being and Time*, 222.

44. Groarke, "Psychoanalysis and Structuration," 569. For Heidegger, the primary nothingness of the world perceived in the mode of anxiety is precisely what constitutes the human in relation with the world, with fellow beings, in care and concern. To describe the radically ethical constitution of the self, Butler likewise resorts to the distinction between "fear" and "anxiety" Lévinas finds in commentaries on Genesis. Jacob, "troubled by the news that his brother Esau—enemy or friend—is marching to meet him 'at the head of four hundred men . . . was greatly afraid and anxious.'" Jacob, we learn from a series of interpreters, was "frightened of his own death but was anxious he might have to kill." See Butler, *Precarious Life*, 136.

45. Also see Butler, *The Psychic Life of Power*, for a critique of identity and a distinction between identity and identification. Citing Jacqueline Rose, Butler argues that "the unconscious constantly reveals the failure of identity. . . . There is a resistance to identity at the very heart of psychic life" (97). See also Lévinas, *Alterity and Transcendence*, 135; and Butler, *Precarious Life*, 136.

46. On "affect," see Green, "Conceptions of Affect." On anxiety as an affect, see Harrari, *Lacan's Seminar on "Anxiety"*; and Lacan, *Anxiety*.

47. Giddens, *Modernity and Self-Identity*, 43–46.

48. For Lacan's strong criticism of this purported relation between anxiety and fear, see Lacan, *Television*; and Harrari, *Lacan's Seminar on "Anxiety."*

49. See Lacan, "Function and Field of Speech"; and Freud, *Beyond the Pleasure Principle*.

50. Freud, *Beyond the Pleasure Principle*.

51. Lacan, *Freud's Papers on Technique*, 173.

52. See Hyppolite, "A Spoken Commentary on Freud's *Verneinung*," 296–97.
53. Ibid.
54. For the importance of contact in the mother-infant relationship, see Groarke, "Making Contact."
55. Freud, *Introductory Lectures on Psycho-Analysis*, 505.
56. Lévinas, *Totality and Infinity*.
57. On responsibility and faith, see Kierkegaard, *Fear and Trembling*.
58. According to Lacan, "Man's desire is the desire of the other" (for example, in Lacan, *Freud's Papers on Technique*, 177).
59. "How there is, It gives Being and how there is, It gives time. In this giving, it becomes apparent how that giving is to be determined which, as a relation, first holds the two toward each other and brings them into being." See Heidegger, *On Time and Being*, 5. To illustrate further, the translator, Stambaugh, quotes Heidegger's comments on the "It gives" from his *Letter on Humanism*: "The 'it' which here 'gives' is Being itself. The 'gives,' however, indicates the giving nature of Being granting its truth" (5n).
60. Kapil told me his mother was dead. I have the details from other sources, including at least one instance when years later he went with a cousin to secretly meet his mother, who lives in a neighboring village. Later, both were mercilessly beaten by family members.
61. See Lacan, *The Ethics of Psychoanalysis*. Griffiths says, "Até is a rich and evocative term, especially in tragedy, suggesting both *outcome* (delusion, ruin, misery) and *cause* (often a mixture of human folly and supernatural sabotage) . . . [an] inescapable complex of delusion, error, crime, and ruin." See Gibbons and Segal, *Antigone*, 41.
62. In a translation from Heidegger's German: "Not just now, nor since yesterday, but ever steadfast this prevails. And no one knows from whence it first appeared." Heidegger, *Hölderlin's Hymn*, 116.
63. Lacan, *The Ethics of Psychoanalysis*, 278.
64. Ibid., 300.
65. See Derrida, *Given Time*; and Polanyi, *The Economy as Instituted Process*.
66. See Hegel, *Philosophy of Right*, 82.
67. See Chatterjee, "A Response to Taylor's 'Modes of Civil Society,'" 119–32. See also Meyer, "Taking Risks for Others," 137.

CHAPTER 3
1. See Raheja, *The Poison in the Gift*.
2. See Scheper-Hughes, *Death without Weeping*; Wacquant, "Toward a Dictatorship over the Poor?," "Following Pierre Bourdieu," and "Urban Marginality in the Coming Millennium"; Auyero, "The Hyper-Shantytown" and *Routine Politics and Violence in Argentina*.
3. Benjamin, "Theses on the Philosophy of History," 255.
4. See Mbembe and Roitman, "Figures of the Subject in Times of Crisis"; Bourdieu and Wacquant, "On the Cunning of Imperialist Reason"; See also Mahmood, *Politics of Piety*.
5. See Gaines, *Teenage Wasteland*.
6. I could not agree more with Lacan when he says, "In order to have perhaps a slight chance of conducting a correct ethnographic inquiry, one must, I repeat, not proceed by

way of psychoanalysis, but perhaps, if there is such a thing, be a psychoanalyst" (*The Other Side of Psychoanalysis*, 92).

7. Cartesian individuality then is but one manner of marking a boundary in a phenomenological and temporal continuum. It is particularly important to note this since we exist in a time dominated by teletechnology, relentless bombardment by imageries, discourses, and forces, at once remote and instant, expertly coded to capture and manipulate attention, bodies, and affects. One may think of such subjectivity as suspended between the subject of contemporary affect theory with its conceptual antecedents in the monism of Spinoza and Deleuze on one end and the temporality of being-in-the-world in Heidegger's existential phenomenology on the other. See Clough, *Autoaffection* and "The Affective Turn"; and Singh, "Religion and Neoliberalism."

8. Lacan, *Freud's Papers*, 268.

9. Butler, *Psychic Life of Power*, 47.

10. See also Obeyesekere, *Medusa's Hair*.

11. See Coomaraswamy, *The Dance of Śiva*.

12. *Skanda Purana*, cited in O'Flaherty, *Śiva*.

13. Excerpt from *Śiva Purana* and *Matsya Purana*, cited in Handelman and Shulman, *God Inside Out*, 160.

14. *Śiva Upasana*, 38–39.

15. *Bol Bhole Bum Bum*, 3.

16. See O'Flaherty, *Śiva*.

17. See Sircar, *The Śākta Pīṭhas*; see also Sax, *God of Justice*.

18. See O'Flaherty, *Śiva*.

19. See Lutgendorf, *Hanuman's Tale*.

20. See Erndl, *Victory to the Mother*.

21. On this point, see also Weber's illustration of the significance of the "calling" in *The Protestant Ethic*.

22. See also Jeffrey, Jeffery, and Jeffery, *Degrees without Freedom*

23. See Eck, *Darśana*.

24. He located this hierarchical disposition in the traditional superiority of the Brahman—and thereby the purity he represented—over the worldly power of the king. See Dumont, *Homo Hierarchicus*.

25. Freud, *Beyond the Pleasure Principle*, 65, 42–47.

26. Ibid., 67.

27. Ibid., 46.

28. Freud, "Remembering, Repeating and Working-Through," 154.

29. Benjamin, *On Hashish*, 59.

30. Benjamin, *Selected Writings*, 2:329.

31. Assoun, *Freud and Nietzsche*, 112.

32. See Derrida, "Freud and the Scene of Writing."

33. See also Lacan, "Function and Form of Language."

34. See Freud, "Remembering, Repeating and Working-Through" and "*Beyond the Pleasure Principle*."

35. See also Lacan, "Function and Form of Language," 215.

CHAPTER 4

1. Once consecrated by offering to the gods, the *prasād* is carried back for distribution in the family and neighbourhood.

2. As opposed to Śiva and other deities who are not physically present.

3. See Lochtefeld, *God's Gateway*.

4. Ibid.

5. Western travelers, such as Matheson, *England to Delhi*; Taylor, *A Visit to India*; and Heber, *Narrative of a Journey*, report seeing Kanwarias during the winter, about January or February, which must have been on the occasion of Mahasivratri in the month of Phālgun. Information on the Śrāvaṇa festival is rarer, although this may be attributed to the obvious disinclination to travel during the horrid summer with the inconveniences compounded by the monsoon rains. Accounts of the Kanwar practice in different parts of northern India are also found in Hodges, *Travels in India*; Wright, *Lectures on India*; Hamilton, *The East-India Gazetteer*; Buchanan, *A Journey from Madras*; and Parlby, *Wanderings of a Pilgrim*.

6. Atkinson, *Statistical, Descriptive and Historical Account*, 109.

7. See Lochtefeld, *God's Gateway*.

8. Matheson, *England to Delhi*, 332.

9. Taylor, *A Visit to India*, 117.

10. Heber, *Narrative of a Journey*, 132.

11. *Dainik Jagran*, Dehradun/Hardwar, July 29, 2011, 5.

12. The capitals of both the warring parties, Hastinapur and Indraprastha, are part of the doab, although the actual site of battle, Kurukshetra, is about twenty miles west of the Yamuna River.

13. Zakaria, *The Widening Divide*, 5.

14. A lac or lakh equals one hundred thousand.

15. Timur, "Malfuzat-I Timuri," 455–59.

16. Sarkar, "Historical Pedagogy of the Sangh Parivar."

17. See Benveniste, *Indo-European Language*, 521

18. Weber, *From Max Weber*, 328.

19. See Bellah, "Religious Evolution."

20. Timur, "Malfuzat-I Timuri," 436.

21. Kant, *Religion within the Limits*.

22. See Derrida, "On Forgiveness."

23. *CNBC*, August 17, 2010; *Jagran*, Bareilly, December 18, 2010. There had been another incident in Bareilly a few months earlier over the change in the route of a Muslim procession, Julūs-e-muhammadi. See *Jagran*, Bareilly, March 2, 2010.

24. *Sentinel*, Guwahati, August 8, 2011.

25. Imran Khan, "Religious Brotherhood: Muslims Make 'Kanwars' for Hindu Pilgrims," *Indo-Asian News Service*, August 8, 2011, https://in.news.yahoo.com/religious-brotherhood-muslims-craft-kanwars-hindu-pilgrims-092150436.html.

26. Faisal Fareed, "Moradabad ADM Threatening TV Journalist Fareed Samsi," TwoCircles.net, August 10, 2011, http://twocircles.net/2011aug17/moradabad_adm_threatening_tv_journalist_fareed_shamsi.html#.VvWa5uZn2Wk.

27. Ibid.

28. Vidya Subramaniam, "After Last Week's Riots, Moradabad a Tinderbox," *The Hindu*, August 14, 2011, http://www.thehindu.com/news/national/after-last-weeks-riots-moradabad-a-tinderbox/article2354477.ece.

29. Fareed, "Moradabad ADM."

30. "It was all made up by that person who was accused in the case of sexual assault in order to distract the attention of the people. You will be surprised to know that the community believed the version of a 12 years old girl, who alleged that she had seen the police showing disrespect to the holy Quran," said Fareed Shamsi, a local journalist. Md. Ali, "Moradabad: A City of Communal Riots," TwoCircles.net, August 20, 2011, http://twocircles.net/2011aug20/moradabad_city_communal_riots.html#.VvWoseZn2W.

31. Sahai, *South Asia.*

32. Ghassem-Fachandi, *Pogrom in Gujarat*, 2.

33. See Pandey, *The Construction of Communalism.*

34. See Kakar, "Some Unconscious Aspects of Ethnic Violence."

35. Insofar as the sacrificial violence against this other happens in the arena of the sacred, it shows that "in the object of our desires we try to find evidence for the presence of the desire of" an Other, which Lacan calls *"the dark God."* Lacan, *Four Fundamental Concepts*, 275.

36. Nandy, "The Politics of Secularism," 87.

37. Nandy, *Time Warps*, 85.

38. See, for example, various essays in Bhargava, *Secularism and Its Critics.*

39. Madan, *Modern Myths, Locked Minds*, 6.

40. Ibid., 9. A celebrated elucidation of the early Christian conception of this dichotomy is that by Saint Augustine at the beginning of the fifth century: "Two cities have been formed by two loves: the earthly by the love of self, even to the contempt of God; the heavenly by the love of God, even to the contempt of the self." See Augustine, *The City of God*, 47. Without going into greater historical details, let us note that in western Europe of the Middle Ages, the papacy dominated secular authority but gradually "by the early fourteenth century, towns and secular governments, which had meanwhile grown in size and scope, first found their voice." See Madan, *Modern Myths, Locked Minds*, 9.

41. See, for example, Berger, *The Sacred Canopy*, 106; and Madan, *Modern Myths, Locked Minds*, 12.

42. Madan, *Modern Myths, Locked Minds*, 13.

43. Thus, as Madan says, citing Peter Berger, "'Protestantism cut the umbilical cord between heaven and earth,' and presented secularization as a gift to humankind. . . . 'The Protestant reformation, however, may . . . be understood as a powerful re-emergence of precisely those secularizing forces that had been 'contained' by Catholics, not only by replicating the Old Testament in this, but going directly beyond it.'" Ibid., 12.

44. See also Asad, "The Construction of Religion."

45. For example, in the *Sacred Canopy*, Berger proposes that as an empirical discipline, sociology can view religion only as a human projection. Humans construct and project a world outside them, a world of "mysterious and awesome power" to give order to their emotions and experiences. Whereas the observation seems self-evident at first glance, one needs to revisit the epistemological work done by terms such as "order" and

"projection," which inevitably assume a stable reference, a human being, a world, that may be thought outside this "sacred cosmos"—in terms of a Cartesian rational construction. Thus, the "function," the place, of the sacred cosmos would be derived on the basis of the self-evident truth of a metaphysical, logical conception of the human and the social.

46. Nandy, *Time Warps*, 67.

47. Benveniste, *Indo-European Language*, 516, 517.

48. Ibid., 519.

49. Ibid., 518–19.

50. Ibid., 521.

51. We keep returning to these differences so that we may harbor any hope of relating to the pilgrims who keep returning to what we might continue to provisionally call "religion," not only through their return every year for the pilgrimage but also in the differential texture of everyday life in which there is always a small space, a time, a marked space in the house, or a little scruple or ritual particularly reserved for the divine, the holy Other. Yet beyond these differences, which usually function under the cover of power and political economy—and in which one should always be conscious of the risk, the temptation of extrapolating a type of cultural relativism to which several anthropologists and Indologists happen to succumb—it is important not to neglect (*neg-legere*, disregard, slight) what appears common and integral to the diverse rituals, phenomena, and "subjective attitude" described as "religion."

52. Derrida, "Faith and Knowledge."

53. Although comparative history of Indo-European languages shows across these languages subtle variations in the conception of the sacred and no common word, this aspect of the separation of what is holy and integral, and has to be approached with the greatest punctiliousness, is widely shared among the languages—Greek *hierós*, German *heilig*, Latin *sacer*, and Iranian *spənta*. Equally important, comparative history of language suggests a common structure whereby the notion of the sacred "nearly everywhere" seems to require not one but two terms: positive, "what is charged with divine presence," as seen in the previous terms; "and negative," to designate prohibitions to human access, for example, *yaoždata* (Avestan), *sanctus* (Latin), and *hágios* (Greek). See Benveniste, *Indo-European Language*, 445.

54. Choksy, "To Cut Off."

55. Should we call it a paradox that today "faith," a fiduciary bond, is probably nowhere as critical as when we speak of belief in science or technology, not only in the manner in which a certain know-how—which one trusts without any claim to knowledge, such as how microchips function, telecommunication works, or subways operate—defines the texture if not the possibility of our lives but also the possibility of revolutions (or choice of revolutions) in medical technology, genetic technology, or mass destruction? And thus the risk of this belief is the risk of a violation of the bond (and what bond, how many bonds?) against which there is in the end no indemnity. There is no belief without risk; and which risks will people not take for belief. We live in a time—and the question remains whether there has ever been a time very different in this regard—when the sacrifices people will make for belief are all too alive for us, in so many different forms, at so many places. See Derrida, "Faith and Knowledge."

56. Kant, *Religion within the Limits*, 47.

57. Ibid., 158, 47 (emphasis in original).

58. Can we not hear in the madman's diatribe proclaiming the death of God in Nietzsche's *Gay Science* the echoes of Hegel's depiction of how religious artworks of the past fare in contemporary understanding, where "in place of the inner elements composing the reality of the ethical life, a reality that environed, created and inspired these works, we erect in prolix detail the scaffolding of the dead elements of their outward existence"? Hegel, *Phenomenology of Spirit*, 340.

59. Nandy, *Time Warps*, 85.

60. Ibid., 78, 80.

61. Moreover, this is not a Habermasian analysis that emphasizes the abstract distinction between the sociocultural life world and functionalist systemic logic that, though derived from the former, threatens to colonize it. This would imply a cognitive understanding of religion as an institutionalized system of faith and belief outside the political and economic battlefields, outside people's lived conditions, responsibilities, and sufferings.

62. Heidegger, *Being and Time*, 78.

63. Ali, citing the shahar qazi, the chief clerical authority of the city and a local journalist, "Moradabad: A City of Communal Riots."

64. See Kakar, "The Time of Kali."

65. Ali, "Moradabad: A City of Communal Riots."

66. See Wilkinson, *Votes and Violence*.

CHAPTER 5

1. See, for example, Waghorne, *Diaspora of the Gods*.

2. See Hansen, *The Saffron Wave*.

3. For contests over pilgrimages, see Eade and Sallnow, *Contesting the Sacred*; Maclean, *Pilgrimage and Power*; and Khan, *Conversions and Shifting Identities*.

4. For Latin American pilgrimages, see Crumrine and Morinis, *Pilgrimage in Latin America*; for European, Jansen and Kuhl, "Shared Symbols"; for African, Schramm, "Coming Home to the Motherland"; and for New Zealand, Sinclair, "Mission to Waitangi." On pilgrimages in India, see Karve, "On the Road"; Bharati, "Pilgrimage in the Indian Tradition"; and Gold, *Fruitful Journeys*.

5. See, for example, Sarkar, *Hindu Wife, Hindu Nation*. Also see Jaffrelot, "Hindu Nationalist Reinterpretation of Pilgrimage," 324–42.

6. See, for example, Jatinder Sethi, "Maha Shivratri, Kovad Mela and a Long Weekend," Ghumakkar, March 6, 2012, http://www.ghumakkar.com/2012/03/06/mahashivratri-kovad-mela-long-week-end/.

7. "Street Eternity," Hard News, accessed July 15, 2012, http://www.hardnewsmedia.com/2008/09/2335 (emphasis added).

8. "Kanwarias Distorting Hinduism," *Hindustan Times*, August 11, 2007, https://www.highbeam.com/doc/1P3-1318516921.html.

9. See, for example, Marty and Appleby, *Fundamentalisms Comprehended*; and Bauman, "Postmodern Religion?," 55–78.

10. Weber, *From Max Weber*, 277, 289.

11. Ibid., 270.

12. See Weber, *The Protestant Ethic*, 356 (emphasis in original).

13. Breuer and Freud, *Studies in Hysteria*, 131.

14. "Kanwarias to Follow the Usual Route," *Hindustan Times*, July 18, 2007, http://global.factiva.com.

15. On the T-Series business model, see Sundaram, *Pirate Modernity*, 120.

16. See Hansen, *The Saffron Wave*.

17. See Freud, *The Uncanny*, 121–58.

18. S. K. Deshwal, "One Response to Handling Kanwaria Rush," MetroNow, July 23, 2008, http://metronow.wordpress.com/2008/07/21/handling-Kanwaria-rush/.

19. Shantanu Dutta, "Kanwaria: The Lumpen on the Pilgrim Trail," *Merinews*, August 10, 2007, http://www.merinews.com/article/kanwaria-the-lumpen-on-the-pilgrim-trail/125905.shtml.

20. "Kanwarias May Be Termed Non-tourists," *Pioneer*, July 21, 2010, http://global.factiva.com.

21. Kristeva, *The Portable Kristeva*, 230.

22. Ibid., 232.

23. On the juxtaposition of opposite affects in Śiva, see O'Flaherty, *Śiva*. On the subversive symbolism of Śiva, see Wakankar, *Subalternity and Religion*.

24. Freud, "Remembering, Repeating and Working-Through." Also see Freud, *Beyond the Pleasure Principle*.

25. See White, *The Alchemical Body*.

26. See Guru, *Humiliation*; Ilaiah, *Why I Am Not a Hindu*.

27. See Chapter 1, note 39.

28. See also Böröcz, "Informality Rules."

29. Purnima S. Tripathi, "The Long Walk for Worship," *Frontline* 21, no.17 (2004), http://www.frontline.in/static/html/fl2117/stories/20040827000206600.htm.

30. Shobhit Mahajan, "I Grew Up in Sleepy Small Town on the Outskirts of Delhi," accessed July 17, 2012, people.du.ac.in/~sm/smweb/ARTICLES/kanwarias.doc.

31. Dutta, "Kanwaria: Lumpen on the Pilgrim Trail."

32. "Kanwarias Distorting Hinduism."

33. Tripathi, "The Long Walk for Worship."

34. Rent seeking is seeking personal gains in return for access to the public services one may control.

35. Dutta, "Kanwaria: The Lumpen on the Pilgrim's Trail."

36. *Bhagavad Gita*, 18.28.

37. Kant, *Critique of Judgement*, 174.

38. See Hansen, *The Saffron Wave*.

39. See *Bhagavad Gita*, 4.13. See also Weber, *Religion of India*.

40. Śankara, *The Vedanta Sutras*, 1.3.34–38.

41. Manu, *Manu's Code of Law*, 1.91.

42. From the *Sāṃkhyakārikā* (23):

adhyavasāyo buddhir
dharmo jñānaṃ virāgo aiśvaryam
sāttvikam etadrūpaṃ
tāmasam asmād viprayastam

"The buddhi [will or intellect] is [characterized by] ascertainment or determination / Virtue, knowledge, non-attachment, and lordliness / are its *satvika* [truth/light] form / Its *tamas* [dark] form is the inverse." See Īśvarakṛṣṇa, *Sāṃkhyakārikā of Īśvarakṛṣṇa*.

43. See Weber, *Religion of India*.

44. See Becker, "Nobel Lecture"; Bourdieu, "Essence of Neoliberalism"; Foucault, *Birth of Biopolitics*; Goldberg, *Threat of Race*.

45. See Foucault, *Birth of Biopolitics*.

46. As capital normatively defines not just work and social status but the mode of being itself, as much in working as in consuming, as much in economic as cultural terms, behavioral disposition is perhaps the best marker of race. Race marks the lack of appropriate or worthy disposition.

47. Young, *The Vertigo of Late Modernity*, 20.

48. Maloney, *Language and Civilization*, 85.

49. *Bahujan*, "majority" or "many," is how Dalit political groups in India's electoral context have framed their political constituency. The successful mobilization of group interests and identities behind a vanguard of the caste oppressed may be explained as political pragmatics, but it also indicates that the "excluded"—the Sudras and the "untouchables," as some commentators call them—are indeed *many*. In Uttar Pradesh, the North Indian state perhaps most radically divided on caste lines, for the last two decades political power has alternated between the Bahujan Samaj Party and the Samajwadi Party. The former is the party of those who are caste oppressed, while the latter consolidates "lower" caste groups with Muslims, another abject social group of modern India.

50. Guru and Chakravarty, "Who are the Country's Poor?," 262.

51. Goldberg, *The Threat of Race*, 348 (emphasis in original).

52. Manu, *Manu's Code of Law*, 12.33, 12.29. Quite early in the *Bhagavad Gita*, we hear from Lord Kṛṣṇa: "cāturvarṇyaṃ mayā sṛṣṭaṃ guṇakarmavibhāgaśaḥ" (4.13). That is, "the four varnas of society (viz., Brahmin, Kshatriya, Vaishya and Sudra) I created, classifying them according to the *gunas* (*satva*, *rajas*, and *tamas*) and *karmas* (behaviors) predominant in each and apportioning corresponding duties to them." And in accordance with the nature of the text, the concluding chapter is almost exclusively devoted to the ontological merit of the three gunas and castes to which they apportion.

> The work of Brahmans, Kshatriyas, Vaishyas, and Sudras, O thou Slayer of thy Foes, is determined by the *gunas* born of their own natures. Serenity, self-restraint, austerity, purity, forgiveness, and uprightness indeed and faith in knowledge and realization of truth are the activities born of a Brahmana's nature. Valor, splendor, firmness and skill in battle, and also not to flee, and generosity and lordliness, such are the activities born of a Kshatriya's nature. Agriculture, cattle rearing and trade are activities in the nature of the Vaishya, furthermore, service to others is action proper to the nature of the Sudra. (18.41–44)

Ideally of a *satvika* nature, the Brahmana has a fine, discriminating intellect; he is a seeker of metaphysical truths, a believer, and is well behaved and compassionate. In the Kshatriya and the Vaishya, different aspects of the *rajasika* predominate, which makes them cherish power and material wealth and reflects a level of ignorance (18.38). To the Sudra, and a fortiori to the outcasts, however, is assigned the *tamasika*, which is an absolute lack of goodness.

CHAPTER 6

1. See Freud, *General Psychological Theory*.
2. See Freud, *Beyond the Pleasure Principle*.
3. Lacan, *Ego in Freud's Theory*, 154–55.
4. Freud, *The Interpretation of Dreams*, 89.
5. Ibid., 88–104; and Lacan, *The Ego in Freud's Theory*, 146–72.
6. See Raj and Harman, *Dealing with Deities*, 250–51. Again, I think the reason for the popularity of such ideas lies in the dominance of market rationality and an ego psychology tradition agreeable to it. See Maslow, "A Theory of Human Motivation."
7. See Freud, *Interpretation of Dreams*; and Lacan, *Ego in Freud's Theory*.
8. See chapters 13 and 14 on the dream "Irma's Injection" in Lacan's second seminar. Lacan, *Ego in Freud's Theory*, 146–74.
9. Freud, *Interpretation of Dreams*, 403; and Lacan, *Four Fundamental Concepts*, 34.
10. Freud, *Interpretation of Dreams*, 403 (emphasis in original).
11. Maslow, "A Theory of Human Motivation."
12. Lacan, *Ego in Freud's Theory*.
13. Kierkegaard, *Fear and Trembling*, 113 (emphasis in original).
14. Derrida, *The Gift of Death*, 67.
15. Lacan, *Ego in Freud's Theory*, 151.
16. Lacan, *Freud's Papers*, 45.
17. Ibid., 44 (emphasis in original).
18. See Mahmood, "Secularism, Hermeneutics," 323.
19. Scott, *Domination and the Arts of Resistance*.
20. See Guha, *Elementary Aspects of Peasant Insurgency*.
21. Lacan, *Freud's Papers*, 36.
22. For an excellent illustration of the limitations of ethnographic practice, see Clough, *The End(s) of Ethnography*.
23. See Hall and Jefferson, *Resistance through Rituals*; and Hebdige, "Subculture."
24. Abu-Lughod, "The Romance of Resistance"; and Gal, "Language and the 'Arts of Resistance,'" 407.
25. Kellner, *Media Culture*; and Gal, "Language."
26. Seymour, "Resistance," 305.
27. Ortner, "Resistance," 190.
28. See Ahearn, "Language and Agency"; and Bilge, "Beyond Subordination vs. Resistance."
29. Butler, *Psychic Life of Power*, 13.
30. See Mahmood, *Politics of Piety*.
31. See Derrida, "Structure, Sign, and Play."
32. Abu-Lughod, "Romance of Resistance."
33. See Heidegger, *Being and Time*; Lacan, "Function and Form of Language" and *The Other Side of Psychoanalysis*; and Derrida, *Dissemination* and "Structure, Sign, and Play."
34. See Derrida, "Structure, Sign, and Play"; Fabian, *Time and the Other*; Heidegger, *Being and Time*; and Foucault, "Truth and Power."

35. See Mahmood, *Politics of Piety*. For greater analytical engagement with this concern, see, for example, Derrida, "Structure, Sign, and Play."

36. To appreciate the profound coincidence that must be posited here, one need only look at the Herculean labor it takes Hegel to establish the conformity between self-consciousness and the object-world in the form of the spirit. See Hegel, *Phenomenology of Spirit*. Yet this powerful proposition cannot by any means be taken as final. For pathbreaking critiques of Hegel, see, for example, Heidegger, *Being and Time*, especially the last chapter; Kierkegaard, *Fear and Trembling*; Derrida, "From Restricted to General Economy"; Lacan, *The Other Side of Psychoanalysis* and "The Function and Field of Speech"; Lévinas, *Totality and Infinity*; and of course Marx and Engels, *German Ideology*.

37. In the essay "Intentional Structure of the Romantic Image," Paul de Man provides a fine analysis of the power and fascination of the romantic image. Patricia Clough's *End(s) of Ethnography* is a compelling criticism of ethnographic realism. Clifford, *The Predicament of Culture*, also provides a strong critical reflection on ethnography. Also see Derrida, "Structure, Sign, and Play."

38. "It temporalizes world-time, within the horizon of which 'history' can 'appear' as historicizing within-time." Heidegger, *Being and Time*, 486.

39. See Derrida, *Dissemination*.

40. See, for example, Emirbayer and Mische, "What Is Agency?" For a compelling critique, see Wang, "Agency."

41. Kant, *Critique of Practical Reason*.

42. Foucault, "Truth and Power."

43. See Lacan, *Freud's Papers*; and Freud, "The Dynamics of Transference."

44. Lacan, *Freud's Papers*, 36.

45. Ibid., 41.

46. See Lacan, "Function and Form of Language," 314.

47. Ibid., 348.

48. Sered, *Women as Ritual Experts*, 86.

49. Jansen and Kuhl, "Shared Symbols."

50. King, "Pilgrimages, Promises"; and Obeyesekere, *The Work of Culture*, 3.

51. Spivak, "Can the Subaltern Speak?"

52. Lacan, *Freud's Papers*, 21.

53. Lacan, *Ego in Freud's Theory*, 243.

54. Lacan, "Function and Form of Language" and *The Other Side of Psychoanalysis*.

55. Lacan, *The Other Side of Psychoanalysis*, 12–13.

56. Ibid., 79, 21. As an example, Lacan challenges, "*I defy you to prove in any way* that descending 500 meters with a weight of 80 kilos on your back and, once you have descended, going back up the 500 meters with that it is nothing, no work at all. Make the effort, give it a try, you will find proof to the contrary" (48–49).

57. Ibid., 90–91.

58. Ibid.; and Lacan, "Function and Form of Language," 242–43. Also see Kierkegaard, *Fear and Trembling*, for a critique of Hegel's focus on the Universal and exteriority, especially on the question of religious responsibility and ethics. It is important to note that

Kierkegaard is a constant presence in Lacan's observations on ethics, repetition, and the death drive. See also Lévinas's excellent commentary on Kierkegaardian ethics in "Existence and Ethics."

59. See Lacan, *The Other Side of Psychoanalysis*, for compelling observations on the play of the master's perspective in the dominant discourse and in Western philosophy in general. Lacan posits the analyst's discourse as a structural subversion of the master's discourse. In *Being and Time*, Heidegger is likewise critical of the Cartesian notion (followed through from Plato to Hegel) of the subject, which relates to entities as present-at-hand. Derrida provides an expansive elaboration of this "metaphysics of presence" in several texts. But see his analysis of Socrates's discourse in "Plato's Pharmacy" (in *Dissemination*), which shows how Socrates's dialectic in the *Phaedrus* sets out to give reason and logic to the self-pronounced word of the mythical king. Working on the authority of the king, the *logos* comes to translate, replace, and disseminate the king's *manteia*. Foucault's critique of power/knowledge, although more disjointed and institutionally oriented, demonstrates the relation between power and discourse in "concrete," historical terms.

60. See Lacan, "Function and Form of Language," 242. In reading "his desire," one may never forget Lacan's refrain that one's desire is the desire of the other.

61. See Crapanzano, *Imaginative Horizons*; O'Flaherty, *Śiva*; Obeyesekere, *Medusa's Hair*; and Roberts, "Symbols, Sacrifice."

62. See Derrida, "Structure, Sign, and Play."

63. Lacan, *The Other Side of Psychoanalysis*, 110.

64. *Śiva Upāsanā*, 37–39.

65. Ibid., 30–51.

66. The *Hanumāna Calisa* is a eulogy to Hanumāna in forty couplets.

67. Lacan, *Écrits*, 87.

68. Lacan, *Ethics of Psychoanalysis*, 212.

69. See Hegel, *Phenomenology of Spirit*, 91.

70. Lacan, *Écrits*, 85.

71. Ibid.

72. On the play of "force" and "form," see Derrida's excellent essay "Force and Signification."

73. Lacan, *Ethics of Psychoanalysis*, 212.

74. At this point Lacan warns, "Don't put the emphasis on the term 'will' here. Whatever interest may have been aroused in Freud by an echo in Schopenhauer, it has nothing to do with the idea of a fundamental Wille." Ibid., 212.

75. Scott, *Domination and the Arts of Resistance*, 21.

76. Ibid., 113.

77. Ibid., 82.

78. Mahmood, *Politics of Piety*.

79. Mahmood, "Secularism, Hermeneutics," 856, 857.

80. Ibid., 846.

81. Ibid., 851.

82. Ibid., 860.

CHAPTER 7

1. Foucault, *"Society Must Be Defended,"* 51.

2. See, for example, Wacquant, "Urban Marginality"; and Alexander, *The New Jim Crow.*

3. Marty and Appleby, *Fundamentalisms Observed,* vii–x (emphasis in original).

4. Thus, an anonymous Western man's diatribe against a female friend (apparently Muslim) on Facebook: "Load of shit! They treat you like a possession, a piece of furniture that needs covering up to be protected and you go along with that bull shit. Rebel against those bigots."

5. Plato, "Timaeus," 18c, 94.

6. Marty and Appleby, *Fundamentalisms Observed,* x.

7. See also Singh, "Definite Exclusions."

8. Bauman, "Postmodern Religion?," 74.

9. Lévinas, *Totality and Infinity,* 88.

10. "If Hegel had constructed his whole systematic edifice, just as he did, and then at the end appended a footnote saying that the whole thing, after all, was only a 'thought-experiment,' he would have been the greatest thinker who ever lived; as it is, he is 'merely comic.'" Kierkegaard, quoted in Bretall, *A Kierkegaard Anthology,* 191.

11. "Faith is precisely this paradox, that the individual as the particular . . . is not subordinate but superior . . . to the universal, *inasmuch as the individual as the particular stands in an absolute relation to the absolute.*" Kierkegaard, *Fear and Trembling,* 130 (emphasis in original).

12. Heidegger, *Being and Time,* 75.

13. Derrida, "Structure, Sign, and Play," 248.

14. Derrida, *Dissemination,* 135.

15. Marx, *Wage Labor and Capital,* 14.

16. See Butler, *Precarious Life*; Mahmood, *Politics of Piety.*

17. See Śaṃkara, *Vedanta Sutras,* 1.3.34–38, quoted in Chapter 5.

18. Lacan, *The Other Side of Psychoanalysis.*

19. See Bourdieu and Wacquant, "On the Cunning of Imperialist Reason."

20. See Hansen, *The Saffron Wave*; Rajagopal, *Politics after Television*; and Van der Veer, *Religious Nationalism.*

21. See Pandey, *Construction of Communalism*; and Varshney, *Ethnic Conflict and Civic Life.*

22. See Pandey, *Construction of Communalism*; Anderson, *Imagined Communities*; and Chatterjee, "Whose Imagined Community?," 521–27.

23. Ghassem-Fachandi, *Pogrom in Gujarat.*

24. See Pandey, *Construction of Communalism*; and Hansen, *The Saffron Wave.*

25. Hansen, *The Saffron Wave,* 18.

26. See Chandra, *Why Ethnic Parties Succeed.*

27. Brosius, *Empowering Visions,* 310; Eck, *India.*

28. Davis, "The Cultural Background of Hindutva," 129.

29. Bhambhri, *Bharatiya Janata Party.*

30. Such politics of pilgrimage and the contests over forms, spaces, and powers of the

sacred have been important currents in pilgrimage research. See, for example, MacLean's study of how Allahabad's *Pragwal* Brahmins, a community out of favor with the British for their role in the 1857 revolt, surreptitiously applied the nomenclature *Kumbh* to the existing annual Magh Mela in Allahabad. See Maclean, *Pilgrimage and Power*. Bal Gangadhar Tilak's historic organization of Maharashtra's now famous Ganpati procession, an anticolonial cultural motif of much political consequence, out of popular Gaṇeśa fondness and festivities is an example from the late nineteenth and early twentieth centuries. See Courtright, *Lord of Obstacles*. Another example of such inventiveness is the institution of the *Ban-Yātra* at Braj in the sixteenth century. See Entwistle, *Braj*; and Shah, "Braj." So too in Ramdevra, the popular Tantric cult was framed by the Rajput rulership as its own extension. See Khan, *Conversions and Shifting Identities*. Likewise, the Catholic Church, in all likelihood, encouraged and influenced the appearance of Marian apparitions in Lourdes and actively promoted pilgrimages to Santiago to win back its popular following, driven no less by the anxiety of maintaining its relevance in a secularizing age. See Dahlberg, "The Body as a Principle of Holism"; Reader, "Pilgrimage Growth"; and Harris, *Lourdes*. As another example, Bauer and Stanish show, using extensive historical and archaeological evidence, how the Incas conquered and translated the ancient pilgrimage to the islands of the sun and the moon in Lake Titicaca and the crucial importance of this control of the religious shrine in the legitimation and consolidation of their power. See Bauer and Stanish, *Ritual and Pilgrimage in the Ancient Andes*.

31. See Eade and Sallnow, *Contesting the Sacred*.

32. Benford and Snow, "Framing Processes and Social Movements."

33. Similar dynamics of identity definition may be witnessed in the "Hinduization" of the "indigenous peoples" by Hindu rightist forces in central India. See Baviskar, "Indian Indigeneities." Both pilgrimage and social movement literature describe these processes where different meanings, or worldviews, overlap as contentious or contested. The conflict terminology, to the extent that it is seen to be a function of definite group interests, seems to overdetermine social processes by drawing lines where possibly none exist and imputing to them separate coherent intentionalities. While the social analyst invested in her own ethic and practice may see an obvious conflict, it is undoubtedly a reduction of the historically spread subtleties of the performed rapport between divergent worldviews. We find it hard to distinguish moments of contention from processes of co-constitution. This is evident in the cultural dramas that the BJP is so adept in. The important aspect of BJP's framing of Hinduness is not that it is contested by other political parties or groups but that it creates its Hindu only so far as a subject identifies with the frame. Hinduness is primarily constructed by virtue of a superimposition of meaning, whatever its provenance, on existing cultural (or identity) performances, not through contests over "who a Hindu is," a problem that emerges only consequently. Of course, following the structuralists, we may reason that meaning itself is an assemblage of signifiers defined by difference with one another and lacks a given signified. Without following deeper into that conversation, here I am only arguing against stabilizing, or fixing, this play of difference at the level of social identity. For contestation in the pilgrimage literature, see Eade and Salnow, *Contesting the Sacred*; for the social movement literature, see Tilly, *Contentious Performances*; McAdam, "Tactical Innovation"; and Tarrow, *Power in Movement*.

34. See, for example, Ghassem-Fachandi, *Pogrom in Gujarat.*

35. See Jaffrelot, *Religion, Caste, and Politics in India.*

36. Reader, "Pilgrimage Growth."

37. Yet, obviously, alluding to the RSS and the BJP as agencies that instituted this massive pilgrimage, as Lochtefeld argues in *God's Gateway*, is to go too far. This gives them an overarching agency that they are simply incapable of.

38. Kierkegaard, *Fear and Trembling*, 63.

39. Pandey, *Construction of Communalism*; and Hansen, *The Saffron Wave.*

BIBLIOGRAPHY

Abu-Lughod, Lila. "The Romance of Resistance: Tracing Transformations of Power through Bedouin Women." *American Ethnologist* 17, no. 1 (1990): 41–55.

Agamben, Giorgio. *Homo Sacer: Sovereign Power and Bare Life.* Stanford, CA: Stanford University Press, 1998.

Ahearn, Laura M. "Language and Agency." *Annual Review of Anthropology* 30, no. 1 (2001): 109–37.

Alexander, Michelle. *The New Jim Crow: Mass Incarceration in the Age of Colorblindness.* New York: New Press, 2012.

Alker, Hayward R. "A Typology of Eco-logical Fallacies." In *Quantitative Ecological Analysis in the Social Sciences,* edited by M. Dogan and S. Rokkan, 64–86. Cambridge: Massachusetts Institute of Technology Press, 1969.

Anderson, Benedict. *Imagined Communities: Reflections on the Origin and Spread of Nationalism.* London: Verso, 1983.

Asad, Talal. "The Construction of Religion as an Anthropological Category." In *Genealogies of Religion: Discipline and Reasons of Power in Christianity and Islam,* 27–54. Baltimore: Johns Hopkins University Press, 1993.

Assoun, Paul-Laurent. *Freud and Nietzsche.* London: Athlone Press, 2006.

Atkinson, Edwin T. *Statistical, Descriptive and Historical Account of the North-Western Provinces of India.* Vol. 2, pt. 1. Allahabad: North-western Provinces' Government Press, 1875.

Augustine. *The City of God.* Edited by Marcus Dods. Edinburgh: T & T Clark, 1878.

Austin, J. L. *How to Do Things with Words.* Cambridge, MA: Harvard University Press, 1962.

Auyero, Javier. "The Hyper-Shantytown: Neo-liberal Violence(s) in the Argentine Slum." *Ethnography* 1, no. 1 (2000): 93–116.

———. *Routine Politics and Violence in Argentina: The Gray Zone of State Power.* Cambridge: Cambridge University Press, 2007.

Bataille, Georges. *The Accursed Share: An Essay on General Economy.* Vols. 2 and 3. New York: Zone Books, 1993.

Bauer, Brian S., and Charles Stanish. *Ritual and Pilgrimage in the Ancient Andes: The Islands of the Sun and the Moon.* Austin: University of Texas Press, 2001.

Bauman, Zygmunt. 1998. "Postmodern Religion?" In *Religion, Modernity, and Postmodernity,* edited by Paul Heelas, 55–78. Malden, MA: Wiley-Blackwell.

Baviskar, Amita. "Indian Indigeneities: Adivasi Engagements with Hindu Nationalism in India." In *Indigenous Experience Today,* edited by Marisol De la Cadena and Orin Starn, 275–304. Oxford: Berg, 2007.

Bayly, Christopher A. *Recovering Liberties: Indian Thought in the Age of Liberalism and Empire*. Cambridge: Cambridge University Press, 2012.

Becker, Gary. "Nobel Lecture: The Economic Way of Looking at Behavior." *Journal of Political Economy* 101, no. 3 (1993): 385–409.

Bellah, Robert. *The Broken Covenant: American Civil Religion in Time of Trial*. Chicago: University of Chicago Press, 1992.

———. "Civil Religion in America." *Daedalus* 96, no. 1 (1967): 1–21.

———. "Religious Evolution." In *The Robert Bellah Reader*, edited by Robert Bellah and Steve Tipton, 23–50. Durham, NC: Duke University Press, 2006.

Bendle, Mervyn F. "The Crisis of 'Identity' in High Modernity." *British Journal of Sociology* 53 (2002): 1–18.

Benford, Robert D., and David A. Snow. "Framing Processes and Social Movements: An Overview and Assessment." *Annual Review of Sociology* 25 (2000): 611–39.

Benjamin, Walter. "Critique of Violence." In *Reflections: Essays, Aphorisms, Autobiographical Writings*, by Walter Benjamin, 277–300. New York: Schocken Books, 2007.

———. *On Hashish*. Cambridge, MA: Belknap Press of Harvard University Press, 2006.

———. *Selected Writings, Volume 2, Part 1, 1927–1930*. Cambridge, MA: Harvard University Press, 1999.

———. "Theses on the Philosophy of History." In *Illuminations: Essays and Reflections*, by Walter Benjamin, translated by H. Zohn, 253–64. New York: Schocken Books, 1968.

Benveniste, Emile. *Indo-European Language and Society*. Coral Gables, FL: University of Miami Press, 1973.

———. *Problems in General Linguistics*. Coral Gables, FL: University of Miami Press, 1971.

Berger, Peter. *The Desecularization of the World: Resurgent Religion and World Politics*. Washington, DC: Ethics and Public Policy Center, 1999.

———. *The Sacred Canopy: Elements of a Sociological Theory of Religion*. Garden City, NY: Anchor, 1990.

Beyer, Peter. *Religions in Global Society*. Oxford: Routledge, 2006.

Bhagavad Gita. Translated by Edwin Arnold. 1885. http://www.sacred-texts.com/hin/gita/index.htm.

Bhambhri, Chandra Prakash. *Bharatiya Janata Party: Periphery to Centre*. Delhi: Shipra Publications, 2001.

Bharati, Agehananda. "Pilgrimage in the Indian Tradition." *History of Religions* 3, no. 1 (1963): 135–67.

Bhardwaj, Surinder Mohan. *Hindu Places of Pilgrimage in India: A Study in Cultural Geography*. Berkeley: University of California Press, 1983.

Bhargava, Rajeev, ed. *Secularism and Its Critics*. Oxford: Oxford University Press, 1998.

Bilge, Sirma. "Beyond Subordination vs. Resistance: An Intersectional Approach to the Agency of Veiled Muslim Women." *Journal of Intercultural Studies* 31, no. 1 (2010): 9–28.

Blumer, Herbert. *Symbolic Interactionism: Perspective and Method*. Berkeley: University of California Press, 1969.

Bol Bhole Bum Bum. Delhi: B. S. Praminder, n.d.

Böröcz, Jozsef. "Informality Rules." *East European Politics & Societies* 14, no. 2 (2000): 348–80.

Bourdieu, Pierre. "The Essence of Neoliberalism." *Le Monde diplomatique*, December 1998. https://mondediplo.com/1998/12/08bourdieu.

———. "Vive la Crise!" *Theory and Society* 17, no. 5 (1998): 773–87.

Bourdieu, Pierre, and Loic Wacquant. "On the Cunning of Imperialist Reason." *Theory, Culture & Society* 16, no. 1 (1999): 41–58.

Bretall, Robert K. *A Kierkegaard Anthology*. Princeton, NJ: Princeton University Press, 1973.

Breuer, Josef, and Sigmund Freud. *Studies in Hysteria*. London: Penguin Books, 2004.

Brosius, Christiane. *Empowering Visions: The Politics of Representation in Hindu Nationalism*. London: Anthem Press, 2005.

Bruce, Steve. *God Is Dead: Secularization in the West*. Oxford: Blackwell, 2002.

Buchanan, Francis. *A Journey from Madras through the Countries of Mysore, Canara, and Malabar*. Cambridge: Cambridge University Press, 2011.

Butler, Judith. *Gender Trouble: Feminism and the Subversion of Identity*. New York: Routledge, 1989.

———. *Precarious Life: The Powers of Mourning and Violence*. London: Verso, 2004.

———. *The Psychic Life of Power: Theories in Subjection*. Stanford, CA: Stanford University Press, 1997.

Casanova, José. *Public Religions in the Modern World*. Chicago: University of Chicago Press, 1994.

Cerulo, Karen A. "Identity Construction: New Issues, New Directions." *Annual Review of Sociology* 23 (1997): 385–409.

Chandra, Kanchan. *Why Ethnic Parties Succeed: Patronage and Ethnic Head Counts in India*. Cambridge: Cambridge University Press, 2007.

Chatterjee, Partha. "A Response to Taylor's 'Modes of Civil Society.'" *Public Culture* 3 (1990): 119–32.

———. "Whose Imagined Community?" *Millennium: Journal of International Studies* 20, no. 3 (1991): 521–27.

Choksy, Jamsheed K. "To Cut Off, Purify, and Make Whole: Historiographical and Ecclesiastical Conceptions of Ritual Space." *Journal of the American Oriental Society* 123, no. 1 (2003): 21–41.

Clifford, James. *The Predicament of Culture*. Cambridge, MA: Harvard University Press, 1988.

Clifford, James, and George E. Marcus, eds. *Writing Culture: The Poetics and Politics of Ethnography*. Berkeley: University of California Press, 1986.

Clough, Patricia. "The Affective Turn: Political Economy and the Biomediated Body." *Theory, Culture & Society* 25, no. 1 (2008): 1–24.

———. *Autoaffection: Unconscious Thought in the Age of Technology*. Minneapolis: University of Minnesota Press, 2000.

———. *The End(s) of Ethnography: From Realism to Social Criticism*. New York: Peter Lang, 1998.

Coleman, Simon, and John Eade, eds. *Reframing Pilgrimage: Cultures in Motion*. London: Routledge, 2004.

Cooley, Charles H. *Social Organization: A Study of the Larger Mind.* New York: Schocken Books, 1909.

Coomaraswamy, Ananada Kentish. *The Dance of Śiva: Essays on Indian Art and Culture.* New York: Dover Publications, 2011.

Courtright, Paul. *Lord of Obstacles, Lord of Beginnings.* New York: Oxford University Press, 1985.

Craib, Ian. *Experiencing Identity.* London: Sage Publications, 1998.

Crapanzano, Vincent. *Imaginative Horizons: An Essay in Literary-Philosophical Anthropology.* Chicago: University of Chicago Press, 2004.

Crumrine, N. Rose, and Alan Morinis, eds. *Pilgrimage in Latin America.* New York: Greenwood Press, 1991.

Dahlberg, Andrea. "The Body as a Principle of Holism: Three Pilgrimages." In *Contesting the Sacred: The Anthropology of Pilgrimage,* edited by John Eade and Michael Sallnow, 30–50. Urbana: University of Illinois Press, 2000.

Davis, Richard H. "The Cultural Background of Hindutva." In *India Briefing: Takeoff at Last?,* edited by Alyssa Ayres and Philip Oldenburg, 107–40. Armonk, NY: M. E. Sharpe, 2005.

De Man, Paul. *The Rhetoric of Romanticism.* New York: Columbia University Press, 2013.

Demerath, N. J., III. *Crossing the Gods: World Religions and Worldly Politics.* New Brunswick, NJ: Rutgers University Press, 2003.

Derrida, Jacques. *Dissemination.* Translated by Barbara Johnson. Chicago: University of Chicago Press, 1981.

———. "Faith and Knowledge." In *Acts of Religion,* edited and translated by Gil Anidjar, 1–40. New York: Routledge, 2002.

———. "Freud and the Scene of Writing." In *Writing and Difference,* by Jacques Derrida, translated by Alan Bass, 196–231. Chicago: University of Chicago Press, 1978.

———. "From Restricted to General Economy: A Hegelianism without Reserve." In *Writing and Difference,* by Jacques Derrida, translated by Alan Bass, 251–277. Chicago: University of Chicago Press, 1978.

———. *The Gift of Death.* Chicago: University of Chicago Press, 1995.

———. *Given Time. I. Counterfeit Money.* Translated by Peggy Kamuf. Chicago: University of Chicago Press, 1992.

———. "On Forgiveness." In *On Cosmopolitanism and Forgiveness,* by Jacques Derrida, translated by Mark Dooley and Michael Hughes, 27–60. New York: Routledge, 2001.

———. "Plato's Pharmacy." In *Dissemination,* by Jacques Derrida, translated by Barbara Johnson, 61–172. Chicago: University of Chicago Press, 1981.

———. "Structure, Sign, and Play in the Discourse of the Human Sciences." In *Writing and Difference,* by Jacques Derrida, translated by Alan Bass, 278–94. Chicago: University of Chicago Press, 1978.

Dumont, Louis. *Homo Hierarchicus: An Essay on the Caste System.* Chicago: University of Chicago Press, 1970.

Durkheim, Émile. *The Elementary Forms of Religious Life.* Translated by Karen Fields. New York: Free Press, 1995.

———. *The Rules of Sociological Method.* New York: Macmillan, 1982.

Eade, John, and Michael J. Sallnow, eds. *Contesting the Sacred: The Anthropology of Pilgrimage*. Urbana: University of Illinois Press, 2000.

Eck, Diana. *Banaras: City of Light*. New York: Columbia University Press, 1999.

———. *Darśana: Seeing the Divine Image in India*. New York: Columbia University Press, 1996.

———. "The Goddess Ganga in Hindu Sacred Geography." In *Devī: Goddesses of India*, edited by John Hawley and Donna Wulff, 137–53. Berkeley: University of California Press, 1996.

———. *India: A Sacred Geography*. New York: Harmony, 2012.

Emirbayer, Mustafa, and Ann Mische. "What Is Agency?" *American Journal of Sociology* 103, no. 4 (1998): 962–1023.

Entwistle, Alan W. *Braj, Centre of Krishna Pilgrimage*. Vol. 3. Leiden, Netherlands: Brill Academic Publishers, 1987.

Erndl, Kathleen M. *Victory to the Mother: The Hindu Goddess of Northwest India in Myth, Ritual, and Symbol*. New York: Oxford University Press, 1993.

Eze, Emmanuel C. "Introduction: Philosophy and the (Post)colonial." In *Postcolonial African Philosophy: A Critical Reader*, edited by Emmanuel Eze, 1–22. Cambridge, MA: Blackwell, 1997.

Fabian, Johannes. *Time and the Other: How Anthropology Makes Its Object*. New York: Columbia University Press, 2002.

Feldhaus, Anne. *Connected Places: Religion, Pilgrimage, and Geographical Imagination in India*. New York: Palgrave Macmillan, 2003.

Foucault, Michel. *The Birth of Biopolitics: Lectures at the Collège de France, 1978–1979*. Translated by Graham Burchell. Basingstoke, UK: Palgrave Macmillan, 2010.

———. *"Society Must Be Defended": Lectures at the Collège de France, 1975–1976*. New York: Macmillan, 2003.

———. "Truth and Power." In *The Essential Foucault*, edited by Paul Rabinow and Nikolas Rose, 300–318. New York: New Press, 2003.

Freud, Sigmund. *Beyond the Pleasure Principle*. Translated by James Strachey. New York: Norton, 1959.

———. "The Dynamics of Transference." In *Essential Papers on Transference Analysis*, edited by Gregory P. Bauer, 5–18. Northvale, NJ: Aronson, 1994.

———. *General Psychological Theory: Papers on Metapsychology*. New York: Touchstone, 2008.

———. *The Interpretation of Dreams*. Translated by A. A. Brill. New York: Macmillan, 1913.

———. *Introductory Lectures on Psycho-Analysis*. Edited by Peter Gay. Translated by James Strachey. New York: Norton, 1989.

———. "On Narcissism." In *The Standard Edition of the Complete Psychological Works of Sigmund Freud*, vol. 14, *1914–1916*, edited by James Strachey, 73–102. London: Hogarth Press, 1957.

———. "Remembering, Repeating and Working-Through." In *The Standard Edition of the Complete Psychological Works of Sigmund Freud*, vol. 12, *1911–1913*, edited by James Strachey, 147–56. London: Hogarth Press, 1958.

———. *The Standard Edition of the Complete Psychological Works of Sigmund Freud.* Vol. 14, *1914–1916.* Edited by James Strachey. London: Hogarth Press, 1957.

———. *The Uncanny.* New York: Penguin, 2003.

Gaines, Donna. *Teenage Wasteland: Suburbia's Dead End Kids.* Chicago: University of Chicago Press, 1998.

Gal, Susan. "Language and the 'Arts of Resistance.'" *Cultural Anthropology: Journal of the Society for Cultural Anthropology* 10, no. 3 (1995): 407–24.

Gay, Peter. *The Enlightenment: The Rise of Modern Paganism.* Vol. 1. New York: W. W. Norton, 1995.

Geertz, Clifford. *The Interpretation of Cultures: Selected Essays.* New York: Basic Books, 1973.

Ghassem-Fachandi, Parvis. *Pogrom in Gujarat: Hindu Nationalism and Anti-Muslim Violence in India.* Princeton, NJ: Princeton University Press, 2012.

Gibbons, Reginald, and Charles Segal. *Antigone.* New York: Oxford University Press, 2003.

Giddens, Anthony. *The Consequences of Modernity.* Stanford, CA: Stanford University Press, 1990.

———. *Modernity and Self-Identity: Self and Society in the Late Modern Age.* Stanford, CA: Stanford University Press, 1991

———. *Runaway World.* London: Profile Books, 2002.

Giddens, Anthony, and Will Hutton. *On the Edge: Living with Global Capitalism.* London: Jonathan Cape, 2000.

Goffman, Erving. *Asylums: Essays on the Social Situation of Mental Patients and Other Inmates.* London: Penguin, 1961.

———. *The Presentation of Self in Everyday Life.* Garden City, NY: Doubleday, 1959.

Gold, Ann G. *Fruitful Journeys: The Ways of Rajasthani Pilgrims.* Berkeley: University of California Press, 1998.

Goldberg, David Theo. *Racist Culture: Philosophy and the Politics of Meaning.* Malden, MA: Blackwell, 1993.

———. *The Threat of Race: Reflections on Racial Neoliberalism.* Oxford: Blackwell, 2009.

Green, A. "Conceptions of Affect." *International Journal of Psycho-Analysis* 58, no. 2 (1977): 129–56.

Groarke, Steven. "Making Contact." *Infant Observation* 13, no. 2 (2010): 209–22.

———. "Psychoanalysis and Structuration Theory: The Social Logic of Identity." *Sociology* 36 (2002): 559–76.

Guha, Ranajit. *Elementary Aspects of Peasant Insurgency in Colonial India.* Durham, NC: Duke University Press, 1999.

Guru, Gopal. *Humiliation: Claims and Context.* New Delhi: Oxford University Press, 2011.

Guru, Gopal, and Anuradha Chakravarty. "Who Are the Country's Poor? Social Movement Politics and Dalit Poverty." In *Perspectives on Modern South Asia: A Reader in Culture, History, and Representation,* edited by Kamala Visweswaran, 254–68. Malden, UK: Wiley-Blackwell, 2011.

Hall, Stuart, and Tony Jefferson. *Resistance through Rituals.* London: Hutchinson, 1976.

Hamilton, Walter. *The East-India Gazetteer: Containing Particular Descriptions of the Em-*

pires, Kingdoms, Principalities, Provinces, Cities, Towns, Districts, Harbours, Rivers, Lakes, &c. of Hindostan, and the Adjacent Countries, India beyond the Ganges and the Eastern Archipelago. London: Parbury, Allen, 1828.

Handelman, Don, and David Dean Shulman. *God Inside Out: Śiva's Game of Dice*. Oxford: Oxford University Press on Demand, 1997.

Hansen, Thomas Blom. *The Saffron Wave: Democracy and Hindu Nationalism in Modern India*. Princeton, NJ: Princeton University Press, 1999.

Harari, R. *Lacan's Seminar on 'Anxiety': An Introduction*. New York: Other Press, 2001.

Harman, William. "Negotiating Relationships with the Goddess." In *Dealing with Deities: The Ritual Vow in South Asia*, edited by Selva J. Raj and William P. Harman, 25–42. Albany: State University of New York Press, 2006.

Harris, Ruth. *Lourdes: Body and Spirit in the Secular Age*. London: Penguin UK, 2008.

Hausner, Sondra L. *Wandering with Sadhus: Ascetics in the Hindu Himalayas*. Bloomington: Indiana University Press, 2007.

Hebdige, Dick. "Subculture: The Meaning of Style." *Critical Quarterly* 37, no. 2 (1995): 120–24.

Heber, Reginald. *Narrative of a Journey through the Upper Provinces of India: From Calcutta to Bombay, 1824–1825, (with Notes upon Ceylon,) an Account of a Journey to Madras and the Southern Provinces, 1826, and Letters Written in India*. London: J. Murray, 1828.

Hegel, Georg W. F. *The Phenomenology of Spirit*. Translated by J. B. Baillie. Digireads.com Publishing, 2009.

——. *Philosophy of Right*. Translated by S. W. Dyde. London: G. Bell and Sons, 2008.

Heidegger, Martin. *Being and Time*. Translated by John Macquarrie and Edward Robinson. New York: Harper, 1962.

——. *Hölderlin's Hymn "The Ister."* Bloomington: Indiana University Press, 1996.

——. *On the Way to Language*. New York: Harper and Row, 1971.

——. *On Time and Being*. Translated by Joan Stambaugh. 1972. Reprint, Chicago: University of Chicago Press, 2002.

Hobsbawm, Eric, and Terence Ranger, eds. *The Invention of Tradition*. Cambridge: Cambridge University Press, 1983.

Hodges, William. *Travels in India: During the Years 1780, 1781, 1782, & 1783. by William Hodges* London: Printed for the author, and sold by J. Edwards, Pall-Mall, 1793.

Hume, David. "National Characters." In *Essays and Treatises on Several Subjects, Vol.1*, 244–57. London: A. Millar, 1767.

Hyppolite, Jean. "A Spoken Commentary on Freud's Verneinung." In *Freud's Papers on Technique 1953–1954*, by Jacques Lacan, edited by Jacques-Alain Miller, translated by John Forrester, 289–98. New York: W. W. Norton, 1988.

Iannaccone, Laurence. "Introduction to the Economics of Religion." *Journal of Economic Literature* 36, no. 3 (1998): 1465–96.

Ilaiah, Kancha. *Why I Am Not a Hindu*. Calcutta: Samya, 1996.

Īśvarakṛṣṇa. *Sāṃkhyakārikā of Īśvarakṛṣṇa: Text, Translation and Commentary—Yuktidīpikā*. Edited and translated by S. S. Sastri, Suryanarayana, and N. C. Panda. Delhi: Bharatiya Kala Prakashan, 2009.

Jaffrelot, Christophe. "The Hindu Nationalist Reinterpretation of Pilgrimage in India: The

Limits of Yatra Politics." In *Religion, Caste, and Politics in India*, by Christophe Jaffrelot, 324–42. New York: Columbia University Press, 2011.

———. *Religion, Caste, and Politics in India*. Delhi: Primus Books, 2010.

Jansen, Willy, and Meike Kuhl. "Shared Symbols: Muslims, Marian Pilgrimages and Gender." *European Journal of Women's Studies* 40, no. 3 (2008): 295–311.

Jeffrey, Craig, Patricia Jeffery, and Roger Jeffery. *Degrees without Freedom? Education, Masculinities, and Unemployment in North India*. Stanford, CA: Stanford University Press, 2008.

Kakar, Sudhir. *Shamans, Mystics, and Doctors: A Psychological Inquiry into India and Its Healing Traditions*. Chicago: University of Chicago Press, 1991.

———. "Some Unconscious Aspects of Ethnic Violence in India." In *Mirrors of Violence*, edited by Veena Das, 135–45. Delhi: Oxford University Press, 1990.

———. "The Time of Kali: Violence between Religious Groups in India." *Social Research* 67, no. 3 (2000): 877–99.

Kant, Immanuel. "An Answer to the Question: What Is Enlightenment?" In *Practical Philosophy*, edited and translated by Mary Gregor, 17–22. Cambridge: Cambridge University Press, 1999.

———. *Critique of Judgement*. Translated by James Creed Meredith. Oxford: Clarendon Press, 1952.

———. *Critique of Practical Reason*. 1909. Reprint, Mineola, NY: Dover Publications, 2004.

———. *Essays and Treatises on Moral, Political, and Various Philosophical Subjects*. Vol. 2. London: William Richardson, 1799.

———. *Religion within the Limits of Reason Alone*. La Salle, IL: Open Court Publishing, 1960.

Karve, Irawati. "On the Road: A Maharashtrian Pilgrimage." *Journal of Asian Studies* 22, no. 1 (1962): 13–29.

Kellner, Douglas. *Media Culture: Cultural Studies, Identity, and Politics between the Modern and the Postmodern*. Oxford: Routledge, 1995.

Khan, Dominique-Sila. *Conversions and Shifting Identities: Ramdev Pir and the Ismailis in Rajasthan*. New Delhi: Manohar, 1997.

Kierkegaard, Søren. *Fear and Trembling; Repetition*. Edited and translated by Howard V. Hong and Edna H. Hong. Princeton, NJ: Princeton University Press, 1983.

King, Lindsey C. "Pilgrimages, Promises, and Ex-votos." In *Pilgrimage and Healing*, edited by Jill Dubisch and Michael Winkelman, 49–68. Tucson: University of Arizona Press, 2005.

Kinnvall, Catarina. *Globalization and Religious Nationalism in India: The Search for Ontological Security*. London: Routledge, 2006.

Kristeva, Julia. *The Portable Kristeva*. Edited by Kelly Oliver. New York: Columbia University Press, 2002.

Lacan, Jacques. *Anxiety: The Seminar of Jacques Lacan, Book X*. Cambridge: Polity Press, 2014.

———. *Écrits: The First Complete Edition in English*. Translated by Bruce Fink. New York: W. W. Norton, 2005.

————. *The Ego in Freud's Theory and in the Technique of Psychoanalysis, 1954–1955, Book II.* New York: W. W. Norton, 1988.

————. *The Ethics of Psychoanalysis, 1959–1960.* New York: W. W. Norton, 1997.

————. *Four Fundamental Concepts of Psychoanalysis.* London: W. W. Norton, 1981.

————. *Freud's Papers on Technique: Seminar of Jacques Lacan, Book I.* Edited by Jacques Alain-Miller. Translated by John Forrester. New York: W. W. Norton, 1988.

————. "The Function and Field of Speech and Language in Psychoanalysis." In *Écrits: The First Complete Edition in English*, edited and translated by Bruce Fink, 197–268. New York: W. W. Norton, 2005.

————. *On Feminine Sexuality: The Limits of Love and Knowledge, 1972–1973.* Translated by Bruce Fink. New York: W. W. Norton, 1999.

————. *The Other Side of Psychoanalysis.* Translated by Russell Grigg. New York: W. W. Norton, 2007.

————. *Television.* Translated by Denis Hollier, Rosalind Krauss, and Annette Michelson. New York: W. W. Norton, 1990.

Lechner, Frank J. "Global Fundamentalism." In *The Globalization Reader*, edited by Frank J. Lechner and John Boli, 338–41. Malden, MA: Blackwell Publishers, 2000.

Lévinas, Emmanuel. *Alterity and Transcendence.* New York: Columbia University Press, 1999.

————. "Existence and Ethics." In *Kierkegaard: A Critical Reader*, edited by Jonathan Rée and Jane Chamberlain, 27–34. Oxford: Blackwell, 1998.

————. *Totality and Infinity: An Essay on Exteriority.* Translated by Alphonso Lingis. Pittsburgh: Duquesne University Press, 1969.

Lochtefeld, James. *God's Gateway: Identity and Meaning in a Hindu Pilgrimage Place.* Oxford: Oxford University Press, 2010.

Lockman, John, and Jesuits. *Travels of the Jesuits, into Various Parts of the World: Particularly China and the East-Indies.* London: T. Piety, 1762.

Luckmann, Thomas. *The Invisible Religion: The Problem of Religion in Modern Society.* New York: Macmillan, 1967.

Lutgendorf, Philip. *Hanuman's Tale: The Messages of a Divine Monkey.* Oxford: Oxford University Press, 2006.

Lyotard, Jean-François. *The Postmodern Condition: A Report on Knowledge.* Minneapolis: University of Minnesota Press, 1984.

Maclean, Kama. *Pilgrimage and Power: The Kumbh Mela in Allahabad, 1765–1954.* New York: Oxford University Press, 2008.

Madan, Triloki Nath. *Modern Myths, Locked Minds: Secularism and Fundamentalism in India.* Delhi: Oxford University Press, 1997.

Mahmood, Saba. *Politics of Piety: The Islamic Revival and the Feminist Subject.* Princeton, NJ: Princeton University Press, 2005.

————. "Secularism, Hermeneutics, and Empire: The Politics of Islamic Reformation." *Public Culture* 18, no. 2 (2006): 323–47.

Maloney, Clarence. *Language and Civilization Change in South Asia.* Leiden, Netherlands: E. J. Brill, 1978.

Manu. *Manu's Code of Law: A Critical Edition and Translation of the Manava-Dharmasastra.*

Edited by Patrick Olivelle and Suman Olivelle. Oxford: Oxford University Press, [2005].

Marriott, McKim. *Hindu Transactions: Diversity without Dualism*. Chicago: University of Chicago, Committee on Southern Asian Studies, 1976.

Martin, Bernice. "From Pre-to Postmodernity in Latin America: The Case of Pentecostalism." In *Religion, Modernity, and Postmodernity*, edited by Paul Heelas, 102–46. Malden, MA: Wiley-Blackwell, 1998.

———. "Pentecostal Conversion and the Limits of the Market Metaphor." *Exchange* 35, no. 1 (2006): 61–91.

Marty, Martin, and Scott R. Appleby, eds. *Fundamentalisms Comprehended*. Chicago: University of Chicago Press, 1995.

———, eds. *Fundamentalisms Observed*. Vol. 1. Chicago: University of Chicago Press, 1994.

Marx, Karl, and Friedrich Engels. *The German Ideology, Parts I & III*. Mansfield, CT: Martino Publishing, 2011.

———. *Wage-Labor and Capital*. Melbourne: Workers' Literature Bureau, 1942.

Maslow, Abraham. "A Theory of Human Motivation." *Psychological Review* 50, no. 4 (1943): 370–96.

Matheson, John. *England to Delhi: A Narrative of Indian Travel*. London: Longmans, Green, 1870.

Mauss, Marcel. *The Gift: The Form and Reason for Exchange in Archaic Societies*. Translated by W. D. Halls. 1954. Reprint, London: Routledge, 2002.

Mbembe, Achille, and Janet Roitman. "Figures of the Subject in Times of Crisis." *Public Culture* 7, no. 2 (1995): 323–52.

McAdam, Doug. "Tactical Innovation and the Pace of Insurgency." *American Sociological Review* 48, no. 6 (1983): 735–54.

McGee, Mary. "Desired Fruits: Motive and Intention in the Votive Rites of Hindu Women." In *Roles and Rituals for Hindu Women*, edited by Julia Leslie, 71–88. Madison, NJ: Fairleigh Dickinson University Press, 1991.

Meyer, Gerd. "Taking Risks for Others: Social Courage as a Moral Virtue." In *On Behalf of Others: The Psychology of Care in a Global World*, edited by Sarah Scuzzarello, Catarina Kinnvall, and Kristen R. Monroe, 52–105. Oxford: Oxford University Press, 2009.

Monier-Williams, Monier. *Sanskrit-English Dictionary*. Delhi: Motilal Banarsidass, 2002.

Moreno Arcas, Manuel. "Murugan, a God of Healing Poisons: The Physics of Worship in a South Indian Center for Pilgrimage." PhD diss., University of Chicago, 1984.

Morinis, Alan, ed. *Pilgrimage in Latin America*. New York: Greenwood Press, 1991.

Nancy, Jean-Luc. "The Unsacrificeable." *Yale French Studies* 79 (1991): 20–38.

Nandy, Ashis. "The Politics of Secularism and the Recovery of Religious Tolerance." In *Mirrors of Violence: Communities, Riots, and Survivors in South Asia*, edited by Veena Das, 69–93. Delhi: Oxford University Press, 1990.

———. *Time Warps: Silent and Evasive Pasts in Indian Politics and Religion*. New Brunswick, NJ: Rutgers University Press, 2002.

National Commission for the Enterprises in the Unorganized Sector. *Report on Conditions of Work and Promotion of Livelihoods in the Unorganised Sector*. New Delhi: Academic Foundation, 2008.

Obeyesekere, Gananath. *Medusa's Hair: An Essay on Personal Symbols and Religious Experience*. Chicago: University of Chicago Press, 1981.

———. *The Work of Culture: Symbolic Transformation in Psychoanalysis and Anthropology*. Chicago: University of Chicago Press, 1990.

O'Flaherty, Wendy D. *Dreams, Illusion, and Other Realities*. Chicago: University of Chicago Press, 1986.

———. *Śiva: The Erotic Ascetic*. Oxford: Oxford University Press, 1981.

Olivelle, Patrick. *The Āśrama System: The History and Hermeneutics of a Religious Institution*. Oxford: Oxford University Press, 1993.

Ortner, Sherry B. "Resistance and the Problem of Ethnographic Refusal." *Comparative Studies in Society and History* 37, no. 1 (1995): 173–93.

Pandey, Gyanendra. *The Construction of Communalism in Colonial North India*. New Delhi: Oxford University Press, 2006.

Parlby, Fanny P. *Wanderings of a Pilgrim in Search of the Picturesque: During Four-and-Twenty Years in the East*. London: P. Richardson, 1850.

Pearson, Anne Mackenzie. *"Because It Gives Me Peace of Mind": Ritual Fasts in the Religious Lives of Hindu Women*. Albany: State University of New York Press, 1996.

Pintchman, Tracy. *Women's Lives, Women's Rituals in the Hindu Tradition*. Oxford: Oxford University Press, 2007.

Plato. "Timaeus." In *Timaeus and Critias*, translated by A. E. Taylor, 13–100. New York: Routledge, 2013.

Polanyi, Karl. "The Economy as Instituted Process." In *The Sociology of Economic Life*, edited by Mark Granovetter and Richard Swedberg, 29–51. Boulder, CO: Westview Press, 1992.

Pritchett, Lant. "Who Is Not Poor? Dreaming of a World Truly Free of Poverty." *World Bank Research Observer* 21, no. 1 (2006): 1–23.

Raheja, Gloria Goodwin. *The Poison in the Gift: Ritual, Prestation, and the Dominant Caste in a North Indian Village*. Chicago: University of Chicago Press, 1988.

Raj, Selva J., and William Harman, eds. *Dealing with Deities: The Ritual Vow in South Asia*. Albany: State University of New York Press, 2006.

Rajagopal, Arvind. *Politics after Television: Religious Nationalism and the Reshaping of the Indian Public*. Cambridge: Cambridge University Press, 2001.

Reader, Ian. "Pilgrimage Growth in the Modern World: Meanings and Implications." *Religion* 37, no. 3 (2007): 210–29.

Roberts, Michael. "Symbols, Sacrifice, and Tamil Tiger Rites." *Social Analysis* 49, no. 1 (2005): 67–93.

Robertson, Roland, and JoAnn Chirico. "Humanity, Globalization, and Worldwide Religious Resurgence: A Theoretical Exploration." *Sociology of Religion* 46, no. 3 (1985): 219–42.

Robinson, William S. "Ecological Correlations and the Behavior of Individuals." *International Journal of Epidemiology* 38, no. 2 (2009): 337–41.

Rousseau, Jean Jacques. *The Social Contract*. London: Hafner Press, 2010.

Sahai, Shashi B. *South Asia: From Freedom to Terrorism*. New Delhi: Gyan, 1998.

Śaṃkara. *The Mandukyopanishad with Gauḍapāda's Kārikās and the Bhāshya of Śaṃkara*. Translated by M. N. Dwivedi. Bombay: Bombay Theosophical Publication Fund, [1894].

————. *The Vedanta Sutras with the Commentary of Sankaracharya.* Vol. 1. Translated by George Thibaut. Oxford: Clarendon Press, 1904.

Sarkar, Tanika. *Hindu Wife, Hindu Nation: Community, Religion, and Cultural Nationalism.* Bloomington: Indiana University Press, 2001.

————. "Historical Pedagogy of the Sangh Parivar." *Seminar: A Monthly Symposium* 522 (February 2003): 51–56. http://www.india-seminar.com/2003/522/522%20tanika%20sarkar.htm.

Sax, William S. *God of Justice: Ritual Healing and Social Justice in the Central Himalayas.* Oxford: Oxford University Press, 2008.

Schechner, Richard. *Performance Studies: An Introduction.* New York: Routledge, 2002.

Scheper-Hughes, Nancy. *Death without Weeping: The Violence of Everyday Life in Brazil.* Berkeley: University of California Press, 1993.

Schramm, Katharina. "Coming Home to the Motherland: Pilgrimage Tourism." In *Reframing Pilgrimage: Cultures in Motion,* edited by Simon Coleman and John Eade, 133–49. London: Routledge, 2004.

Scott, James C. *Domination and the Arts of Resistance: Hidden Transcripts.* New Haven, CT: Yale University Press, 1990.

Sered, Susan S. *Women as Ritual Experts: The Religious Lives of Elderly Jewish Women in Jerusalem.* Oxford: Oxford University Press, 1996.

Seymour, Susan. "Resistance." *Anthropological Theory* 6, no. 3 (2006): 303–21.

Shah, Behulah. "Braj: The Creation of Krishna's Landscape of Power and Pleasure and Its Sixteenth Century Construction through the Pilgrimage of the Groves." In *Sacred Gardens and Landscapes: Ritual and Agency,* edited by Michel Conan, 153–72. Washington, DC: Dumbarton Oaks Research Library & Collection, 2007.

Sinclair, Karen P. "Mission to Waitangi: A Maori Pilgrimage." In *Sacred Journeys: The Anthropology of Pilgrimage,* edited by Alan Morinis, 233–56. Westport, CT: Greenwood Press, 1992.

Singh, Vikash. "Definitive Exclusions: The Social Fact and the Subjects of Neo-liberalism." In *The Unhappy Divorce of Psychoanalysis and Sociology,* edited by Lynn Chancer and John Andrews, 380–400. New York: Palgrave, 2014.

————. "Religion and Neoliberalism: TV Serial Rāmāyaṇa and the Becoming of an Ideology." *International Journal of Žižek Studies* 6, no. 2 (2012): 1–17.

Sircar, Dineschandra. *The Śākta Pīṭhas.* Vol. 8. Delhi: Motilal Banarsidass, 1998.

Śiva Upasana [Praying to Śiva]. Delhi: Lakshmi Prakashan, n.d.

Spivak, Gayatri C. "Can the Subaltern Speak?" In *Marxism and the Interpretation of Culture,* edited by Cary Nelson, Lawrence Grossberg, and Henry Lefebvre, 271–316. London: Macmillan, 1988.

Springett, James. "Religious Fundamentalism and Primitive Projective Processes." *Psychoanalytic Psychotherapy* 17, no. 4 (2003): 325–41.

Stark, Rodney. "Micro Foundations of Religion: A Revised Theory." *Sociological Theory* 17, no. 3 (1999): 264–89.

Stark, Rodney, and William Bainbridge. *A Theory of Religion.* New Brunswick, NJ: Rutgers University Press, 1996.

Sundaram, Ravi. *Pirate Modernity: Delhi's Media Urbanism*. London: Routledge, 2010.

Tarrow, Sidney G. *Power in Movement: Social Movements and Contentious Politics*. Cambridge: Cambridge University Press, 1998.

Taylor, Bayard. *A Visit to India, China, and Japan, in the Year 1853*. New York: G. P. Putnam, 1855.

Tilly, Charles. *Contentious Performances*. Cambridge: Cambridge University Press, 2008.

Timur. "Malfuzat-I Timuri or Tuzak-I Timuri: The Autobiography of Timur." In *The History of India, as Told by Its Own Historians. The Muhammadan Period*, vol. 3, edited by H. M. Elliot and John Dowson, 389–477. London: Trübner, 1871.

Turner, Bryan. "Reshaping the Sociology of Religion: Globalization, Spirituality and the Erosion of the Social." *Sociological Review* 57, no. 1 (2009): 186–200.

Turner, Victor W. *Dramas, Fields, and Metaphors: Symbolic Action in Human Society*. Ithaca, NY: Cornell University Press, 1974.

Turner, Victor W. T., and Edith L. B. Turner. *Image and Pilgrimage in Christian Culture: Anthropological Perspectives*. New York: Columbia University Press, 1978.

Van der Veer, Peter. *Religious Nationalism: Hindus and Muslims in India*. Berkeley: University of California Press, 1994.

Van Poppel, Frans, and Lincoln H. Day. "A Test of Durkheim's Theory of Suicide— without Committing the 'Ecological Fallacy.'" *American Sociological Review* 61, no. 3 (1996): 500–507.

Varshney, Ashutosh. *Ethnic Conflict and Civic Life: Hindus and Muslims in India*. New Haven, CT: Yale University Press, 2003.

Vyasa. "Book 3: Vana Parva: Tirtha-yatra Parva." In *The Mahabharata*, translated by Manmath Nath Dutt. Delhi: Parimal Publication, 2001.

Wacquant, Loic. "Following Pierre Bourdieu into the Field." *Ethnography* 5, no. 4 (2004): 387–414.

———. "Toward a Dictatorship over the Poor? Notes on the Penalization of Poverty in Brazil." *Punishment and Society* 5, no. 2 (2003): 197–205.

———. "Urban Marginality in the Coming Millennium." *Urban Studies* 36, no. 10 (1999): 1639–47.

Waghorne, Joanne P. *Diaspora of the Gods: Modern Hindu Temples in an Urban Middle-Class World*. New York: Oxford University Press, 2004.

Wakankar, Milind. *Subalternity and Religion: The Prehistory of Dalit Empowerment in South Asia*. Abingdon, UK: Routledge, 2010.

Wang, Yong. "Agency: The Internal Split of Structure." *Sociological Forum* 23, no. 3 (2008): 481–502.

Weber, Max. *From Max Weber: Essays in Sociology*. Edited and translated by Hans H. Gerth and C. Wright Mills. New York: Oxford University Press, 1946.

———. *The Protestant Ethic and the "Spirit" of Capitalism and Other Writings*. New York: Penguin, 2002.

———. *The Religion of India: The Sociology of Hinduism and Buddhism*. Edited and translated by Hans H. Gerth and Don Martindale. Glencoe, IL: Free Press, 1967.

White, David Gordon. *The Alchemical Body: Siddha Traditions in Medieval India*. Chicago: University of Chicago Press, 2012.

Wilkinson, Steven I. *Votes and Violence: Electoral Competition and Ethnic Riots in India.* Cambridge: Cambridge University Press, 2006.

Wilson, Bryan. *Religion in Secular Society.* London: C. A. Watts, 1966.

Wright, Caleb. *Lectures on India.* Boston: Caleb Wright, 1851.

Yamane, David. "Secularization on Trial: In Defense of a Neosecularization Paradigm." *Journal for the Scientific Study of Religion* 36, no. 1 (1997): 109–22.

Young, Jock. *The Exclusive Society: Social Exclusion, Crime and Difference in Late Modernity.* London: Sage, 1999.

———. *The Vertigo of Late Modernity.* Los Angeles: Sage, 2010.

Zakaria, Rafiq. *The Widening Divide: An Insight into Hindu-Muslim Relations.* New Delhi: Penguin, 1995.

INDEX

The authorized representative in the EU for product safety and compliance is:
Mare Nostrum Group
B.V Doelen 72
4831 GR Breda
The Netherlands

www.ingramcontent.com/pod-product-compliance
Lightning Source LLC
Chambersburg PA
CBHW030359270326
41926CB00009B/1181